Everyday Revolutionaries

Genocide, Political Violence, Human Rights Series

Edited by Alexander Laban Hinton, Stephen Eric Bronner, Aldo Civico, and Nela Navarro

Everyday Revolutionaries

Gender, Violence, and Disillusionment in Postwar El Salvador

IRINA CARLOTA SILBER

RUTGERS UNIVERSITY PRESS

NEW BRUNSWICK, NEW JERSEY, AND LONDON

LIBRARY OF CONGRESS CATALOGING-IN-PUBLICATION DATA

Silber, Irina Carlota
  Everyday revolutionaries : gender, violence, and disillusionment in postwar
El Salvador / Irina Carlota Silber.
      p. cm. — (Genocide, political violence, human rights)
  Includes bibliographical references and index.
  ISBN 978-0-8135-4934-7 (hbk. : alk. paper) — ISBN 978-0-8135-4935-4
(pbk. : alk. paper)

    1. Postwar reconstruction—Social aspects—El Salvador.   2. Revolutionaries—
El Salvador—Case studies.   3. Political activists—El Salvador—Case studies.
4. El Salvador—History—1992–   5. El Salvador—Social conditions.
6. El Salvador—Politics and government—1992–   7. El Salvador—Emigration
and immigration—Social aspects.   I. Title.
  F1488.5.S55   2011
  972.8405′4—dc22   2010013766

A British Cataloging-in-Publication record for this book is available
from the British Library.

Visit our Web site: http://rutgerspress.rutgers.edu

Manufactured in the United States of America

For Antonio, Cenzo, and Inés

Dispatches from the Frontlines

AROUND THE WORLD; Salvadoran Police Report 50 Dead in Political Strife
SAN SALVADOR, July 6

The police said today that at least 50 people were killed over the weekend in El Salvador.

Ten of the bodies were in the northern town of Las Vueltas, an area where leftists who have been fighting the ruling junta are concentrated. Residents of the town said that the victims had been pulled from their homes Friday night by unidentified men, and that when the bodies were found the next day, they showed signs of having been tortured.

Meanwhile, the Salvadoran military reported guerrilla attacks on installations in the northern town of Chalatenango and in the eastern department of Cabanas [*sic*]. A military spokesman said the attacks were minor and discounted them as "desperate acts of extremists."

—Associated Press, July 7, 1981

CONTENTS

ACKNOWLEDGMENTS

This book has taken me some time. In the process of assembling it I have been inspired, pushed, challenged, and supported by mentors, colleagues, family, and friends. While time has changed the questions I pose, the stories I weave, and the analysis I develop, what has remained constant is my deep respect for the men, women, and children of repopulated communities in Chalatenango, El Salvador, who welcomed me into their homes and shared so much about their lives in the past and in the present. Their power of reflection and their analysis of loss and possibility is what I privilege in this book. Though I provide pseudonyms, in particular, I must thank Elsy, who opened up a path for this research and whose children I did not expect to thank over *pupusas* in the United States. Much of this book is for this next generation of Chalatecos, whose stories, whose genealogies, force us to rethink the meaning of postwar and to people our accounts upon which so much policy is forged. For so many hours of conversation, company, and distraction, I thank Chayo, her family, and Chavela and the women from the arts and crafts workshop. I am grateful to Aquilino for his patience in explaining postwar processes to me, and to Kasandra for her companionship and *café listo.* This book would not be possible without the assistance of the many directors and staff of the Chalatenango offices of two organizations, CORDES and CCR, who opened up their doors to me in 1993 and granted me access to repopulated communities. Throughout the book I seek to discuss, faithfully and fairly, events organized by these groups, whose overarching labor is to promote a dignified life for historically marginalized citizens in El Salvador.

After nearly two decades of engagement with Salvadoran processes, the list of individuals and institutions to thank are many. For their intellectual guidance at different stages of his project, I thank Roger Rasnake, who first pushed me to research the politics of Salvadoran migration when I was still an undergraduate, Connie Sutton for her early guidance, Aldo Lauria-Santiago for shaping the field, and Elisabeth Wood for her model scholarship and her engagement with my work. I am indebted to Bambi Schieffelin for helping me theorize narrative language practices and for her long-standing support of my scholarship and career. Thomas Abercrombie supported this project when I needed it most. His vision allowed me to frame the demoralization of a social movement through an analysis that incorporated the reconstruction of social memory. I also thank Meg McLagan and Lok Siu for providing me with thoughtful comments from which to build on, social mobilizing and gender theorizing, respectively. It is, however, with great sadness that I write about William Roseberry, a mentor who generously guided me during my doctoral research in the 1990s, but who tragically died shortly before its completion. I hope that this book honors his legacy.

My ethnographic research began at a time when ethnographies of postwar were new and when few anthropologists formed in the U.S. academy had conducted fieldwork in El Salvador. I thank the many funding agencies whose generous support made this research possible. I am grateful to New York University for granting me preliminary research money through the Tinker Research Fellowship, Center for Latin American and Caribbean Studies, which steered me ultimately to a doctoral project on Chalatenango's postwar reconstruction. I also thank the institutions that made my doctoral research possible: the Fulbright-Hays Doctoral Dissertation Fellowship, the Inter-American Foundation Fellowship, and the Organization of American States Dissertation Fellowship. My dissertation writing was supported by the Woodrow Wilson National Fellowship Foundation's Charlotte W. Newcombe Dissertation Fellowship, and by New York University's Dean's Dissertation Fellowship. Serving as a post-doctoral fellow at Rutgers University's Center for Historical Analysis, led by Matt Matsuda, provided the intellectual community and professionalization that a recent PhD so needed. I was lucky to share this position with Zvi-Ben D'Or. A Rockefeller Fellowship at the Virginia Foundation for the Humanities Institute on Violence and Survival at the University of Virginia, under the leadership of Roberta Culbertson, allowed me to expand my theoretical framing. I also thank Fred Myers, who generously extended visiting scholar status at New York University's Department of Anthropology so that I could conduct new bibliographic research while I took the time to care for my two small children. As a participant in the Social Science Research Council's Cultural Agency in the Americas workshop, I pushed my thinking on the representation of NGO labors.

Support from the City College of New York (CCNY) allowed me to take this book in new and fruitful directions. While at CCNY I have been fortunate to receive institutional support, including a William Stewart Travel Award grant, a CCNY Presidential Research Award, and two PSC–CUNY Research Awards, which funded new research across the United States. A City University of New York (CUNY) Faculty Fellowship Publication Program award gave me the opportunity to sharpen my writing with a cohort of CUNY colleagues. I am particularly grateful to the program's mentor, Virginia Sanchez-Korrol, and to fellows Cindy Lobel, Peter Vellon, Jodie Roure, Paula Saunders, and Kathy López for their careful reading and thoughtful comments on my work. I thank Harriet Alonso, Daniel Lemons, and Juan Carlos Mercado for their support during my time at CCNY. While at CCNY's Department of Interdisciplinary Arts and Sciences at the Center for Worker Education, I have been fortunate to work with an interdisciplinary group of scholars whom I can count as friends, making the balance between scholarship, teaching, and institution building a pleasant pursuit. In particular, many thanks go to Marlene Clark, Kathy McDonald, and Martin Woessner. To my colleague Carlos Aguasaco, I extend a great thanks for his expertise and dedicated correction of the Spanish orthography in the text. I must also thank the students in my Social Science Core I course in the fall of 2009 for taking the time to read several chapters and ask for points of clarification.

Initial review of the manuscript by anonymous readers strengthened this project's theorizing and narrative analysis. Ethel Brooks was a reader for the entire book, and I thank her for her close read, her thoughtful recommendations, and her insights—theoretically broad and agile yet grounded in the practices of everyday. I also thank Mike Siegel for his precise and elegantly crafted maps. I extend great thanks to Rutgers University Press for its support of this project. In particular, I thank Adi Hovav for first acquiring this manuscript while she was at the Press, and Leslie Mitchner for her seasoned hand and editing expertise, which made this book possible. Thanks must also go to Katie Keeran and Suzanne Kellam for making the completion of this book such a clear process and Karen Johnson for her careful copyediting.

My friendships in El Salvador, in academia, and much beyond have truly sustained me all these years. In El Salvador, Serena Cosgroves's long-term knowledge of the country and her rock of a friendship kept me rooted. Ralph Sprenkels and his work on disappeared children through the organization Pro-Búsqueda during the 1990s was a constant reminder of what important work must be done in El Salvador. More than a decade later, I thank him for these years of friendship, for his engaged scholarship that continues to inspire me, and for the permission to use his beautiful photographs. Victoria Sanford worked in neighboring Guatemala, and her groundbreaking project on human rights pushed this project. Her ongoing work, her solidarity, and her friendship have provided invaluable pillars of support during the process of writing a book. In the San Salvador of the 1990s, I befriended a new generation of international volunteers. Thanks to Holly Smith, Paula Grace, and Rhonda Chapman, in particular. A special thanks to Federico Julián Gonzalez and, especially, his mother, Margarita Julián Gonzalez, for their friendship and *cariño*.

Over the last few years I have been lucky to meet a new generation of anthropologists working in El Salvador whose work has grounded my own. I thank Ellen Moodie, Jocelyn Viterna, and, particularly, Brandt Peterson for his insights and his humor. I owe so many thanks to other friends and colleagues along the way who created opportunities for me to develop my work or who simply leant an ear and their thoughts (apologies for any omissions): John Jackson, Brian Larkin, Paul Garrett, Diana Wells, Sarah Teitler, Anupamo Rao, Asale Angel-Ajani, Lisa Maya Knauer, Katherine Gordy, Peter Platt, Nancy Fee, Rebecca Colesworthy, Linda Basch, Horacio Sívori, Cristina Fangmann, and Alan Courtis. As we are former dancers, gym dates with Deborah Thomas got me writing. Deborah's expertise in diasporic studies, among many others, has been invaluable. For nearly two decades Ayala Fader has been an extraordinary friend and colleague. I thank her for listening to my ideas, for becoming almost a Salvadoranist as a result, and for pushing me to always try and polish my work. She has the uncanny ability to say just the right thing, whether it is about teaching, scholarship, or motherhood. To Jordan Pavlin and Ari Haberberg, I thank you for the love, joy, and support you radiate. My time writing was inspired by the books you provided and lightened by countless family dinners with good wine, excellent company, exuberant children, and abundant laughter. I also thank Marta Soledad Aguilar, who with a loving hand helped me care for my children and keep my house in order.

Finally, I must thank my family. My parents supported me in countless ways during this journey, and I will be forever grateful to them for the ways I was taught to ask questions about Latin America, histories of violence, inequality, migration, and making lives anew. My mother, Rosita Silber, has been my first advocate and Nona par excellence to my children when they were young. I don't know who needed that grandmother's touch more so that I could finish my writing. I thank my father, Tomas Silber, a tireless and critical reader who offered seemingly effortless and creative advice on the manuscript on multiple occasions. To the memory of his father, poet and intellectual Hans Silber, I dedicate my poems. My brother Dan Silber helped me theorize questions of ethics and morality, and my brother Ariel Silber provided me with coffee care packages that kept me going while in El Salvador. My husband's family, particularly his parents, Mario and Maria Rossi, have treated me as one of their own with long, rich, and decadent meals. I hope that this book honors the memory of my sister-in-law, Rita Rossi, who did not live to see its completion but who was fiercely supportive of my endeavors even if she would not have chosen them as her own.

This book is for my husband, Antonio Rossi, and our two children, born at very different stages of this project. I dedicate it to them. For Antonio, who gently encouraged me to keep at it, to write something new, I hope you can see it here. Besides his love and kindness, I also thank him for all his help in preparing the images for this book. My son, Cenzo, arrived at the tail end of my dissertation writing and made me finish it. At the time his journey toward health was a constant reminder to impart the immediacy of everyday struggles in postwar Chalatenango, to portray the human ability to heal and live amidst continued injustice. At ten, Cenzo has tracked it all. Picking up strewn manuscript pages, reading my passages aloud, he has earnestly announced, "That was a long sentence, Mama!" Inés, now six, has come to know of Chalate through the young adults she meets in our travels across the United States. Researching with her by my side made me rethink practice, my own positioning, and the too many stories of motherhood loss I collected before I had experienced it. These joys in my too small New York City apartment rub up against the upturned lives, the interrupted possibilities, the arcs of revolutionary projects, and my desire to think through the everyday kind of revolutionary where calls for participation, for *adelante, adelante que la lucha es constante,* do not ring hollow. With all this guidance and support, the faults in this book are entirely my own.

ORGANIZATIONS

ARENA — Alianza Republicana Nacionalista (National Republican Alliance)

BPR — Bloque Popular Revolucionario (Popular Revolutionary Block)

CCR — Coordinadora de Comunidades en Desarrollo Chalatenango (Coordinator of Communities in Development in Chalatenango)

CEMUJER — Instituto de Estudios de la Mujer "Norma Virginia Guirola de Herrera" (Institute of Women's Studies "Norma Virginia Guirola de Herrera")

CO-MADRES — Comité de Madres y Familiares de Presos, Desaparecidos y Asesinados de El Salvador (Committee of the Mothers of the Disappeared)

CONAMUS — Coordinadora Nacional de la Mujer Salvadoreña (National Coordinating Committee of Women in El Salvador)

CORDES — Fundación para la Cooperación y el Desarollo Comunal (Foundation for the Cooperation and Community Development of El Salvador)

CRIPDES — Asociación para el Desarrollo de El Salvador (Association for the Development of El Salvador)

ERP — Ejército Revolucionario del Pueblo (People's Revolutionary Army)

FECCAS — Federación Cristiana de Campesinos Salvadoreños (Christian Federation of Salvadoran Peasants)

FENASTRAS — Federación Nacional de los Trabajadores Salvadoreños (National Federation of Salvadoran Workers)

FESPAD — Fundación de Estudios para la Aplicación del Derecho (Foundation for the Study of the Application of the Law)

FMLN — Frente Fabarbundo Martí para la Liberación Nacional (Fabarbundo Martí National Liberation Front)

FPL — Fuerzas Populares de Liberación (Popular Liberation Forces)

ISDEMU — Instituto Salvadoreño para el Desarrollo de la Mujer (Salvadoran Institute for Women's Development)

Las Dignas   Asociación de Mujeres por la Dignidad y la Vida El Salvador,
                Centroamérica (Women's Association for Dignity and Life El
                Salvador, Central America)
MAM   Movimiento de Mujeres Mélida Anaya Montes (Mélida Anya
                Montes Movement)
MOLID   Movimiento de Liberación y Desarrollo (Movement of
                Liberation and Development)
ONUSAL   Misión de Observadores de las Naciones Unidas (United
                Nations Observer Mission)
ORDEN   Organización Democrática Nacionalista (Democratic
                Nationalist Organization)
PCN   Partido de Conciliación Nacional (National Conciliation Party)
PCS   Partido Comunista de El Salvador (Salvadoran Communist
                Party)
PDC   Partido Demócrata Cristiano (Christian Democratic Party)
PNC   Policía Nacional Civil (National Civilian Police)
PROCHALATE   The Rehabilitation and Development Project of Areas Affected
                by Conflict in the Department of Chalatenango
PRTC   Partido Revolucionario de los Trabajodres Centroamericanos
                (Central American Workers Revolutionary Party)
RN   Resistencia Nacional (Armed Forces of National Resistance)
USAID   United States Agency for International Development
UTC   Unión de Trabajadores del Campo (Rural Workers Union)

CAST OF CHARACTERS

ELSY A central protagonist in this ethnography whose life cycle coincides with the life cycle of wartime organizing, experiences in refugee camps, and postwar rebuilding in the department of Chalatenango. During the postwar period she was an active community representative for "women's issues." She also became an active member of internationally funded but locally implemented gendered development projects. She is partnered with Avel and is the mother of four children. Her relationships with her eldest daughter, Flor, and her third child, Miguel, are the most salient for this text. She lives in the community of El Rancho, a key site in this book.

AVEL Elsy's partner and father of Elsy's youngest child, who is an adolescent. A former political prisoner, human rights worker, and National Civilian Police officer (the police force was created with the United Nations' brokered peace agreements), he migrated to the United States in 2003 and is responsible for sending remittances to Elsy as well as his extended kin network. He works in the service industry.

FLOR Elsy's daughter resides in Los Angeles with a new partner and infant daughter born in the United States. Her young son lives in El Rancho and is raised by Elsy. Flor works three jobs in the service industry.

MIGUEL Elsy's third child. Miguel migrated to the United States in 2007 at the age of eighteen. He lives with Avel and works double shifts for national fast-food chains.

CHAYO Former rank-and-file member of the FPL (Popular Liberation Forces), one of the organizations that comprised the FMLN (Farabundo Martí National Liberation Front), the oppositional, guerrilla group during the Salvadoran civil war. She resided in Mesa Grande, a refugee camp in Honduras, for part of the war. She was an active member of community projects in El Rancho during the early and intermediate postwar period, an adult literacy teacher, and a student herself. She migrated to the United States in 2003, joining her husband, Chico, in New Jersey.

CHICO   Former tailor for the FPL. He resided in Mesa Grande, a refugee
              camp in Honduras, for part of the war. He is Chayo's husband
              and father of all three of her children. He devoted himself to
              agricultural labor during the early and intermediate postwar
              period. He migrated to the United States in 2000 after Hurricane
              Mitch. He is also one of the few Chalatecos in this study with
              temporary legal status (TPS) in the United States, while most
              others are unauthorized migrants.

AQUILINO   Armed combatant for the guerilla forces during the Salvadoran
              civil war. He did not spend time in Honduran refugee camps.
              He spent the entirety of the war in combat and later was a
              demobilized combatant. After the war, he was reunited with his
              family and has become a valued local leader at the community
              and municipal level. He is a vocal community member who
              contributes his analysis to political organizing and postwar
              development programs. At the municipal level, he was charged
              with overseeing the land transfer process, a key aspect of the
              peace accords.

HUGO   Recruited into oppositional organizing in the early 1970s.
              He typifies the early beginnings of the political and military
              oppositional forces. He continued his political organizing from
              inside the Mesa Grande refugee camp. He was not a demobilized
              combatant during the peace process and, as a result, did not
              receive postwar benefits for this category of survivor. He is no
              longer active in political or community organizing.

ROLANDO   Formerly a guerilla platoon leader. Like Aquilino, he was not a
              refugee during the war but rather joined the FMLN military
              and political forces. Unlike the individuals mentioned above,
              he is not originally from the Department (like a state) of
              Chalatenango. This, however, is not rare as during the war
              people were internally displaced or moved around as the
              demands of battle dictated. In the postwar period, Rolando is an
              important member of a grassroots organization, CCR, dedicated
              to helping communities garner development projects and
              organize for their human rights.

ESPERANZA   Former FPL combatant. As the director of CCR's Secretaría de la
              Mujer, she is responsible for organizing the work of regional
              women's representatives. She continues to be an active leader in
              CCR labors, in particular, anti-mining campaigns in the first
              decade of the twenty-first century.

DAYSI   Foreign national who moved to El Salvador during the civil war
              to support the Salvadoran peasantry against military repression.

She was captured and tortured during the war. In the postwar period she became the charismatic executive director of the CORDES regional office in Chalatenango.

PADRE JOSÉ Born to peasant farmers in Northern Chalatenango. He served as the parish priest of Las Vueltas during the period of early intermediate reconstruction. A proponent of liberation theology, alongside his religious service, his work with Chalateco communities focused on critiques of capitalist development.

Everyday Revolutionaries

FIGURE I. Map of El Salvador, the department of Chalatenango, and the northeastern communities discussed in the book.

Maps by Michael Siegel.

Introduction

Country, El Salvador; Department, Chalatenango; Municipality, Las Vueltas; Community, El Rancho; Year, 1997

From late afternoon until evening on most days, a group of men kneel, squat, and sit as they play cards and gamble a bit of their money in front of a family-run store (*tienda*) which also serves as a bus stop. Some smoke Salvadoran cigarettes, some drink community-produced grain alcohol, and there is a lot of talk amidst the thumping of the cards onto the cement floor. Their mothers, sisters, and wives are home finishing up the day's labors, after which they, too, visit neighbors, chat and gossip at other nearby tiendas, or watch Mexican soap operas on TV. These are gender-divided evening spaces of community life, and conversations are topically varied across these spaces.[1]

One afternoon, before the card game, I waited for a local bus to take me to the capital city of Chalatenango, a trip that, depending on the condition of the road and the condition of the bus, takes between forty and sixty minutes. As I waited, Aquilino, a thirty-five-year-old former guerilla troop leader and present-day mayoral council member also waited, but for the card game to begin. After we exchanged formulaic greetings he asked me exactly what it was that I was doing spending so much time in a former war zone in the municipality of Las Vueltas, a municipality controlled by guerilla forces during the Salvadoran Civil War (1980–1992) and a municipality attacked by the Salvadoran government's military forces. With three research trips under my belt and a solid ten months of fieldwork underway, I responded with what I thought was a cogent sound-bite of my project on El Salvador's ongoing postwar reconstruction and efforts at national reconciliation after a bloody civil war between insurgents and the government that had claimed the lives of seventy-five thousand people, "disappeared" another seven thousand Salvadorans, and displaced five hundred thousand civilians. I told Aquilino that I was trying to understand what happens after wars to the everyday warriors and supporters of an insurgency. How is this aftermath lived through under new economic, social, and political pressures and when battles were not necessarily won? For on January 16, 1992, United Nations–brokered peace accords were signed by the political leaders of the guerilla forces, FMLN (Farabundo Martí National Liberation Front), and the Salvadoran government. This officially ended the civil war. In doing so, it opened up a series of steps in the nation's transition to democracy.

While El Salvador continues to receive international acclaim as a successful model for negotiating a revolution, I explained to Aquilino that there was more to this story, evident at the local level. By this point in my research, I knew that Aquilino was a gifted public speaker and an important local leader. I still, though, had not found my way into his social circle, and I wanted to impress him. I took the opportunity to show him that I had a beat on the pulse of the situation, and so I continued by offering him one of my preliminary findings: postwar El Salvador in formerly revolutionary regions was characterized by a palpable disillusionment and waning activism among the master organizers of the past— rural men and women who were the backbone of the militant popular organizing of the war. This was a striking and perplexing legacy of the war, and one that I hoped to help clarify. Aquilino tilted his straw cowboy hat back on his head, paused, looked at me with a slight smile, and suggested that, indeed, what I was studying was a "spectral" rebuilding process where oppositional people, places, and struggles continued to be marginalized in the postwar. A few weeks later, during an audio-taped interview, Aquilino clarified his theory,

> Yo dije reinserción fantasma. (I said a spectral reintegration). And we're talking about a reintegration into civil society. And according to what's said, the problems are being resolved, every day a bit more. But that is in theory. In reality reintegration does not exist. Reintegration has not been resolved because the problems continue. We organized because of these; it is what motivated us, what drove us to an armed struggle, for issues that are still not resolved. I think the challenge for those of us that formed part of the FMLN in the armed sector is that we have to become part of the political sector. To see if there we can win and gain total power, and be able to, let's not say end poverty, because it is just too great and every country has poverty, but try to resolve a large part of that situation. That is why I said the word "spectral."

Aquilino's metaphor has come to guide my thinking on postwar El Salvador, specifically, for the northeastern region of Chalatenango comprised of former revolutionary combatants and civilian supporters of the insurgency who live in repopulated communities. Twelve years later, with the first FMLN president elected to office, will the seed planted by Aquilino's call for oppositional struggle bear fruit?

Country, United States; States, New York and Virginia; Year, 2008

My phone rings on a late Sunday afternoon. I was expecting Miguel's weekly check-in but not his tears. On his way to work in a fast-food restaurant in Virginia he calls from his mobile phone and speaks in remarkably fluent English given his eighteen months in the United States. Dating Spanish- and English-speaking U.S.-born young women of Salvadoran descent, as well as attending English classes at a community center, have paid off. I have known Miguel since he was a spry, four-year-old boy in the rural countryside of El Rancho, Chalatenango, El Salvador. He was Aquilino's neighbor and was always bright, energetic, funny, and affection-ate. I was immediately struck by him in 1993. He was the type of child that easily becomes endearing and everyone's favorite. Nearing twenty, his charm, wit, and intellect have not diminished. But on this day he sounds devastated. During the conversation Miguel sobs on and off. "I am a bit sad today, Lotti," he tells me. My mind races. What could have happened? Does he need an immigration lawyer? What is going on in El Rancho? Trying to contain my panic, I ask him to tell me what has happened. He responds, "My girlfriend broke up with me yesterday." I breathe and pause, stunned by the cause of his sorrows. After years of collect-ing stories of loss, from the murder of partners in war to the everyday violence of postwar poverty that propelled Miguel to the United States in the first place, I am not expecting matters of the heart. Relieved that it is "just" love, I fumble to find words that do not sound clichéd. I am not so successful. Somehow I get him to stop crying and he laughs saying, "Tal vez tenga que regresar a El Rancho y buscarme una Chalateca." (maybe I need to go back to El Rancho and find a Chalateca).[2] He laughs, not because he does not miss El Rancho and his life there, particularly working with cattle as a hired hand. But after so much sacrifice, the trials of crossing borders, and the seven thousand dollars recently repaid to make the journey, returning for a girl is simply impossible.

Miguel exemplifies a recent postwar migration to the United States by Chalatecos and their now young adult children who stayed and fought in El Salvador during the civil war or fled to Honduran refugee camps. It is only at the turn of the twenty-first century, after the signing of peace accords and well into the transition to democracy, that these former fighters, broadly defined, take up the strategy of (undocumented) migration. I wonder if Aquilino, quoted previously, would have predicted Miguel's young journey.

Much has been written on the plight of the undocumented in the United States and the ways in which their exit from their homeland has become a key aspect of El Salvador's development planning—not unlike other countries such as Mexico, Nicaragua, and Guatemala. While I do not forward a celebratory account, here I wish to point out how in the unexpected temporal and physical distance produced by postwar there are possibilities (Tsing 2005). From the spectacle of armed struggle to the disillusioned and spectral reconciliation of Aquilino's experiences, there is also a story about a fatherless child-survivor of war who cries for unrequited love—an expected angst of youth, though a luxury in times of war. Is this a new possibility? Is this part of the fruit of democratization? Is it enough or does it point to more layers of injustice? Again, I think about Aquilino's analysis of phantom postwar possibilities.

There is also the joyful story Miguel tells me about buying a used car for five hundred dollars to commute to work, a fiction had he stayed in Chalatenango. Like his older sister living in Los Angeles, Miguel is a self-taught driver, without a license. I worry about the implications of Miguel having a vehicle and being an undocumented migrant. The risk of deportation, for example, increases with a traffic infraction. I ask about Miguel's knowledge of driving laws and encourage him to drive accordingly. I have trouble reconciling the image I still carry with me of a tiny tot with cropped hair with the teen behind a wheel. Miguel is one step ahead of me, letting me know that he is working toward getting a driver's license in the neighboring state of Maryland. To date, Maryland is the only East Coast state, one of four states in the country (others are New Mexico, Washington, and Hawaii), that enables undocumented migrants to receive driving licenses without the need to show proof of legal residence in the United States.[3] Technologies of surveillance run deep in the lives of Chalatecos, in the past and present and across nations.

Our phone call lasts close to twenty minutes and ends as Miguel wishes my husband and two children well. Months before, we each snapped photos onto our cell phones, documenting our *reencuentro* after more than a decade. This time I was married and traveled with my family, my son, eight, the age Miguel was when I last saw him, and my daughter, four, the age Miguel was when I first met him.

I BEGIN THIS BOOK by juxtaposing two ethnographic vignettes of everyday life in and out of El Salvador and over a decade of research to highlight the longitudinal and multi-sited nature of my project. These snapshots also foreshadow what this book is about: an analysis of how the hopes for social, political, and economic justice that carried a generation of Salvadorans to mobilize for social change jut up against an increasingly neoliberal postwar economy that remarginalizes newly reincorporating oppositional citizens. As such, this study falls squarely within what has become an important topic in the anthropological study of much of Latin America: the aftermath of violence in post-conflict societies. Recent research has shown that transitions from war to peace, from state-sponsored violence to internationally observed, democratic elections, bring with them new modalities of violence that continue to marginalize the subaltern (Rojas Pérez 2008). From Aquilino, peasant revolutionary and community leader, to Miguel, the generation for whom the revolution was waged, we can trace the ways in which a "continuum of violence" (Bourgois 2002) entangles the lives of self-identified former revolutionaries, their kin, neighbors, followers, and leaders. Theirs is a story of precarious lives lived, of multiple losses, and of battles hard won. This is a story that moves from the broken promises and bankrupt dreams of revolution to the broken hearts and new cars of postwar migrations.

Overview

A series of questions guide this book and are elaborated in ethnographic chapters that privilege the complexities of people's lives. These questions include the following: How have people moved from participatory models of revolutionary action to the difficult task of nation-building while still inhabiting the margins? How do their emergent identities—gendered and historically based simultaneously in locality and displacement—as oppositional citizens in the making, conflict with the state's neoliberal agendas, the Left, and their own visions for the future? And, ultimately, what are the possibilities of socioeconomic and political justice for the everyday revolutionaries turned undocumented migrants? In parsing these questions, I explore the limits of a transition to democracy, what Philippe Bourgois terms the lies of democracy (2006). I do so in El Salvador through the practices of survivors of a civil war who carry the legacies of both their wartime activism and postwar fatigue. The everyday practices of democratization are entangled by the legacies of revolutionary activism.

This entanglement is seen vividly through a close study of the region, specifically, in observing the lived experiences of every day life. Ethnography is best suited for this endeavor, and as a result I focus on the residents of a repopulated community that I call El Rancho in the municipality of Las Vueltas and in the Department of Chalatenango (see figure 1, country and region map). During the war throughout the region, residents fled their small communities, either joining the insurgency or becoming displaced peoples in refugee camps in Honduras. Many returned to reclaim their communities beginning in 1987, though a majority were unable to settle back to their places of origin. Meaning, while many returned to a familiar region, most could not rebuild their former homes, cultivate their fields, and so on. Throughout the book I introduce several postwar protagonists and seek to illuminate the complexities of their lives and the analysis they bring with them. In all cases, I provide pseudonyms to ensure confidentiality. For example, readers will come to know Elsy from El Rancho, who in the early 1990s typified the "peasant revolutionary woman." She was a former combatant, medic, cook, mother of four, outspoken, energetic, always volunteering to travel not only to the capital of Chalatenango but to San Salvador to participate in demonstrations or educational workshops. Her experiences, exhilaration, fatigue, her "fearless talk," and her transgressions become a metaphor for postwar processes. Readers will also come to know several of her children and their migration stories.

An organizing theme of my analysis of postwar entanglements is a play with time and perspective, my own and the subjects of this book. This allows me to trace and reanalyze unfolding events. Along with this foregrounding of individual trajectories, also notable is the book's experimentation with structure. Borrowing from reflexive anthropology and feminist praxis, this book draws on recent innovative ethnographic texts (Biehl 2005; Nordstrom 2004; Tsing 2005), most clearly evidenced in the sections that I describe as "interstitials," writings that fall between the more conventional ethnographic chapters that build arguments around ethnographic data and social theory. These are positioned pieces aimed to reveal, highlight, position, or direct the reader toward upcoming chapters in terms of images, emotion, critique, perplexity, and so on. Because of the richness of the book's form, below I provide a roadmap for upcoming chapters.

Chapter 1 provides an overview of what I term the entangled aftermaths of war and displacement. Here I introduce larger theoretical issues on gender and war, development, democracy and displacement, and the politics of memory. I also provide the larger ethnographic setting of El Rancho and the ethico-politics of my research positioning. To further contextualize entanglements of postwar, in chapter 2 I briefly summarize the Salvadoran war. This chapter serves to set up chapter 3, "Rank-and-File History," which offers the words and lives of several men and women who "walked and fell through those mountains" during the war, as one survivor so poignantly put it. These war stories support, amplify, and open up more questions about the past through the narratives and memories of differently positioned men and women who participated in the armed struggle and popular organizing beginning in the 1970s. Specifically, this chapter juxtaposes the grander rhetorics of war (i.e., prewar organizing histories, armed struggle, the peace accords) with the everyday accounts of gendered suffering. Theoretically, an analysis of social memory structures this chapter as history is told through the selective tellings of several grassroots activists and residents of El Rancho.

The interstitial "NGO War Stories" introduces not only the importance of non-governmental organizations (NGOs) in postwar politics and economies but specifically highlights the importance of the charismatic leadership of Daysi, a central protagonist of NGO processes in Chalatenango. As I offer two narratives of gendered violence and motherhood in war, I illustrate how oppositional NGOs are also keepers of the past. I do so in order to foreshadow chapter 4, "NGOs in the Postwar Period," a presentation of the explosion of NGOs in post-conflict areas. This chapter locates the emerging relationships, practices, and discourses of local development historically absent in Chalatenango. I introduce the grassroots group CCR (Coordinator of Communities in Development in Chalatenango) and the NGO CORDES (Foundation for the Cooperation and Community Development of El Salvador). A longitudinal and textual perspective that tracks NGO circuits through their different forms of activism and priorities and through different methodological perspectives frames the chapter. It does so, however, not as a story about a development industry but rather in order to flesh out the social field for the majority of Chalatecos who continue to carve out lives marked by political, economic, and social uncertainty.

"Stitching Wounds and Frying Chicken" is a positioned piece that sets up a critical chapter (5), "Not Revolutionary Enough?" which is the apex of the book's argument on the plight of residents of repopulated communities. In this interstitial I introduce Chayo, a vocal thinker, activist, and critic who finds herself in the early 2000s in New Jersey. This account also foregrounds the silences that must be respected. It is in chapter 5 that I explicitly explore a decline in gendered community participation that emerges in the transition to democratization. The chapter highlights the formation of disillusionment through the circulation of a moral discourse of heroic, sacrificing participation and the resistance to it in the discourse of lies. A discourse of blame and a language of crisis circulates and juts up against the material reality of emerging stratification as residents are accused of being either too revolutionary—failing in neoliberal development— or not revolutionary enough, "losing" their oppositional identities and "forgetting" the past of wartime organizing and the unity of struggle. Strikingly, this is only five years into the transition to peace-building. Why the anxiety over forgetting and with such immediacy? In part I demonstrate how wartime social relations, activism, and survival are held up as the model and voiced as the ideal for community life. But important questions remain: How can the wartime sacrifice of home, family, community, and bodies be expected to move into the postwar present? How much community participation can be asked of people? Are the answers to these questions found in highlighting former participants' couched words and hushed critiques? Are they found in later undocumented migration?

As will become clear, Chalatenango's postwar arc is highly politicized. "FMLN Snapshots" offers several ethnographic encounters of the ways in which party politics infuse development practices via the fluidity of leaders' bodies that inhabit party, NGO, and community spaces. Indeed, development in the region is intimately linked to oppositional electoral politics (voting for the FMLN) and an everyday practice that espouses the ideals of community-led and participative democracy. In the early to intermediate postwar period, northeastern Chalatenango's repopulated communities were homogenously FMLN supporters. This interstitial provides a bridge from which to theorize the time and space of transitions where the struggle is one that could be posed as a question: How to carve out oppositional politics, create alternative productive economies, push gender equity, and struggle against an agentless-appearing global capitalism that sweeps over El Salvador with the name of poverty?

Chapter 6, "Cardboard Democracy," brings an ethnographic attention to discussions of democracy and details how democracy is fragile and shallow.

In particular, I seek to show how postwar political subjects are regulated and disciplined in El Salvador and across its borders through NGO functions previously held by the state. In doing so, I build from an interest in governmentality and root this literature in a history of popular education and contemporary reeducation, which I argue spawns "flip-chart development," a form of technology that focuses on bottom-up training. A central aim of this chapter is to show the specificity of the Chalateco case as distinguished precisely by the legacy of revolutionary empowerment. Ultimately, I suggest that development be understood as a resocialization of survivors of the civil war into contentious citizens who engage in a politics of resistance to continued processes of exclusion.

Following this chapter, "Aftermaths of Solidarity" is a poem that is intended to do various things. First, it builds on the theme of forgetting that is part of the postwar landscape. Second, it positions the author and makes transparent the historically under-theorized place of family in ethnographic research. Third, most importantly, the chapter that follows, chapter 7, "Conning Revolutionaries," discusses the invisibility and spaces of corruption that open up in the postwar period for women in the transition to democracy. Building on the literature on women's social movements under democratization, I expose the underbelly of this process: waning social movements for justice and the impact of the shrinking state in women's lives. More importantly, in the context of the post-Beijing international women's movement, this chapter uncovers the spaces of corruption as women survivors of a civil war appropriate the new language of women's rights while tragically becoming victims of a political scam by a group named MOLID. Women's framing of *"mucho más perdimos en la guerra"* (we lost so much more in the war) addresses humanistic questions of suffering.

Key questions guide this chapter: How could a group of savvy former activists get caught up in an increasingly obvious economic fraud masked under the legitimizing rubric of "women's movement"? Why would this create such strife within politically homogenous communities? As I seek to answer these questions, I also discuss the ethics of an engaged research agenda, as my participation in blocking MOLID arguably caused more harm than good as community schisms escalated. The chapter also contributes to our understanding of why in El Salvador the struggle for economic justice that framed prewar and wartime organizing, though marginalized in the postwar period, trumps human rights practices, discourses, and use of legal mechanisms at the grassroots level.

A final poem, "Postwar Dance," opens up a conversation on the generation socialized in and through war, the children of the protagonist generation. It is followed by chapter 8, "The Postwar Highway." Open leading Salvadoran newspapers and one will find entire sections devoted to the "15th department," which refers to the Salvadoran diaspora in the United States. As the most recent human development report by the United Nations Development Programme argues, El Salvador's human development indicators must include Salvadorans building communities in the United States. This chapter builds from the exciting field of transnational migration but is uniquely positioned in its longitudinal depth, unraveling a migratory puzzle from the mid 1990s, when migration was not a primary option, an unimagined path for the Chalatecos at the heart of this book. This chapter offers the provocative analysis that it is through migration that material and ideological revolutionaries deterritorialize the Salvadoran transition to democracy and work against the demoralization of their postwar pasts, the inability to find redress for war and postwar injustices, while confronting the structural inequalities of their participation in the U.S. labor market. Methodologically, this chapter also addresses the ways in which the ethnographer becomes a repository for migrants' social memories first recorded in El Salvador.

I conclude the book with an epilogue, "Amor Lejos, Amor de Pendejos" (Long distance love is for fools), the lingering words voiced by Elsy one late evening as we talked about love and politics in El Salvador. The chapter plays with the ideas of distance, time, sacrifice, and battles for love. I weave a story about the difficulties of building a historical memory site to commemorate El Rancho's dead with the hopes and dreams of migrants and those who are stuck in El Salvador. The book ends by suggesting the importance of temporality, how this story could not be told without multiple narrative arcs told across time and space.

Taken together, *Everyday Revolutionaries* offers that it is imperative to examine the analytically expected structural traumas (i.e., the challenges of healing the social fabric of war-torn societies, the damages of uneven global capitalism). But also, it is important to give voice to the unexpected joys, those unexpected productive frictions (Tsing 2005) that come about as Chalateco migrants recreate their "warrior" pasts and present and earn their never quite enough dollars. In somber stories of war and postwar we must also seek to interpret, though not romanticize, the experiences of joy, agency, resistance, and the pleasure of things—Miguel's new car. Ultimately, my hope is that the ethnographic insights developed regarding the dynamics of postwar rebuilding, community development, historical memory, and the politicized issue of migration can shed light on what has now become a global postwar development and peace-building industry. For now, I spotlight one case as it unfolds.

1

Entangled Aftermaths

Postwar El Salvador is defined by what I term the *entangled aftermaths* of war and displacement, aftermaths that have produced postwar deception and disillusionment. I use the metaphor of entanglement to theorize postwar lives as enmeshed, ensnared, confused, and intertwined yet deeply involved.[1] It is in this material, physical, and internal space that Chalatecos live with their embodied trauma and speak for a generation lost to war and for the next generation socialized through it. In this enmeshing people reflect upon the lies of revolution and democracy and remake their worlds in fraught spaces and times. For in the transition from war to peace, larger processes discursively and materially reframe Chalatenango's "subversives," "communists," and "terrorists" of the Cold War's proxy war into legitimate neoliberal subjects. In different contexts community members are asked contradictorily to relinquish their identities as "revolutionaries" and to develop a new sense of themselves as productive yet marginalized postwar citizens via the same rubric of "participation" that fueled their revolutionary action. This policy of participation shapes and is shaped by various actors—local grassroots organizations, nationally driven neoliberal development, and international donors.

Central to my analysis is a long-term view of what happens in the aftermath of protracted war. This is a call for extending ethnographies of reconciliation (i.e., Sanford 2003; Theidon 2007) across time and space. In this case, I trace the lives of the rank-and-file members of El Salvador's historic struggle for justice and reconstruction by following community members along their journey from revolutionary activists to postwar development recipients and ambivalent grassroots actors and to, in many cases, now undocumented migrants. In juxtaposing these cartographic shifts, I render more visible the vulnerabilities and possibilities for the everyday participants who moved both in and out of armed and political combat and in and out of postwar development and nation-building projects, often to the chagrin of those in various levels of command.

Ethnographically and theoretically, the book is structured around two moments: the immediate postwar period of reconstruction (1993–1998) and the more recent period of emigration from El Salvador to the United States (2000–2008). As a result, the book is necessarily multi-sited and longitudinal. In the first period, I concentrate on the rebuilding of repopulated communities—areas destroyed during the war and reclaimed by the depopulated civilian population and protected to a fair degree by the FMLN revolutionary forces. Reconstruction during the 1990s in these formerly revolutionized communities took place through the close association between residents and two leading organizations in Chalatenango, an under-funded human rights grassroots group (CCR, Coordinator of Communities in Development in Chalatenango) and a relatively well-funded development non-governmental organization (CORDES, Foundation for the Cooperation and Community Development of El Salvador). Thus, in order to unpack local rebuilding, I take on an analysis of grassroots spaces. Like Mark Schuller (2008), I am not interested in pursuing an analysis of "failed NGOs" or failed revolutions as they become entangled. Rather, "instead of *having* failed, these NGOs *have been* failed by the same neoliberal policies and institutions that are ostensibly working toward their participation and empowerment" (Schuller 2008, 68, emphasis in original). I suggest turning to the politics of NGO development through the perspectives of residents of a particular repopulated community, which I call El Rancho. El Rancho is served by CCR and CORDES and during the 1990s was deemed in "organizational crisis"—not quite at the activist level expected of longtime warriors and of neighboring, more "advanced" repopulated communities such as Guarjila and San José Las Flores.

The second phase of this project emerges unexpectedly at the turn of the twenty-first century when residents from El Rancho begin immigrating for the first time to the United States in large numbers. Analyzing this migration rematerializes the field of this study and begs for a reconceptualization that deterritorializes the possibility of democracy in formerly revolutionized spaces. For in part this book will argue that a failure of democracy in El Salvador is embodied both in the undocumented, unauthorized, or prohibited migration of its citizens (Coutin 2007) whose labor keeps the nation afloat and in the lives of those who are stuck, who cannot move and rely on the economic remittances and capital of their migrating kin in order to survive (Gregory 2006). In other words, I demonstrate the ways in which the impact of neoliberal structural adjustment policies pursued by the Salvadoran state, the economic concessions made by the FMLN, and the often-romanticized spaces of NGOs and grassroots development politics conspire to remarginalize members of destroyed communities, subordinating them to a neoliberal, conservative political agenda.

Several thematic and theoretical frameworks guide this book. In the section that follows I highlight key ideas that will be developed ethnographically in subsequent chapters. First, I situate the Salvadoran case in relationship to discussions of violence in war and peace. This sets up my later theorizing on postwar processes saturated with disillusionment as emerging from the extremes or the excess of mobilization. Second, the expansive literature on practices of memory, individual, collective, national, and so on, is introduced in order to privilege the words of survivors. Chalateco narratives serve as key sites to pursue an analysis of disillusionment that shapes this book. A focus on memory becomes a methodological tool for understanding the gendered experiences of violence in war and peace. A third thematic interest explores the connections between NGOs, development, and democratization. When I first started this project, scholarship and policy on gender and development were emerging as central concerns in the literature on transitions to democracy throughout the global south. I tackle this subject in depth in chapter 7, but first, in this chapter, I set up the ethnographic setting in which development unfolds. I also introduce how displacements continue after war as I build from the literature of migration. The chapter ends with a discussion of feminist and engaged research practices, which highlights the entanglements of representation, storytelling, and accountability.

Violence, Gender, and Memory

The anthropology of Latin America has taken on the study of violence and its aftermath. In particular, the field has developed insights into local social movements that contest oppression and to the lived experience of suffering. I build on this wave of anthropological scholarship on political violence (i.e., Daniel 1996; Feitlowitz 1998; Feldman 1991; Nordstrom 1997, 2004; Paley 2001; Poole 1994; Sanford 2003; Scheper-Hughes 1992) in its pursuit of how the everyday of aftermath is lived by those who attempt to rebuild their lives under democracy.

As will become clear in the stories I weave together, my analysis builds deeply from Philippe Bourgois's elaboration of a "continuum of violence" (2002) and Paul Farmer's work on structural violence (2001).[2] Like Bourgois, I provide instances of the ways in which symbolic violence "normalizes" structural violence attributing the seemingly "everyday interpersonal violence that the poor visit on each other to their alleged character flaws" (Bourgois 2002, 222). Complementing Farmer's concept of structural violence, Bourgois calls for explaining how this violence is "experienced by its victims through its various interfaces with other forms of violence—symbolic, everyday, and political" (2002, 222). Salient for my case study is Bourgois's thesis on how subjects theorize this violence. They place blame locally, most intimately on the self. Indeed, this is the symbolic violence that discursively constructs, as we will come to see, revolutionaries in places like El Rancho as simultaneously too revolutionary or not revolutionary enough. This is a violence that "weighs down heavily" (Bourgois 2002, 229) and that produces often paralyzing demoralization. NGOs blame local peoples, and local peoples blame NGOs and their community leaders for the violence of neoliberal democracy that is felt in the failed economic development projects of peace. Years later, the local is exploded as residents from the northeast of Chalatenango begin their journeys into the United States.

A contradiction of peace is that violence has continued. Making sense of this fact has been the subject of much public discussion in the media, in national and international scholarship, in government policy, and in international development, not to mention people's everyday talk where violence is hierarchized (Moodie 2006). Ellen Moodie's expertly crafted analysis of people's postwar crime stories illuminates the ways in which the transition to democracy is "stunted" and how it is that so many Salvadorans narrate their postwar lives as "worse than the war" given that experiences and understandings of violence have shifted since the war (2010, 10). Recent figures estimate the homicide rate at fifty-four murders per one hundred thousand people, leading Central America in homicide rate for 2006 (Henríquez 2006). Organized crime, depicted in the body of gangs, now infused with the specter of transnational reach, is at the center of these conversations as gangs are seen as both the product and cause of the violence (see Coutin 2007; Moodie 2009; Zilberg 2007). Anna and Brandt Peterson synthesize the postwar experiences of violence as follows: "The sense that violence is an omnipresent and arbitrary threat, unmappable and so unavoidable, pervades everyday life. Unlike martyrs during the war, those who die in these conditions do not knowingly choose a path whose likely end is death" (2008, 532).

What research in the last decade also makes clear, throughout Latin America as well as in other democratizing regions such as Eastern Europe and South Africa, is that wartime violence and people's memories of that violence are gendered though not necessarily in "common-sensical ways" (Theidon 2007, 454). Much research has explored violence against women during wars and has been critical in unmasking rape as a weapon of war, indeed, a war crime (see Moser and Clark 2001). A new field of transitional justice has developed alongside this attention to women and war as, in many countries undergoing a transition from conflict to peace, Truth Commissions have been created that often contest official versions of history (Hayner 2001). These Truth Commissions seek to uncover wartime human rights violations. In doing so, a central goal is to hold violators accountable, end impunity, and suggest paths for national reconciliation. These are victim-centered approaches that attempt to write a more "inclusive history" (Theidon 2007, 456). Inherent to Truth Commissions is a therapeutic model, where the need for victims to talk is naturalized as a key component of the healing process in democracy making. These processes involve a complicated balance between remembering and forgetting. Indeed, in the Peruvian case, Theidon repeatedly remarks that women themselves called for forgetting. This is striking and in stark contrast with Sanford's groundbreaking work in Guatemala, where widows of war and indigenous men and women survivors of genocide claim universal human rights discourses and practices in order to fight for truth and justice as they continue to call for the exhumations of clandestine graves (Sanford 2003).

While not all Truth Commissions have been explicitly gendered, the Salvadoran case was not, though some Truth Commissions like those in South Africa, Guatemala, and Peru have; in most cases women's testimonies have been sought (Hayner 2001; Theidon 2007). Analyses of these efforts further expose gendered experiences and accountings of war. Kimberly Theidon, working on Peru's Truth and Reconciliation Commission (PTRC), opens up the assumptions that underscore a "gender-sensitive" approach to reconciling wartime violence. One of her aims is to "offer a more nuanced understanding of the gendered dimensions of war" (Theidon 2007, 454). While the PTRC efforts created a space for the accounting of women's experiences of wartime violence, they did so in search of particular kinds of truths and types of sexualized violence—rape against women. In contrast, Theidon suggests that women's experiences of war were broader but that also memories of violence themselves are gendered (2007, 459).

This analysis complements my ethnographic findings. In the chapters that follow readers will find that narratives about the past and memories of violence depend upon many factors such as gender, the actor's positioning in the revolutionary social movement, and prewar and postwar poverty and activism. Like Theidon, I did not seek out women's narratives of sexualized violence nor construct the category of woman sufferer or survivor of rape. In some cases these stories emerged, as will be seen in chapter 3, where rape, mutilation, and death commingle, but in most narratives I collected from men and women, after El Salvador's Truth Commission, I am struck by the ways in which surviving the everyday indecencies of war—the "ordinary" heroism of saving babies from hunger, illness, of finding ways to school them, the daily struggle of survival, fight, and flight—was lived differently by men and women. Like Theidon I am also attentive to what she terms the "economics of memory" and what I see as another aspect of a politics of memory that I describe further in a subsequent section on my position as a researcher. Theidon writes, "There is a tacit agreement in the giving and receiving of testimonies, an implicit promise that some form of justice will be forthcoming" (Theidon 2007, 474). Perhaps Aquilino would describe this agreement also as spectral.

Central to the Salvadoran case, then, particularly for the region of Chalatenango, is the heroic capital attributed to war. Narratives of war are deployed to make sense of not only the past, but the present and the future. Daily life is marked by acts and relationships of social memory. Through public

events, festivals, and everyday practices, Chalatecos of all ages engage in a bal-
ancing act of trauma and pain, hope and healing. A key finding is that many
Chalatecos experience the postwar as full of deceit and disillusionment. They
seek to identify what is true (*verdad*) and what is a lie (*mentira*) about a postwar
world that many interpret as a constant battle against deception (*engaño*). For a
call to "rescue the past" circulates across Chalatenango, in contradistinction to
a national rebuilding policy predicated on amnesia. As a result, I am attentive
to how the present is shaped by the negotiation of remembering and forgetting both personal and collective trauma, and the ways this continues to socialize and structure life. In doing so, I privilege men's and women's narratives,
their theories of explanation (Ochs et al. 1994; Polkinghorne 1988). The following chapters illuminate how this call to remember, this discipline to remember,
is resisted and accommodated.

Analyzing a call for historical memory and a discourse of disillusionment is
a central concern of this book. The protagonists of this story are called upon to
build from their heroic collective memories of battles, sacrifice, and suffering.
Specifically, I build from Thomas Abercrombie's cogent definition of social memory where he uses the term to "convey the embodied ways by which people constitute themselves and their social formations in communicative actions and
interactions, making themselves by making rather than inheriting their pasts.
Recollecting and commemorating the past always takes place in contingent
contexts where power is at play. As a result, alternative forms of social memory
and alternative possibilities for construing the social are always in contention"
(1998, 21).

Speaking on the condition of anonymity, an NGO critic of postwar rebuilding processes in Chalatenango, whom I will call Victor, offers a way to understand how people make their pasts rather than inheriting them. Sitting in the
San Salvador home I shared with three international development volunteers,
away from the gaze of Chalatenango's NGO sphere, he agreed to an interview.
With two Pilsners fresh out of the refrigerator and my rather large Sony tape
recorder placed on a white plastic coffee table between us, small Lavalier micro-
phones properly pinned onto our shirts, Victor suggests another way to think
about the demoralization of former rank-and-file revolutionaries and the place
of NGO leadership in reproducing marginalization.[3] He proposes that we look at
the idea, the capacity, the emotion of "happiness." He tells me the postwar is
characterized by a political and economic shift away from sacrifice and toward a
search for happiness:

> The people are no longer willing to sacrifice their happiness, *entre comillas*
> (in quotes), of today for a "happiness" in one hundred years—or keep sac-
> rificing today for the future generations. In reality, I believe that people
> have understood that the struggle is a struggle to be happy today and

tomorrow, tomorrow but also today. . . . The historic leaders cannot continue to demand the same type of sacrifice as in that period. And not only
because the conditions are different, but because subjectively the people
feel that they should not have to keep doing that kind of sacrifice. . . . So,
I believe that the historic leaders, among other errors, make a daily one,
and that is to believe that they can keep having the vertical control and
discipline of that period.

From sacrifice to happiness, in and out of discipline. And in quotes, *entre
comillas*. Why exactly? What can we find in between those quotes? His words
echo Anna and Brandt Peterson's analysis that in the postwar, the call for
memories of sacrifice is "replaceing the call to arms of the war years"; in this
context, "suffering is no longer part of a collective struggle, their agents are no
longer identifiable oppressors, and death is most often rendered as simply
what is" (2008, 536; emphasis in original).

Development and Diasporic Lives

An attention to gender, violence, and the politics of memory in aftermaths must
be contextualized by the larger political and economic forces that characterize
El Salvador's transition from war to peace. After the war, El Salvador entered
into a phase of national reconstruction. While policy analysts and scholars have
discussed a lack of a cogent, long-term development plan, it is ironic that the
decade of the 1990s conflated reconstruction and development both within the
Salvadoran government and in NGO sectors. In places like Chalatenango, long
marginalized, development entered repopulated communities in the form of
new roads, electrification, cement-block houses, and an array of gender-specific
community micro-enterprise projects such as chicken and pig farming projects.
In subsequent chapters I pay special attention to these programs and the discourse around them. As I do so I build upon analyses that foreground processes
of uneven capitalist development and highlight development as a discourse
and technology that constructs marginalized places as problems to be fixed via
modern, capitalist projects (Escobar 1995, Ferguson 1994).

I did not predict that the former revolutionaries chastised for forgetting their
lived history in the mid to late 1990s and simultaneously for not getting development "right" would by the turn of the twenty-first century join a fourth wave of
Salvadoran migrants primarily moving into the United States.[4] Anthropology as
a discipline inherently throws its practitioners into the midst of things and as a
general rule does not train for the making of predictions. In retrospect, I should
have seen it coming. As will be further elaborated in the next chapter, the peace
accords did not establish a cogent development plan or address the underlying
economic inequalities that underscored the war. As economic policy analysis

further elaborates (Gammage 2006; Stephen et al. 2001), neoliberal reforms instituted by the ARENA (National Republican Alliance) government produced new inequities, creating a situation where the nation's primary mode to engage globalization is through the emigration of its citizens (UNDP 2005). Development cannot be discussed outside of migration. It is in this context that the men and women with whom I worked in Chalatenango, and their now adult children, find themselves, I argue, "obligated" to journey to the United States. As Sarah Gammage further asserts, El Salvador's development plan is located in the "exporting" of its people (2006). Of El Salvador's 6.8 million people, 1.5 million Salvadorans are estimated to live in the United States (Gammage 2006, 75).

A significant body of literature has explored migratory experiences and the formation of what has come to be understood as transnational processes. Some of these analyses are more celebratory than others, but most contextualize experiences within the insecurity of crossing borders. As first articulated, this field is predicated on an understanding that bodies, identities, goods, capital, and so on move bi-directionally, creating new diasporic identities and social relationships. For example, Lynn Stephen (2007) builds from Levitt and Glick Schiller's (2004) notion of a "transnational social field" in order to theorize the diversity of migrants and nonmigrants who inhabit new modes of mobility and immobility across generations. Stephen explores the challenges, political, cultural, and economic, that they incur in the multiple borders crossed. Robert Smith, in perhaps the clearest elaboration of the modalities of migration, describes the "transnational life," at once global and local for a "mature migrant community" (2006, 47). Like Stephen he is attentive to questions of gender, generation, and the agency of migrants' political lives. Comparatively, the Chalatecos in this study are recent migrants. They do not join kin networks with a long history of migration, and, in general, they leave their history of political mobilization behind. They are not the actors, for example, involved in advocating for immigration rights in the United States.

As Susan Bibler Coutin makes clear, Salvadorans in the diaspora, and in the United States in particular, defined as El Salvador's "15th Department" (there are fourteen departments, like states, in the territory of El Salvador), are "physically present but legally absent, existing in a space outside of society, a space of 'nonexistence,' a space that is not actually 'elsewhere' or beyond borders but that is rather a hidden dimension of social reality" (2007, 9). In their journeys they may aspire for the "American Dream" but "at best most rise merely from penniless greenhorn to working poor, and that *is* an accomplishment" (Mahler 1995, 137, emphasis in original). It is the lives of the undocumented, the unauthorized, and the prohibited (Coutin 2007) that interest me in this book. The entanglements of a clandestine past within the "shadows" of legality and illegality (Nordstrom 2004) constitute the everyday reality for a majority of recent Chalateco migrants.[5]

This leads me to ponder the ways in which local or regional calls for revolutionary identities rub up against a "Salvadoran national identity" that "includes migration and mobility as one of its central characteristics" (Baker-Cristales 2004, 98). For as nations "leak" (Coutin 2007), citizens redefine borders, but states just as quickly create new tactics of control, first evidenced in the monument commemorating the exile (*el hermano lejano*) and later in the creation of new state apparatuses such as the Dirección General de Atención a las Comunidades en el Exterior (Baker-Cristales 2004; 2008; Gammage 2006). It is on this state Web site that I find the municipality of Las Vueltas detailed as one of the thirty poorest municipalities in the nation and in need of development support. I think back to the many NGO and grassroots meetings of the 1990s that I attended in Las Vueltas asking for more development from and for oppositional citizens. Today, this is a call beyond the state, as multinational lending institutions such as the Inter-American Development Bank and the World Bank are also "encouraging government programs to channel individual and collective remittances" (Gammage 2006, 76).[6]

Through these thematic areas: gender, violence, memory, development, and diaspora, I ethnographically interpret postwar processes in a former conflict zone in terms of the complexities and contradictions that *campesinos* (peasants) face in their everyday lives through time.[7] Throughout the book I will be using the term *campesino* to talk about people who live in rural places in Chalatenango (who engage in various forms of labor practices, not only subsistence agriculture). Like Jeffrey Gould (1990) I suggest using categories that are meaningful to people and used by them. And like William Roseberry, I believe that "peasants" should be located in specific contexts and formations. Roseberry explains, "I retain the word *peasant* as a matter-of-fact way of talking about rural villagers, agriculturalists, tenants and smallholders, making no claims and drawing no inferences about their historical trajectories, moral and ethical dilemmas, political capacities and incapacities" (1993, 362 emphasis in original).

I trace my interest to a long interdisciplinary history of "peasant studies" and "agrarian conflict" (see Stern 1987).[8] Scholarship, both historical and anthropological, has since heeded Stern's call to approach peasantries as agents who "resist, ameliorate or survive the destructive effects of capitalism" (1987, 5).[9] Roseberry's analyses on the formation of peasantries through time, on state-formation, and on uneven capitalist development and the need to understand processes locally and regionally ground my thinking on political economy, defined as a complex reading of the tensions between global and local processes and structure and agency as it situates peasantries through time within regional, national, and global structures or systems of power (see Roseberry 1988, 1993). As Roseberry states, "unless we move toward detailed local studies, we are left with the romance of resistance rather than 'the manifold ways whereby peasants have continuously engaged their political worlds'" (1993, 359). Mine is a conscious attempt to resist the romance of counter-hegemonic mobilizations. I make this clear shortly as I elaborate my research practices. For the anthropologist is also entangled. But first, we need a bit more context.

Ethnographic Setting: The White Indians in a Forgotten Land

They are white and rosy skinned, with blond or light brown hair and light eyes, either green or blue. They are the Chalatecos who are "relatively pure descendents of the Spanish colonizers" assures the Lic. Concepción Clara de Guevara.

Orsy Campos, "Somos Una Mezcla de Colores"

Chalatenango, located in the northeast of the country, is a rural, mountainous region, historically a frontier land and a marginalized department of the nation. The classic and prevailing depiction of Chalatenango is one of a department settled by small-scale Ladino farmers cultivating indigo for commercial production and simultaneously engaging in subsistence practices (Browning 1971, 162). This is a picture of Chalatecos living in dispersed sites in the mountains, with generally poor quality soils and with only some areas adequate for cattle. Chalatenango's "resources," then, are its people, a steady labor reserve. A daily newspaper in 1965 documents the "problems" of the department: "(Chalatenango) with its thin soils, deforested, misused, exhausted and eroded, its primitive agriculture unassisted by capital investment or modern supervision, and its social cohesion weakened by economic decline, dispersal of settlement and migration, gradually became the country's poor, backward and neglected *tierra olvidada* of the present century" (*La Prensa Gráfica*, November 23, 1965, in Browning 1971, 163).

As the director of Chalatenango's UN-funded PDHS (Programa de Desarrollo Humano Sostenible [Program on Sustainable Human Development]) explained to me, the department was and continues to be *"una tierra expulsadora"* (a land that expels). By 1961, Chalatenango had the highest rate of internal migration in the nation (Pearce 1986, 49). The 1971 census indicates that 10 percent of farms covered 75 percent of the land. Thus, 90 percent of farms that are smaller than ten hectares each cover only 25 percent of the land (Pearce 1986, 53). More dramatically, the 1971 census reports that of the 18,989 of these small-scale land plots (*minifundios*), 8,325 were less than one hectare in size (Pearce 1986, 55)— unable to provide subsistence. A recent monograph by Carlos Lara Martínez (2005) corroborates this data. He suggests that there was a range of small landholdings where people pursued subsistence agriculture, planting corn, beans, and different types of squash, and where some peasants also survived by horticultural plots of land, growing tomatoes and cucumbers and raising chickens and pigs. Some peasants had between six and fifteen *manzanas* of land and were able to have cattle, whereas the majority owned no land or only had one-quarter or one-half of a manzana (Lara Martínez 2005, 31–32).[10]

The legacies of generations of Chalatecos mixed survival strategies of labor migration for coffee and cotton picking, cane cutting, and domestic work are evidenced daily in the still too high illiteracy rate, lack of access to health care and education, and so on (author interview with PDHS member, December 1997). This depiction resonates with my own data on prewar settlement patterns. In my discussions with repopulated residents and in the collection of life histories, as older residents described their childhood and their early engagement with oppositional organizing, they portrayed everyday life in these demographic terms. They portrayed the Chalatenango landscape as one comprised of distant communities with a dispersed population living in municipal *cantones* and even smaller residential clusterings (*caseríos*) surrounding a municipal seat, which was the village center. This has changed dramatically in postwar times, resulting from the military's wartime depopulation strategies and the subsequent resettlement patterns dictated by war conditions. Centralization of people has been privileged also because of the entrance of development projects. Smaller and more isolated communities tend to receive less development monies.

Much has been written, some journalistic, some academic, on the civil war that wracks Chalatenango, beginning in the 1970s. The next chapter situates Chalatenango within national processes and is followed by chapter 3, "Rank-and-File History," that is dedicated to understanding the war through the perspective of those who lived it. Many rural peoples from Chalatenango experienced the war deeply as political organizers, armed insurgents, community activists, paramilitary forces, or refugees. From the regional capital to remote, rural hamlets, communities became battlefields as many men and women across generations responded to state-sponsored repression. Thus, central to understanding the ethnographic context of postwar Chalatenango is the fact that, particularly in the northeast of the department, it was a conflict zone, a site of ongoing battle between state military forces and the FMLN that displaced the civilian population while they fought along with the guerilla forces.

Scholarship on the war has documented civilian participation and the gendered experiences of war and concurs with recent studies that suggest "the fact that families even survived the war is due to the courage, ingenuity and grit of women" as they carried the "triple load of family, community, and productive responsibilities" (Cosgrove 1999, 89).[11] Leigh Binford's analysis of wartime Morazán, a department under FMLN control (ERP rather than FPL) is also insightful. He explores FMLN hegemony in the region through the strategy of *"poder de doble cara"* (power of the double-face) that was critical for civilian survival in the campaign of low-intensity warfare. This was a strategy that involved civilians performing a "politically neutral (false) face" to government troops and a "politically committed (true) face" to the FMLN forces. Binford theorizes that this was a way

FIGURE 2. Photograph of painting on 12 × 12 inch thin piece of wood created by Chilango, Chalateco, *campesino* artist. The inscription on the back of the painting explains that it represents El Rancho during a bombing by the Armed Forces of El Salvador.

Painting by Chilango, Chalateco artist. Photograph by Antonio Rossi.

to incorporate more "resistant followers—*los atrasados*" (1998, 12). He suggests that consciousness-raising practices were successful precisely because few of these practices "penetrated to the core of inhabitants' daily practices, leaving the pre-existing *habitus* more or less unchallenged" (Binford 1998, 17, emphasis in original).

After the war these repopulated communities (*repoblaciones*) became for the first time primary targets of national and international reconstruction, evidenced in the surge of development projects in the area: electrification, potable water, housing, roads, and a host of women's projects such as literacy and microcredit. This brief summary of the formation of Chalatenango applies to the municipality of Las Vueltas and the community of El Rancho, the site of my ethnographic research.

The Municipality of Las Vueltas and the Community of El Rancho

Las Vueltas was one of the areas hardest hit during the war and was one of the original sites of a repopulation movement in 1987. The majority of residents reclaimed the municipality of Las Vueltas during a historic repatriation movement that began in October 1987 amidst the war as Salvadorans organized a mass return to El Salvador from the Mesa Grande refugee camp across the border in Honduras and run by UNHCR (United Nations High Commissioner for Refugees). Displacement defines the municipality. In 1977, the prewar population of the municipality was 5,081 (Hernández Rodríguez and Méndez 1996), and an estimated 44 percent of the department was displaced by the war (an estimated 8,301 people) (Halsband 1996, 10). Data from 1997 described the municipality as consisting of a municipal head and six surrounding cantones with a total population of 1,486 (more women than men), a 47.78 percent decrease resulting from the war (Funde 1997). I spent a significant amount of time in a large community I call El Rancho, in the municipality of Las Vueltas. In the mid to late 1990s there were seventy-nine houses and 319 people in El Rancho (Unidad de Salud Las Vueltas 1997). Residents did not repopulate to their original place of origin, in fact, there are only three families (*originarias*) originally from El Rancho who resettled there. Most residents are from nearby cantones and smaller caseríos. Others, through marriage, war ties, and refugee experiences, come from such distant departments as Usulután. In general, however, in the postwar period the municipality is comprised almost entirely of residents who define themselves through wartime oppression and agency as FMLN citizens. Most residents vote FMLN.

There are several factors behind my use of a pseudonym for El Rancho and for its residents. First, although El Salvador has made a transition to democracy, the history of political violence is still relatively recent. Second, because I discuss sensitive points about a leftist past and the challenges of NGO-led development, I do not want my findings decontextualized and used against community residents or grassroots activists. Additionally, many people I spoke with requested I not use their names, particularly when making critiques of the Left and in discussing their postwar moves. I have tried to be consistent in the balance between locating people and places and "protecting" them from the unintended consequences of my research.[12] And so I locate my fieldwork site in the department of Chalatenango, the municipality of Las Vueltas, but provide a pseudonym for the repopulated community that is at the heart of this study—El Rancho. Throughout the book, I provide pseudonyms for all residents of the repopulated communities, many who become the axes upon which I tell this story. While I have provided the actual names of the NGOs and grassroots organizations, I provide pseudonyms for all directors and staff.

Early postwar reconstruction in Las Vueltas addressed infrastructure needs: repairing destroyed homes through projects that brought in new cement-block houses, reestablishing and expanding schools, rebuilding churches, and paving roads. Early national and international funding was invested in urbanizing the municipal head town of Las Vueltas. The *alcaldía* (city hall—with its now multiple-elected FMLN mayor, most recently a woman) was rebuilt, a telephone station was erected to facilitate communication, though no longer needed as so many residents have mobile phones, a Ministry of Health Clinic was staffed, a rehabilitation center was instituted, and electricity was installed, starting from Las Vueltas and trickling to the surrounding cantones.

Along with a slowly moving land transfer program (PTT), a local development plan emphasized gendering reconstruction through the implementation of women's projects such as chicken and pig farming, cattle raising, arts and crafts, sewing workshops, and the creation of day-care centers, enabling women to work. These efforts were intended to incorporate former combatants, injured war veterans, and women (many of whom lost their male kin during the war through death, separation, or abandonment) into the productive economy and the development process. This focus on women was predicated both on the idea of mainstreaming gender and, significantly, on assumptions about women's wartime heroic participation in battle and as civilian support. This NGO-led development was also attractive to institutions like the World Bank and USAID and to critics of hegemonic development practices. As in many parts of the world, NGOs negotiate neoliberal desires, on the one hand, and, on the other, oppositional struggles that seek to politicize what development depoliticizes. However, as the transition from war to peace continued, early optimism gave way to the daily challenges and struggles of rebuilding.

In El Rancho, development "failures" cast the repoblación as *"una comunidad especial"* (a "special" community)—meaning a difficult community to work with—as a representative of an international development organization, Plan Internacional, explained.[13] He was not alone in his critique of El Rancho, for El Rancho is a community mapped out and critiqued by many actors, from community residents themselves to grassroots groups, political NGOs, and other development institutions working in the region. It was precisely this discourse that I wanted to disentangle. During the course of my fieldwork in El Rancho (seventeen months spanning from 1993 to 1997), the physical improvements were striking, yet the community experienced some trying times. Various actors articulated that the popular organizing that characterized the war was in "crisis." Community structures like the community council (*directiva*) were unraveling; coveted "sister city" status was never achieved,[14] and the women's projects placed in Chalatenango as a road to development had in almost all cases collapsed. Even the women's center—intended to serve and unite the region's women through regular meetings aimed at discussing women's issues and continuing with a long-term consciousness-raising project—was unused, closed, and covered with bat feces. Only the arts-and-crafts workshop still operated, providing erratic employment for six marginalized women, as orders for Salvadoran arts and crafts in the international solidarity market were decreasing already by 1996. A grass-roots needs-assessment study conducted in 1996 listed a series of necessities for the region. Lack of organization (*falta de organización*) ranked as a top problem.[15]

Thus, I selected El Rancho as a primary research site not only because of its geographic location in terms of its wartime history, access to other communities, incoming development projects, and so on, but more importantly because of its place in the imaginary of leading NGOs. These were organizations and grassroots groups making the professionalizing turn from emergency relief to internationally funded development work. Their directors, project leaders, and staff, if not from the very rural communities they served, had survived alongside residents during the war. Discursively, this leadership used El Rancho as a powerful and illustrative case. El Rancho epitomized the troubling postwar "organizational" crises taking over historically active, oppositional, and heroic revolutionary communities. Their analysis built upon a few things. One, the well-documented parastate structures communities developed during the war that allowed people to survive; and, two, the expectations of women's historic wartime courage, their participation in all fronts. NGO directors, former wartime leaders, were at a loss. What to make of wartime models in an ever-changing postwar landscape punctuated by some constants: poverty, exclusion, and human loss?

The director of Chalatenango's UN-funded PDHS provided another compelling and lucid analysis of postwar development which still holds. He explained, "One has to begin with a society in crisis and in various levels of crisis."[16] For this director, the key postwar challenge is to unite what he terms the "two maps of Chalatenango": a southern Chalatenango emerging from a *low-intensity* war that was characterized by continuous government and institutional presence with a northern Chalatenango, site of a *high intensity* war with ten municipalities abandoned, entire communities destroyed, and the birth of alternative popular organizing structures. The challenge is to address the double institutionality (*doble institucionalidad*), to coordinate the legacy of these alternative community structures with the post-1994 election return of municipal government bodies. Ultimately, this book focuses on residents of northern Chalatenango who negotiate this doble institucionalidad in their everyday lives: one repoblación, a grassroots group, and an NGO.

The legacies of the war and postwar are layered and unfolding as recent migration from these communities demonstrates. A UNDP study finds that migration from Las Vueltas to primarily the United States can be dated from 2001 to 2004, a time when the agricultural crises deepened (2005, 222). Throughout the municipality the percentage of households with at least one migrant is 30.9 percent (UNDP 2005, 223), though there are differences within the municipality with some communities having less or more experiences with migration. I now turn to my research method and location in both El Salvador and the United States.

Passing Tests of Solidarity: South American/ Gringa Anthropologist in the Making

1993 was a project-defining year. I had been tracking the grassroots activism of a New York City–based Salvadoran solidarity organization (which I at the time did not realize had strong links with the Communist Party of El Salvador [PCS]) when I received summer funding from New York University and traveled to El Salvador in search of revolutionary communities that were building peace. Though I began research with a naïve, romantic idea of peasant resistance, it was fortunately tempered by a budding ethnographer's keen sensibility to absorb the everyday practices of what was beginning to be termed a period of national reconstruction. I was at the right place at the right time.

Through personal contacts carried over from New York and Washington, D.C., three letters of "introduction" from my father's colleague working at the Pan American Health Organization set the course of my study: a letter to a female doctor who was married to a former *comandante* (military commander) of the ERP revolutionary forces based in war-torn Usulután, and who had lived her life in exile only to be abandoned by the ERP; a letter to the vice rector at the Universidad Centroamericana José Simeón Cañas (UCA), which gave me access to Salvadoran bibliographic research; and a letter to a young man who intro- duced me to CORDES. This was before the time of solidified email communica- tion. Writing a book typically does not take into account these intimate paths. Yet, if I had not taken those letters, at the time, completely unaware of the social and political networks I was stepping into with them, this could very well be an entirely different book. However, I was aware that I was focusing on ethno- graphically limited territory both in terms of the themes of postwar, reconcilia- tion, transitional justice, and NGOs, and geographically in terms of El Salvador itself.

I embarked onto an emergent academic interest in non-governmental organizations (NGOs) as key social movement actors and into an interdiscipli- nary conversation on democratization. For the revolutionaries I was in search of had become the postwar development beneficiaries of a variety of grassroots relief organizations and NGOs with strong links to the FMLN. During the Salvadoran rainy season of 1993, I met with the program directors of various NGOs that were either exclusively concerned with women's postwar trajectories (CONAMUS, MAM, CEMUJER, Las Dignas) or had programs on women and development (CORDES, CRIPDES).

I settled on the organization CORDES, but I had to pass a few tests of identity first. With my letters of introduction, a university identity card, and the earnest background reading and research questions that I was posing, my youth helped, along with a tongue-tied though fluent Argentine-inflected Spanish and, perhaps most importantly, a familiar middle-class whiteness associated with so many North American and European solidarity activists. At the CORDES central office in San Salvador I arranged transport with the directors of CORDES's largest regional office in Chalatenango, and I was immediately hooked by the charismatic leadership of Daysi, the director. Gaining entrance into "the field" has been written about in the anthropological literature, but, interestingly, in reading my journal it is clear that I was never quite sure what the field was. Everything was the field, the very process of figuring out that an NGO is an object of study, the field. Everyone I met was a potential project participant as many people were just getting used to wearing their heroic wartime participation on their sleeve. It seemed as though everyone I met on that first trip was a revolutionary. I was in awe, for example, of the young Chalateca with shrapnel in her leg who wore jeans to simultaneously conceal the injury and mark her embodied participation, all the while excusing herself from her campesina colleagues for not wearing like them a skirt just beneath the knees. Two years later she would marry and move to Europe.

I did not realize at the time that in meeting grassroots leadership like the young woman described above, I was indeed being scrutinized, and I was being placed in communities deemed appropriate for me to see and with peasant/ revolutionary women who were "doing development" in these communities. Before I could stay in these communities, I spent the week with CORDES and CCR staff and met the requirements for "being in solidarity." My forays into the field, the first in the summer of 1993, again in July 1994, and for an extended time from October 1996 to December 1997, mark the first seventeen months of ethnographic research in El Salvador. It is followed by longitudinal, more focused, transnational research that begins after my departure with the exchange of letters, then phone calls, and starting in 2006 with trips across the United States to visit recent Chalateco immigrants.

My research design in El Salvador included the following: participant observation in communities (primarily in the community of El Rancho) and of NGO and grassroots practices (CORDES and CCR, respectively); directed interviews with various community residents and CORDES and CCR members; the collection of life histories and conversations across social fields; and audio-taping of structured public events such as community general assemblies, CCR women's meetings, and CORDES's women's literacy workshops. My research design in the United States involved frequent phone calls with various recent migrants, the protagonist generation and the children of former revolutionaries with whom I worked in Chalatenango. Through short research trips, I engaged in their daily life, taking children to doctor's visits, cooking meals, meeting new friends, and conducted open-ended ethnographic interviews that addressed their migration experiences.

In both phases, my recorded and transcribed material is supported by extensive and detailed fieldnotes taken during and shortly after participant observation in the multiple sites of my project.[17] In El Salvador, I regularly visited homes and observed everyday practices. I also regularly attended women's meetings, community council meetings, and various workshops and evaluations sessions held by CORDES' Gender and Training Team and CCR's Women's Secretariat. This methodology enabled me to cover the range of local variation in terms of gender, generation, wartime experiences, and present economic and social differences. It also allowed me to unpack the layered crises that derail reconstruction and development as people debate their sacrificed futures. It is in exploring the points of articulation between community residents and NGO projects and policies that I have been able to evidence the contradictions and unintended consequences of reconstruction. For a while, fieldwork did not feel like fieldwork unless I had two meetings to attend a day.

Although the above is an adequate description of my methodology, it does not portray well the struggles of doing a politically engaged or activist anthropology (see Ramos 2000, Sanford and Angel-Ajani 2006) at a difficult juncture in El Salvador's transition to peace. While 1993 was a hopeful time, as the postwar was a recent phenomenon, when I returned in October of 1996, the Chalateco landscape (and Salvadoran landscape) was significantly different. New shopping malls, fast-food joints, and cinemas physically marked San Salvador's conversion to strip malls in some neighborhoods. Rural areas in Chalatenango were also "developed." A majority of the repopulated communities had received electrification projects, residents had purchased TVs, and as a result evening conversations had diminished. Housing projects had entered many communities and replaced emergency constructed homes with cement block structures with tile roofs in some cases. New roads made distant communities more accessible and there was more movement of people between places. However, by 1997 international development projects (and workers) had moved on to other sites, such as neighboring Guatemala, and there was a sense that El Salvador's issues, from this perspective, were resolved; and the country, on some level, fell off the map.

When I returned to Chalatenango, my nostalgia and, in retrospect, original problematic romance with "the country" and "the people" was quickly replaced by an even more problematic critique of a waning activism. I swallowed whole the local (and international) perspectives that blamed rural people for reconstruction problems because of their lack of participation, an unanticipated factor for areas that had experienced more than a decade of organization. With time, I was able to reframe my object of study but was left with troubling aspects of the romance of fieldwork and fieldworker. Particularly in studies of political violence, researchers' very personal placements deeply inform not only our interpretations but our very object of study. Along with making explicit our own positioning and the assumptions this brings with it (Narayan 1993), it is also important to make visible the ways in which we are read. El Salvador's long history with an international solidarity movement complicated my experiences, as this was how I was read by many Salvadorans, which brought with it a series of expectations that at times I met and at others I did not. Asale Angel-Ajani reminds us that, indeed, "where one works and how one looks when conducting that work factors in significantly. It is an old story that one's race, gender, sexuality, and social position can (and do) determine what kind of information one might receive, and influence the kind of knowledge produced" (2006, 85). I am reminded of the words of an elderly man in Las Vueltas, whose voice both states and questions my presence as he positions me in the recent history of North American and European solidarity activists. He explained to me that people like me come to El Salvador because of "our love for the people. (Vienen por lástima por nosotros.) They come because they pity us. They come to help us, not to swindle us. I think that is good, because we want to be helped." For pity and without deceit. I remember not being able to correct him. What to make of the notion of pity?

Day-to-day events informed by fieldwork practices and in situ theorizing indexed in fieldnotes are at the heart of this book. For example, with increasing violence, with several colleagues attacked in different contexts, with constant stories circulating by Chalatecos about the increasing violence on the highway from San Salvador to Chalatenango and from Chalatenango to Las Vueltas and about masked men pointing guns at busloads of people, and all of this framed by my collection of people's remembrances of wartime violence, my romance with the country was dwindling. There was a time in mid fieldwork when I chose to "input fieldnotes" in a small room in San Salvador rather than return to "the field" and attend that important meeting on women's empowerment. This "down" time (away from the field and "down" on El Salvador) was deeply troubling (I knew it was "wrong") and very isolating (though many scholars in my international network articulated similar thoughts). Yet, my departure from El Salvador and return to the academy was marked by a sense of dislocation. While an activist-inspired-anthropology rooted in the everyday nature of witnessing and engaged listening marked fieldwork, how could I carry this practice with me? Or as Angel-Ajani rightly asks about witnessing, "What and for whom does this form of observation advocate, and who benefits from this mode of engagement?" (2006, 80).

I include these personal transformations not as some sort of confession but rather to extend a conversation on methodology. Although the 1980s saw a critique on representation, I suggest a romance of the fieldworker experience mystifies and even erases how it is that we theorize and fashion our objects of study. This is an attempt to mark the silences that occur before we write. Part of the challenge of doing fieldwork on collective trauma is the important role of bearing witness to people's stories of the war, to their losses, to their fears, and to their continued struggle. Mostly this planted my feet firmly into the importance of my project and reaffirmed my commitment to make sense of postwar times. There were other occasions where I was not so generous. One day in particular, I recall my extreme exhaustion. I was still recovering from dengue fever and had spent the day traveling through Chalatenango, attending various meetings, and completing a very long interview. I walked to the *tienda* in El Rancho to relax, as I did on most days, but I entered into a conversational exchange that at any other time would have had my full attention. The *tienda* owner, Chayo, was recounting one of the times she had to flee from a military operation. I had heard about this *guinda*, this habitual flight into the hills, several times before from the perspective of other speakers, including her older sister. But on that day, my head was full of other people's voices, too many stories of past sufferings and present-day troubles. I could not listen to one more story (and the thought of more fieldnotes to write up on this exchange was overwhelming). As a result, I was an obviously vacant listener and (non)participant, ultimately trivializing this painful rendering of events for Chayo.

I offer this moment to raise the performative aspects of doing fieldwork, the need to "be on" that at times interferes with being present as a human being. Moreover, with distance from the academy, the role, the objective of what an anthropologist "is" or "should do" becomes quite hazy. Thus, my own disillusionment with fieldwork and subsequent critique of my original position greatly influenced the direction of my scholarship. It was at this time that I began to piece together processes in Chalatenango and try to make sense of development practices and discourses in a way that granted agency to Chalatecos and shifted the discussion away from their changing or not changing consciousness.

Gabriel García Márquez's opening words in *Noticia de un secuestro,* a chronicle of the kidnapping of journalists in Colombia in 1990, served as an important reminder as I documented and represented Chalatecos' difficult experiences that I witnessed and the painful stories that they shared. Awed by survivor's disposition to open unhealed wounds, Márquez voices his frustration in only providing a reflection of the horror they lived (1996, 7). I have also come to embrace Michael Taussig's musings on representation. He writes, "What is anthropology but a species of translation made all the more honest, all the more truthful, and all the more interesting by showing showing—i.e., showing the means of its production? The task before us, then, is to see what anthropology has been, all along; namely, telling other people's stories and—in the process—generally ruining them by not being sensitive to the task of the storyteller. We do not have 'informants.' We live with storytellers, whom too often we have betrayed for the sake of an illusory science. The task before us, then, is to cross the divide, scary as it may be, and become storytellers as well" (Taussig 2004, 313–314).

In the chapters that follow I attempt to cross this divide and become a storyteller. In doing so, I foreground the words and analysis of Chalatecos and Chalatecas. Unless otherwise indicated, I include transcribed excerpts from audio-recordings of informal interviews or naturally occurring speech. In many cases I include the original Spanish and then provide an English translation. At times a quoted passage will begin in Spanish, will be followed by the English translation in parenthesis and then continue in English. Sometimes I return to the original Spanish in the midst of a long quote. Readers should note that all conversations occurred in Spanish and that no code-switching into English took place. My intent is to mark the urgency of residents' language, their carefully chosen expressions and the power of their words as social action. I also attempt a stance that is sensitive to a politics of engaged or activist research practice that has emerged as a significant field in anthropology (Hale 2006; Merry 2005; Sanford 2003; 2006). Bourgois reminds us that "ethnographic methods, sensibilities, and politics oblige us to touch, smell and even feel the actual existing social suffering that we may not want to admit to ourselves we have witnessed" (2002, 230). These are practices of engaged listening that ultimately push anthropologists to address questions of accountability. As Charles Hale provocatively discusses, anthropology has concentrated on an engaged practice but remains focused on modes of representation, on cultural critique. He suggests something further. As activist anthropologists attempt to "be loyal both to the space of critical scholarly production and to the principles and practices of people who struggle outside the academic setting" (2006, 104), they should create new research methods that inform social theory. For me, it is in the many years spent, sometimes centrally, sometimes peripherally, invested in the lives and livelihoods of many Chalatecos. Sally Merry raises similar questions in her work on human rights activists. She asks, for example, "Can an activist give up on the rush of outrage and urgency in order to develop complicated analyses? Does the researcher need to streamline analysis and dispense with jargon in order to attract a wider audience that could benefit from these insights?" (Merry 2005, 254). One possible answer for Merry is that anthropologists can clarify "conceptual categories" for activists (2005, 254). In her case, culture, and in this book I offer "revolutionary."

2

Histories of Violence/Histories of Organizing

Scholarship on El Salvador—historical, sociological, comparative, feminist, and ethnographic—has exploded over the last decade, contributing to our understanding of the formation of regional social, political, and economic relationships of power through time. An attention to historical processes provides a window into the multiple factors that shape and are shaped by the broadly defined "everyday revolutionaries" that are at the heart of this book. This chapter points to salient moments and interpretations of the past in order to contextualize what I later develop as the limits of activism and revolution over time and space. The following chapter builds from this presentation in its focus on a localized history through the narratives and memories of several residents from repopulated communities.

Invocations of Revolt

In 1993, a *guerrillero* turned craftsman also made art. Chilango sold polished seeds with depictions of FMLN guerrillas, and on slats of wood he painted representations of battles in communities. One small painting caught my eye back then. It was an illustration of what has become known as La Matanza, the 1932 massacre of indigenous, communist, coffee workers in the western region of El Salvador, far from the northeast of Chalatenango. In Chilango's picture, below the indigenous-looking bodies of men and women with machetes, sticks, and fists in the air, he has written, "*Levantamiento*" (Uprising.) Rather than depict the violence that followed, the massacre of ten thousand people by the Salvadoran state (Gould and Lauria-Santiago 2008), Chilango foregrounds the agency of the people who revolt (see figure 3).

FIGURE 3. Photograph of painting on 6 × 6 inch slat of wood by Chilango resident artist from Chalatenango, depicting the 1932 massacre known as La Matanza.

Painting by Chilango, Chalateco artist. Photograph by Antonio Rossi.

In a recent text, Jeffrey Gould and Aldo Lauria-Santiago (2008) offer a rich analysis of La Matanza, which is echoed not only by Chilango but by many scholars as a pivotal moment that marks Salvadoran history of protest and contention by people who have been systematically excluded politically, economically, and socially through time (Murray et al. 1995, xvii). Gould and Lauria-Santiago predicate their analysis on the processes of *mestizaje* that define the formation of independent Central American nation-states.[1] This is not a facile story of displaced and powerless Indians in the face of elite-led agrarian capitalism for, as Lauria-Santiago's earlier work demonstrates, small-scale producers were actors in the nation-building project, within international economic relations, and in the development of agrarian capitalism (1998, 1999).

What can an interpretation of an uprising and its repression in the early 1930s tell us about the activism, temporally, geographically, and perhaps culturally distant, that takes place in the Chalatenango of the 1970s? While previous work on La Matanza has tended to focus on "political crises, economic collapse, communist agency, and indigenous participation" (Gould and Lauria-Santiago 2008, xviii), Gould and Lauria-Santiago's insights push scholars to interrogate the very categories that have defined the study of this period.[2] While theirs is a call for historicizing the categories of communist and Indian, their insights can be adopted for the study of El Salvador's recent past. In particular, as subsequent chapters will demonstrate, I build from their attention to the blurring of categories and to the diversity of movement actors, and the recollections of their agency. To do so problematizes notions of what it means to be an authentic revolutionary or an Indian (Gould and Lauria-Santiago 2008, xxv).

Fighting to Live, Fighting to Die

In contrast to official national figures of economic growth, by the mid twentieth century, scholars illuminate the increasing disparity of wealth within El Salvador. By the early 1950s, increasingly larger parcels of land dedicated to cash-crop agriculture and grazing compromised subsistence farming (Browning 1971; Dunkerley 1988). This led to a shortage of land available for subsistence farming, which in turn led to land overuse, increasing subdivision of small-scale land plots, seasonal labor migration, and to a growing landless peasantry.[3] The resulting struggles over land, labor and mass underemployment characterized the growing poverty in El Salvador and mark a period of political, economic and social instability which contributed to the formation of oppositional organizations (Dunkerley 1988; Montgomery 1995; Pearce 1986).[4]

Scholarship has coalesced around uncovering the motivations for collective action of a broad spectrum of Salvadoran society: peasants, labor unions, university students, and the clergy. In a recent comprehensive account of collective action through time, Paul Almeida (2008) offers a compelling portrait of "waves of protest" beginning in 1925. He emphasizes the political opportunities that emerge for civil society groups even under authoritarian, military regimes. Significantly, he exposes what he defines as moments of regime liberalization within these environments. For example, Almeida provides evidence that historically clandestine and repressed organizations were able to legally organize from 1962 through 1972. Almeida argues that it is, indeed, subsequent reversals in electoral politics and institutional access that radicalizes and creates what he terms "mobilization by intimidation." Research across conflict zones such as Morazán (Binford 1996), Usulután (Wood 2003), and Chalatenango (Lara Martínez 2005) makes clear that there were diverse responses and historically constituted experiences of prewar organizing and wartime agency amidst paramilitary and military repression. Elisabeth Wood, in a cogent and comprehensive interpretation of insurgent collective action, highlights the importance of what she terms the "pleasure of agency" (2003, 18) to unpack the puzzle of participation, to show how "classic explanations of revolutionary mobilization—class struggle, widening political opportunity, solidary peasant communities, pre-existing social networks, and selective benefits—do not adequately account for patterns of insurgent collective action in El Salvador" (2003, 16). Beyond documenting the widespread and voluntary nature of oppositional participation, Wood demonstrates how "collective action evolved over time" (2003, 17). This attention to shifts in the movement illuminates a changed social, cultural, and political landscape. Carlos Lara Martínez, too, in a rich oral history of northeastern Chalatenango, focuses on the formation of what he delineates as a campesino movement, one he sees very much still in play as it engages in new cultural forms of sociality in opposition to the nation (2005).

Like Lara Martínez and Wood, I in my research underscore the agency of campesino men, women, and children who move in and out of periods of activism that can be dated to at least the mid-1960s with the formation of the Rural Workers Union (UTC) and FECCAS (Federación Cristiana de Campesinos Salvadoreños, Christian Federation of Salvadoran Peasants), which was one of the earliest peasant organizations. Other scholars have sought to understand this precursor to revolution. Jenny Pearce's (1986) *Promised Land* chronicles the transformation of Chalatecos from supporters of a peaceful social movement into grassroots supporters and armed combatants by 1980. This transition must be understood in terms of both an increasingly repressive state regime and an area-wide politicizing process by the progressive Catholic Church. Through the teachings of liberation theology that espoused a "preferential option for the poor" and the social organization, practices, and consciousness-raising of CEBs (Christian Ecclesiastical Base Communities), many people had their first democratic experiences and critiques of social injustice (Berryman 1984; Binford 1998; Peterson 1997).[5] Scholars argue these provided the groundwork for future oppositional struggles (Cabarrús 1983; Dunkerley 1988; Galdámez 1986; Metzi 1988; Montgomery 1995; Pearce 1986).

Early state repression of the progressive church's leadership, nationally (Archbishop Romero was assassinated in 1980) and regionally (Rutilio Grande was murdered in Aguilares in 1977), and of its lay catechists and campesino participants was an important factor in the transformation of a social movement into an armed struggle.[6] Indeed, Archbishop Oscar Arnulfo Romero, assassinated on March 24, 1980, became a martyred symbol for many activists.[7] The practices of liberation theology, the life sacrifices of church leadership, and the early rural organizing, within or outside of the Catholic Church, to contest structures of inequality were met by increasing institutionalized violence. This ignited assertive, combative, and militant anti-government rural movements comprised of committed, courageous, and sacrificing men and women. As one campesino who participated in the armed struggle beginning in 1972 explained, "En todo el trayecto de la lucha, uno no se daba cuenta que iba vivir; during the trajectory of our struggle, you didn't know if you were going to live. You tried to take care of yourself but you didn't know if you were going to die the next day. That was O.K. Uno no tenía esperanza de vivir; one didn't have the expectation of living" (author interview 1997).

Civil War

The growth of national and regional movements struggling for social change functioned within a closed and authoritarian political system operating under the foreign policy concerns of the United States. In the 1960s, El Salvador was part of the Kennedy campaign agenda to develop and democratize Latin America through the USAID's (U.S. Agency for International Development) program, Alliance for Progress. A key Alliance for Progress (counterinsurgency) recommendation to the Salvadoran government was one of land reform, to redistribute land to the landless, which was implemented only in part in 1980.[8] Moreover, in the sphere of politics, El Salvador in the 1970s was marked by a series of electoral frauds (1972 and 1977) by the official ruling party, PCN (National Conciliation Party), which had close links to the military. In 1979 there was a reform attempt. On October 15, 1979, General Carlos Humberto Romero's government was overthrown by La Junta Revolucionaria de Gobierno (the Revolutionary Government Junta, JRG) comprised of young progressive military officers and young intellectuals. However, this attempt was short-lived and unsuccessful as the civilian members were co-opted and soon renounced as they were unable to open up political and economic spaces. Their call to end violence and corruption, to have new elections, and to put an end to paramilitary forces was blocked.

Meanwhile, peasant, student, and labor organizing became increasingly visible. In 1975 the Bloque Popular Revolucionario (BPR) was formed;[9] it was the political wing of the clandestine guerrilla group known as FPL (Fuerzas Populares de Liberación, Popular Liberation Forces). The FPL traces its history to 1970 when it split from the Salvadoran Communist Party. It soon dominated Chalatenango and operated clandestinely, as by the late 1970s confrontations between popular organizations, the military, and paramilitary forces such as ORDEN (Democratic Nationalist Organization) increased. In October 1980 a coalition of clandestine groups, which had been organizing from 1970 to 1979, formed. The FPL became one of five branches of the revolutionary FMLN (Farabundo Martí National Liberation Front).[10] Three of these groups were key military players: the FPL; the ERP (Ejército Revolucionairo del Pueblo, the People's Revolutionary Army), formed in 1971 by former Christian Democrats and other leftists; and the RN (Resistencia Nacional, the Armed Forces of National Resistance), formed in 1975 from former ERP members.[11] A fourth group, the PCS (Partido Comunista de El Salvador-Salvadoran Communist Party), traces its history to 1930. With La Matanza, the Communist Party was banned in 1932; and of the five guerrilla organizations, PCS was the last to support an armed insurrection, agreeing in 1980. Finally, the smallest of the organizations was formed in 1979, the PRTC (Partido Revolucionario de los Trabajadores Centroamericanos, Central American Workers Revolutionary Party).[12]

By 1980, 20 percent of the Salvadoran population controlled 65 percent of the income in contrast to 20 percent of the poorest Salvadorans controlling 2 percent of the income. The disparity of wealth was further evidenced in the unequal distribution of land. In 1987, 70 percent of farmland was distributed among 1 percent of the population and 41 percent of farms were small-scale plots of land covering only 10 percent of arable land. Regarding unemployment, these figures soared in the urban sector to 50 percent, and rural unemployment climbed to 71 percent (Barry 1990, 177–179). The 1980s typify a history of extreme disparities of wealth, of landlessness and land-poor sectors, of under- and unemployment, and of weak state social services such as education and health. It is also a decade marked by a growing national debt which reached $1.825 billion in 1989 (Barry 1990, 177). The United States bolstered the war economy, increasing spending from $25 million in 1980 to an annual assistance of $500 million to $600 million by the mid 1980s (Binford 1998, 11–12). After a decade this figure totaled $6 billion (Murray et al. 1997, 15).

State-committed human rights abuses during this time were rampant. The publication of the United Nation's Truth Commission's final report, *From Madness to Hope*, which was created as part of the peace agreements, found that the Salvadoran state through its systematic institutionalization of violence was the overwhelming agent of terror. Of the twenty-two thousand investigated cases of human rights violations from 1980 to 1991, the Salvadoran Armed Forces were accused of committing 60 percent of the violence, and paramilitary groups and death squads were responsible for 25 percent. The report found that the FMLN was responsible for 5 percent of cases of human rights abuse (United Nations 1993, 41–42). This report was critical since in the past, while journalists, human rights workers, and some scholars documented atrocities during the war, these were often obfuscated, denied, and covered up (i.e., Danner 1994).[13] Recall that this is a war that claimed the lives of seventy-five thousand people, "disappeared" another seven thousand Salvadorans, and displaced five hundred thousand civilians.[14]

From 1980 to 1983, civilian organizing was brutally repressed. By 1980 rural areas were hardest hit by military and paramilitary violence as evidenced in the Rio Sumpul massacre in Chalatenango on May 14–15, 1980,[15] and the El Mozote massacre in the Department of Morazán in December 1981 (Binford 1996). The FMLN's (first unsuccessful) "Final Offensive" in 1981 had the unintended consequence of increasing U.S. military assistance to train, modernize, and increase the number of Salvadoran Armed Forces. It is in this period (1982) that the military strategy was one of *"quitarle el agua al pez"* (take the water from the fish), where civilians were the targets of violence. This period has the highest number of deaths and human rights violations, displacement, and killing by paramilitary rural forces. The number of deaths in 1982 reached 5,962. Death squads had free reign at this time. By 1983 the FMLN had control of the north and east of the country and established its own community organizing infrastructure called Poderes Populares Locales (Local Popular Forces), which oversaw sectors such as education and health in the absence of official government.

In the second phase of the war, state violence decreased (to 1,655 war-related deaths in 1985). Yet civilians remained "legitimate" targets of repression. With the 1984 "democratic" elections of civilian President José Napoleón Duarte of the PDC (Partido Demócrata Cristiano, Christian Democratic Party), which some term a period of façade democracy evidenced by "demonstration elections" (Binford 1998, 11), the United States was able to continue funding the Salvadoran war as U.S. President Ronald Reagan announced a decrease in human rights abuses (however, the number of deaths increased during the Duarte regime). At this time, the networks of international solidarity deepened and attempted to contest the U.S.-funded war that lasted twelve years.[16] By 1984, the FMLN had grown in strength and number, reaching almost ten thousand armed soldiers.[17] Estimates are that they held between 20 and 30 percent of the country. In these conflict zones, battles between the FMLN and the Salvadoran army increased, as did military operations involving air bombings. The FMLN's use of land mines added to civilian casualties.

To address the Salvadoran army's increasing military and aerial presence, the FMLN shifted from a "war of position (large units defending territory) to a war of movement (small-scale guerrilla warfare, hit-and-run operations, sabotage) expanded to previously untouched areas of the national territory" (Binford 1998, 11). My own interviews with former FPL combatants and battalion leaders suggest that it was also the arrival of missiles (and the trainings in Nicaragua) to destroy airplanes that changed the course of the war (interview with Aquilino, November 1997). It is also in this period of increasing terror from military and paramilitary forces that many civilians who supported the FMLN crossed the border to Honduras and into United Nation's refugee camps in the early to mid 1980s, with approximately eleven thousand populating the Mesa Grande refugee camp alone (Lara Martínez 2005).

From 1987 to 1989, efforts by the Duarte regime were made to end the war (i.e., the failed peace meetings of Esquipulas II). Ironically, under this civilian presidency, violence actually increased against labor groups, human rights groups, and the FMLN. It was at this time that displaced peoples from former conflict zones, refugees in Honduras and internally displaced, repatriated amidst the ongoing brutality of the war (Edwards and Sibentritt 1991; MacDonald and Gatehouse 1995; Schrading 1991; Thompson 1995).

The 1989 FMLN offensive brought the predominantly rural-based violence onto the urban and elite streets of the capital of San Salvador. Despite the years of direct U.S. military and economic support, the Salvadoran Armed Forces and government were unable to defeat the FMLN, and both sides realized they were unlikely to win by force. A stalemate was acknowledged by both sides. This created the political opening for dialogue and negotiation between the FMLN and the Salvadoran government. Moreover, international pressure to end the war escalated when on November 16, 1989, the elite U.S. trained Atlacatl Battalion assassinated six Jesuit priests and scholars, their housekeeper, and her daughter at the Central American University (see Whitfield 1994).

Peace accords brokered by the United Nations were agreed upon and signed on January 16, 1992, by ARENA (Alianza Republicana Nacionalista, National Republican Alliance) President Alfredo Cristiani and representatives of the five branches of the FMLN, formerly a clandestine guerilla group and now a political party.[18] This officially ended the civil war.

Transitions to Peace and Neoliberal Democracy

As Elisabeth Wood notes, El Salvador's transition from war to peace and democracy was "forged from below via a revolutionary social movement" (2003, 5). Pursuing peace was characterized by a series of "bargains" between the FMLN and the Salvadoran government. A central bargain was this: elites conceded political democracy and the FMLN conceded a liberalized market economy (2000, 3, 12). The peace accords focused mostly on opening the political system, creating a representative democracy, reducing the armed forces, strengthening the judicial system, and reforming the electoral process. Critically, a Truth Commission was created to investigate human rights abuses. However, in March 1993 a law was passed granting amnesty to all those involved in massacres and war crimes mentioned in the truth report (on both the right and the left).

Briefly, the peace accords privileged the following areas:

1. Military reform which involved dissolving repressive branches of the Salvadoran army: the National Guard, National Police, Treasury Police, civilian police forces, and all elite counter-insurgency battalions. Paramilitary groups were banned and a New Civilian Police (PNC) was created (former FMLN combatants were encouraged to join).
2. The legalization of the FMLN as an official political party and the demobilization and reintegration of FMLN combatants.[19]
3. The creation and strengthening of democratic institutions such as the office of Human Rights Ombudsman.
4. The creation of the Supreme Electoral Tribunal, electoral reform, and the strengthening of the judicial branch.

5. Economic and social reforms concentrated on land through a program termed PTT, Programa de Transferencia de Tierras (Land Transfer Program). Former combatants and their supporters, called *tenedores*, were privileged, and long-term, low-interest loans for land purchases were set up.[20]

To oversee the challenges of massive rebuilding after a violent civil war, a five-year (1992–1997) National Reconstruction Plan (NRP) was created, focusing on war-torn areas, specifically, on the 115 most damaged municipalities in twelve out of fourteen departments.[21] The focus was on the integration of 22,500 ex-combatants on both sides of the conflict and 25,000 tenedores. Reconstruction was understood in terms of rebuilding and repairing destroyed infrastructure—roads, bridges, and buildings—in order to "promote broad citizen participation in the reconstruction effort" (MSI 1996, 1). USAID was a leading international organization overseeing this process, and the agency pledged $302 million for the NRP, a substantial contribution to the international donors' pledge of $800 million, given as both donation and credit (MSI 1996, 2).[22] The NRP has received substantial critique from scholars (see Murray et al. 1994) for the silencing and limiting of alternative development models, of progressive NGOs, of grassroots organizations and their beneficiaries, and of FMLN participation (Foley 1996; UNDP 1995). To its credit, the NRP mapped out assistance at a time when the agricultural economy was stagnant and national growth was occurring in new financial sectors and in places that were historically marginalized. It also attempted to decentralize reconstruction at the local level by continuing with a USAID project operating since 1987, Municipalities in Action (MEA).[23]

The transition to peace is also marked by El Salvador's neoliberal economic policies which privilege market logic (Harvey 2005) and are evidenced in structural adjustment programs that include external trade liberalization, dollarization, privatization of state enterprises, encouragement of foreign investment, and reduction of social spending (Silber and Viterna 2009). USAID's assessment of these measures in the mid 1990s is positive, as they indicate that since 1990 there has been "sustained economic growth" as the fiscal deficit has been reduced, inflation has decreased, investment in the private sector has increased, wartime capital flight has been stopped, and Free Trade Zones have been created, marking El Salvador's export competitiveness (MSI 1996, 3–4).[24]

Scholarship proves otherwise as the nation experiences increasing urbanization and the displacement of the rural poor by these larger forces. By 1996, 57 percent of Salvadorans lived in urban areas and 60 percent of the population worked in the informal, unregulated sector with no basic services (PAHO 1998, 259; Stephen et al. 2001, 6). While urban industries grow, rural folks are working in a shrinking agricultural economy (World Bank 1998).[25] Indeed, Sarah Gammage describes the postwar period as consisting of a "rural exodus" (2006, 78). As wages fell in the 1980s and 1990s, so did the importance of agriculture, decreasing from 32 percent of the GDP in 1960 to 9 percent in 2004 (Gammage 2006, 78). Figures on economic "growth" must be grounded in the entrance of not only foreign aid with the signing of peace accords but the $2.5 billion annual amount of remittances sent to kin by Salvadorans living abroad (UNDP 2005, 7–8). Migration has become the leading development strategy for El Salvador, the primary way in which El Salvador enters into globalization (UNDP 2005). As a result, new state forms, technologies, modes, or institutions have emerged in an effort to control this sector (Baker-Cristales 2004; Coutin 2007; Gammage 2006; UNDP 2005).

Still, undeniably great strides have been made in El Salvador. Since the historic elections of 1994 where the FMLN participated as a legal political party, a space has opened up for oppositional political practices. By 1997, municipal, and legislative elections placed the FMLN as an important political force as the party won twenty-seven legislative seats to ARENA's twenty-eight. Moreover, fifty-two new municipalities covering 45 percent of the population were won by the FMLN, including San Salvador with the election of Hector Silva as mayor. In March 1999 elections, the majority of Salvadorans lived in FMLN-led municipalities while ARENA held the majority of legislative seats and the presidency, with the election of U.S.-educated Francisco Flores. In 2004, Antonio Saca was elected as the third ARENA president since the signing of the peace accords. He has been known for increasing a zero tolerance to violence policy and further implementing antiterrorist legislation that ultimately targeted the civilian social movements of the past (see chapter 4). It was in March 2009 that Mauricio Funes was elected as the first FMLN president. The impact of this historic victory is still unfolding. While this chapter has provided some broad strokes of history for those unfamiliar with El Salvador, the following chapter opens up a window into postwar lives by rooting them in localized memories of war.

3

Rank-and-File History

The postwar is a hard, difficult time. It is like trying to find one's lost voice. It is about trying to make the connection between 1979 and 1997 . . . and since the Chalateco and Salvadoran peasants, they like to live in the present, and not remember the past, because of the pain. And we have to understand that as well. The anguish, the sadness, so much that was lived . . . but historical memory gives us meaning. It helps us put our feet on the ground.

Interview with a Las Vueltas priest, October 1997

The young priest Padre José, the son of peasants from Ojos de Agua, traveled throughout Chalatenango's rural communities in a small white jeep.[1] Usually dressed in jeans and a T-shirt, he put on only a white cloak tied with a simple length of twine to hold mass in churches still half rebuilt, some with benches, some without benches, or sometimes under trees. He celebrated first communions with children dressed in white and led in other ritual celebrations. After a year of attending these different events by Padre José, who was trained in and practiced the teachings of liberation theology, I felt ready, and he agreed to speak candidly with me about the hegemonic discourse circulating at the time: that communities were in crisis, dangerously forgetting their past in the context of encroaching neoliberal capitalism. Implicit in this critique from within leadership in communities, and across NGOs and grassroots groups, is a vision of repopulated communities in the northeast of Chalatenango as uniformly revolutionary. Explicit in this critique is a mourning for this loss and an anxiety over how to reclaim the revolutionary spirit. Specifically, in the region of Chalatenango that I focus on "history," the "past," or the "story" that repatriated residents are called upon to remember as social or collective memory is a heroic representation of the recent struggle.[2]

To be sure, a majority of the people who live in the northeast of Chalatenango, a wartime conflict zone or "liberated" territory, depending on perspective, lived the war deeply. Men and women, young and old, able-bodied or not, infants, toddlers, and children who "missed" their youth, all experienced violence and oppression firsthand. Many organized around their human rights beginning in the early 1970s. In the aftermath of the Salvadoran civil war, what it means to have been a revolutionary carries meaning for individual trajectories, community organizers, political parties, international development organizations, and so on. This chapter foregrounds Chalateco recollections of the past and grants people intellectual agency as makers of their own analyses. To do so, I concentrate on what I see as a process of becoming or "being revolutionary." This process is located in people's practices and talk and is often described as a shift or as a moment of clarity, for some more gradual than others, where a realization takes place, where injustice is reinterpreted, and where people identify their own changed consciousness as born from a feeling of agency that is physical, intellectual, and religious.

For example, Hugo, a longtime participant of the struggle for human rights, what some describe as a *campesino* social movement (Lara Martínez 2005), reflects on the beginning of his own involvement in organizing for justice. Hugo joined the FPL in 1972 but dates his theorizing earlier: "In 1970, I started to understand things. I was already an adult, and those pamphlets started appearing, thrown around by the group that was born the first of April of 1970. The group was the FPL, the first group that would become FPL. I started reading those pamphlets that talked about social classes in the country, who are the poor campesinos, the *jornales,* the middle campesinos, and the rich campesinos. Y éso lo fue iluminando la idea. ¿Verdad? Y pegababa con la realidad que nosotros vivíamos. O sea la hoja era buena. (And that illuminated the issue, right? And it matched the reality of our lives. That was a good pamphlet.)" Being revolutionary, for Hugo and for others, took place in the face of unspeakable horror and the everyday violence of surviving. This history or, perhaps more importantly, people's memories and the resulting expectations born from this relationship to the past come to characterize the regional transition to peace building. It is to this that I turn, a politics of memory, which I frame as rank-and-file history. Specifically, I take up historical recollections of prewar communal life, organizing experiences during the early 1970s and the gendered experiences of violence during this phase of repression and agency. I also weave together stories of collective action and survival during the official periodization of war (1980–1992) which include the violences of displacement: flights to the mountains (or *guindas* as they are called in El Salvador), escapes across the Honduran border to the Mesa Grande refugee camp, to the 1987 return to the northeast of Chalatenango during the midst of war, to finally the signing of peace on January 16, 1992. I am interested in the uses of history—talk and action about the past. As scholarship on social, historical, or collective memory has cogently demonstrated, the past is very much shaped by and for the present and the future.

This chapter, then, does not deploy history, national, regional, or communal, as background or context for the rest of the story. It also does not construct a detailed, localized historiography for the region (see Todd 2007). Given that communities in the northeast of Chalatenango are comprised of displaced peoples, their stories mingle histories from across the region and from other departments. From displacement emerges a new relationship to the past that is very much rooted *in* place. In providing some portraits of the past, my intention is to shift the conversation away from analyses that ask what motivated this collective action, whether or not people's consciousness have changed, or even if people are or were revolutionary. These questions are eloquently addressed by a range of scholars working on both the gendered and peasant-based activism of the armed struggle (see, for example, Kampwirth 2002; Luciak 2001; Shayne 2004; Wood 2003). Instead, I suggest that we focus on how history, refracted as memory, becomes a moral discourse that entangles Chalatecos and Chalatecas, inspiring, vindicating, haunting, or chastising them. These memories are also gendered, and so this chapter intervenes into discussions of memory and Salvadoran history by presenting Chalatecos and Chalatecas as owners of their own history.

Below, I begin with snapshots of the 1970s, a time where many locate their agency, as Elsy, a protagonist of this ethnography, often explained: "Tenía once años cuando me di cuenta de la guerra" (I was eleven years old when I realized there was war). This would have been 1974 or 1975. I underscore the gendered experiences of this period of organizing and trace these perspectives into the apex of war and, finally, locate how versions of the past are mobilized for particular ends. The data for this chapter covers a series of conversation-like interviews where I was the intended addressee and where on many occasions new speakers arrived on the scene and became participating audience members, co-constructing the encounter. I provide excerpts from interviews and conversations with a parish priest, a CCR organizer, a longtime FPL militant, and several former women "supporters" throughout. I do so in order to provide people's theories on both the past and why it is being forgotten or not. In all of these situations I have sought to take Susan Gal's (1991) positioning of the ethnographic interview as a frame for my journeys in and out of ethnographic encounters.[3] For Gal, the ethnographic interview is a linguistic practice where the relationship between silence, speech, gender, and power must be taken into account, where anthropologists must also be aware and theorize on their role in eliciting narratives and seek to find "conditions under which informants can talk" (1991, 191).

Portraits of the 1970s

During the course of my research, Aquilino's movements were constant. We would cross paths on the back of pickups, en route to and from the town of Chalatenango, and at all sorts of meetings held in El Rancho or the larger *alcaldía* of Las Vueltas. But I did not remember him from my earlier visits in 1993

and 1994. A demobilized combatant, Aquilino arrived in El Rancho after a year
of being *encuartelado,* placed in an encampment as a demobilized soldier for the
FMLN as part of the peace accords process. He left El Rancho shortly after being
released in order to find work farther north in La Palma, Chalatenango. He was
partnered during the war and had a young daughter to feed, shelter, and clothe
and nothing to do it with. Aquilino explains how after being demobilized he
could not pursue subsistence agriculture given that he had never quite learned
how to till the land. He had been too busy fighting across it from the age of
thirteen, circa 1975. He characterizes those first years of transition from war
to peace as *"esa época fue triste"* (those were sad times). He explained to me,
"I didn't know what to do. Where was I going to find even thirty *colones?*[4] I felt
desperate." For three years he worked as a driver in La Palma, working for two
thousand *colones* a month: "Ni un sorbete me comía porque sabía que tenía la
mujer, que tenía el hijo, y con ganas de hacer un ranchito." (I didn't even buy an
ice-cream cone knowing that I had my wife, my daughter, and the desire to build
a house.) After three years he joined his family in El Rancho and immediately
became a vital member of the community. He was elected to oversee the land
transfer program not only for El Rancho but for the entire municipality. This is
when I met him and this is when, after a year of chatting, we sat down for two long
interviews in his quite sizable *ranchito* (home). Community gossip suggested that
his home was about to double in size with the addition of an incoming housing
project. Implicit in this rumor is Aquilino's corruption, just one more example
of a *directiva* (community council) member skimming from the top of incoming
aid projects.

I begin with this introduction of Aquilino in the ethnographic present of the
mid to late 1990s in order to situate his reflections on the past. In pondering over
our exchange I note that so much of what Aquilino explained to me is an attempt
to teach me about war in the region. He spoke in generalities: "Here the conflict
emerges from the ongoing injustices, from the crises produced by the government. We organized different sectors [meaning the different groups that went on
to comprise the FMLN] and started a struggle for land for campesinos because we
didn't have where to work the land." He speaks about and as a campesino who
fought for eight years in Chalatenango but who participated for twelve.

Hugo's narratives of early organizing are quite a bit more detailed and personal. It is as if Aquilino's own story is consumed by his daily labor for El Rancho
and he is more comfortable discussing land transfer processes, incoming aid,
and municipal projects. Hugo, a generation older than Aquilino, is a gifted
storyteller and, unlike Aquilino, is not so busy these days. His wife, Dolores,
active in CCR's women's committees, had recently taken him back in after an
undisclosed amount of time womanizing and drinking. In part, he agreed to
speak with me because he had seen me often enough tagging along during
"women's activities"—grassroots meetings with Dolores, literacy classes with

FIGURE 4. Remnants of bomb in Las Vueltas, Chalatenango, that serve as a physical reminder of violence perpetrated by the Salvadoran military forces.

Photograph by Ralph Sprenkels.

Elsy, or buying ice cream for kids at the kiosk in the center of Las Vueltas. I arrived at his house ready to record some of his experiences, stories he was saddened to say that the youth did not know very much about. Our exchange, he hoped, could start making the past accessible to the next generations.

Hugo provided a linear narrative of his participation, his labor history from campesino organizing to armed combatant and political organizer. He told me, "I incorporated in 1972, first with the FPL, as a clandestine group. You had to be quiet about it; you couldn't even tell your wife, your brother, nobody. Dolores knew a little bit, *porque le metía cierta conciencia* (because I was raising her consciousness). When they called me to the first meeting, I didn't go; I was just hanging around. But that is how one starts; at first you don't pay any attention. Then they invited me to another meeting. I didn't go to that one either. But they kept asking me, and the third time I went to the meeting and I never missed one after that. I started by distributing *propaganda rebelde* (revolutionary propaganda)."

I was curious about the size of this early movement, given an early conversation with Elsy's father, Don Vicente, who joined the armed struggle along with his entire nuclear family. According to Don Vicente, a few "*muchachos conquistaban a la gente.*" (A few young men conquered [meaning convinced] the people.) I think about the *muchachos* and how they allowed Don Vicente's son to join them despite his epilepsy. I learn this only from Elsy. She named her son Miguel in her brother's honor. A brother, a son, he died alone in the mountains during a quick retreat by the guerrillas. It is unclear if he was injured or left to be recovered after a particularly long grand mal seizure. His body has never been found.

In any event, Hugo's account corroborates Don Vicente's emphasis of small beginnings: "Where I lived there were only two or three clandestine groups. We were coordinated by a *compañero* (comrade) who died in 1979. That's when the idea came about to start a campesino movement, that's what it was called back then. Here in Chalate, Justo Mejía, who is the father of Marco Tulio [president of CCR and in 1997 elected Chalatenango's FMLN coordinator], started to visit the communities, and call semi-illegal meetings. We went all over, Las Vueltas, El Rancho, everywhere with him. We really liked the talks he gave us. Sometimes even Facundo Guardado would come, and they would talk to us about creating a union for agricultural workers. That was the UTC. And the UTC community councils were formed in 1974."

According to Hugo, he was organized in 1972, before the formation of UTC. In 1974, when the *directivas* were formed, he was sent to work with *la base*—understood as the civilian population that would be a grassroots support. He explained,

> Our method was to help the people *compartir* (share.) When someone was sick, we would all go and help. It was about winning their trust. It was a demonstration of solidarity. That was our idea. And that is when they mistreated us, accused us of being Communists, the *orejas* [literally "ears," meaning "spies"], the civil patrols, the National Guards. Only because we started working together they would say, "There are the Communists." They would threaten us with the armed forces. But we were always

consciente [aware] and incorporating *el evangelio* [the Gospel], talking about how we had to help each other as brothers. We organized various bases and the work went pretty well despite the psychological war by the patrols, local commanders, some reactionary mayors and judges, and the National Guard.

Kasandra, of Hugo's generation, also has much to offer on the past, among other things. I spent many afternoons with her, sipping instant coffee, playing with her grandson, and helping out while she ran her household. Originally from nearby La Laguna, Kasandra sought refuge in Mesa Grande after she got sick and after three years working with the guerrillas. She did not repopulate with the majority of the residents on October 11, 1987, but instead lived and worked outside of El Salvador for several years before settling in El Rancho. She is a soft-spoken woman who lives on the periphery of active community life, taking great care in the raising of her grandson while her daughter and son-in-law live and work in Virginia. After the elections of 1997, I noticed the only undefiled ARENA banner in El Rancho displayed in the inside of her home, something she preferred not to discuss. Her stories of the past provide a window into this quiet shift.

During one of my visits I asked her to talk to me about where she grew up in La Laguna and what the war was like there. Traveling to La Laguna is a hike. The view across the valley is always breathtaking. The community in the 1990s remained depopulated from the war with very few families deciding to return to their community of origin given the distance and lack of services (i.e., no school or clinic), the need to clear the land, build homes, pave roads, put in potable water and electricity. Interestingly, Kasandra takes my question on origins and beginnings beyond the framing or organizing of war. She began, "Two men arrived to La Laguna with their wives. This is the history that they told me. Their names were Alejandro and Tomás Guardado. They were brothers. I don't know their wives' names. And there was an unoccupied hacienda and they bought it."

Kasandra is unclear on how they had the funds, but the story goes that they purchased the hacienda from a family living in Chalatenango, and over time the land was divided along kin lines. Kasandra is quick to add that women always inherited less land. By the 1970s, Kasandra explained that 180 families lived in La Laguna, larger than prewar and postwar El Rancho.

When Kasandra tells me about La Laguna's organizing history, unlike Aquilino and Hugo, her story emphasizes less a shift in consciousness or new understandings of injustices but rather how kinship networks determined political or ideological positions. She explains that not all families in La Laguna supported the guerrillas. Indeed, Kasandra's narratives privilege how retribution by incipient guerrilla forces increased paramilitary forces. However, like Hugo, she states that the mobilization began with just a few men. This was no mass movement early on: "Al principio sólo eran dos personas, después mi hermano, los primeros" (At the beginning there were only two people, then my brother, the first ones). From three to five to then eleven to form a *directiva*. She continues, "Y así fueron consiguiendo un poquito más gente, un poquito más gente hasta que consiguieron bastante gente" (And that is how they got a little bit more people, some more people, until they got a lot of people). In this recollection, "a lot of people" are marked in the formation and mass movement of UTC.

Kasandra is a quiet critic, adamant about the use of a pseudonym and trusting me not to speak about our interview with others in the community while I am living there. I understand why. Her accounts are not the celebratory ones that could mobilize future activism. Neither are they facile indictments of the guerillas. It appears as though the face of neutrality, near impossible during the war, is difficult in its aftermath as well. Her indictments shift from breath to breath, leaving me wondering about the subjects of her story. Her accounts emphasize the inability to be neutral, and how this impossibility was met with violence. Does this speak more to her concerns in the present? She explained, "In La Laguna many people died for that reason, because they stayed in the middle, neutral. The ones that said, 'Yo no les hecho mal a ninguno. Yo no me he metido en nada. Yo estoy libre, me voy a quedar.' (I haven't done anything to anyone. I haven't gotten involved in anything. I am free. I can stay.) Those were the people that died. Entire families died." In analyzing and pouring over this transcript again, so many years later, I am struck by her use of passive voice. People died, but who were they killed by? It is so very unclear in her words. And perhaps that is her message to me.

When I asked her to further elaborate on her experiences of violence, thinking about conversations with neighbors on the role of peasant paramilitary forces such as ORDEN, in part because these people do not live in the repopulated communities, I am surprised when she locates the origins of repression by ORDEN and the military at the community level in the "guerrilla justice" (Taussig 2004) of 1979. According to Kasandra, the guerrillas began calling for the execution of several extremely violent men working in ORDEN, as their weekly killings were increasing. She explained, "And that's when it all started. One day the organization decided to get rid of them. Early one morning, a group of armed guerrillas killed them, and that was in November 1979, I believe. They killed four of them and after that is when things got really difficult. Yes, that was November and already on the thirty-first of December came the first military invasion. They always sent fifty or one hundred soldiers, but they say after that they sent four thousand troops to the department." Kasandra also claims that this is when sides were forced to be drawn; she narrates the killing of eleven family members by guerillas in this time period, an act by the guerillas to incite fear, to draw boundaries, to claim territory and allegiance, and to take ownership of people's goods—corn, cows, pigs, chickens, beans, everything.

Hugo would perhaps acknowledge Kasandra's claim but would not apologize for these actions. He places the need to have a strong fist (*poner mano dura*) as arising from the very repression by local politico-military forces. The increasing repression is what spawned armed resistance: "All those cruel *orejas,* those assassins had to be eliminated. We already had our pistols and we also started using grenades. . . . When we started getting rid of those people the army, the guard would come, but since they were responsible for it, we just couldn't sit there with our arms crossed. We would say, 'Well we've already tried to struggle peacefully, we've tried, so now it's time to arm ourselves—*pues ahorita nos toca armarnos.*'" Hugo dates the formation of militias at this moment in 1979 with the creation of the FMLN in 1980 in pursuit of the "Final Offensive." He reminds me that this action was not successful in overthrowing the government or the "fascist military dictatorship," which Hugo tells me they termed the power structure to topple. Alan Riding, reporting for the *New York Times* on October 25, 1980, describes the paramilitary repression as follows: "Almost daily, 30 or 40 bullet-ridden and mutilated bodies are found throughout the country, most of them of suspected guerrilla sympathizers who were killed by right-wing paramilitary groups or by the much-feared National Guard. The guerrillas, on the other hand, have often seized members of Orden, a pro-Government peasant group, and executed them" (1980, 3).

Thus, many former activists and supporters of the revolutionary social movement tell their history from the early organizing of the 1970s. In an almost origin-myth genealogy of organizing, the protagonists of the past struggle, men and women in their mid-thirties to mid-forties during the 1990s, present a periodization of the past that begins with UTC and FECCAS, before these peasant organizations became involved in the clandestine armed struggle.

A case in point is Rolando's personal organizing history. Rolando is the quintessential guerrilla-turned-grassroots organizer and CCR professional. He often wore a button-down, light blue, short-sleeve shirt, and baseball cap and had legs that just walked on and on from community to community. He never appeared tired. I met him often in his attempts to get the chaos of El Rancho's community *directiva* under control—months vacant without leadership. I emulated his accoutrements and retired my green knapsack and bought a small black canvas satchel to swing over one shoulder and carry my agenda, pens, notebooks, and tape recorder. A black canvas bag signifies a local NGO professional worker. Indeed, many former fighters explained to me that after so many years with a rifle on their shoulders they needed a strap to hook a finger around, something to hold. Satchels for rifles in postwar. I admired Rolando. I was awestruck by this local intellectual who was not a Chalateco by birth but by time spent in the territory. He carried with him a wealth of knowledge, an even temper, and an ongoing energy to struggle for human rights. On a mild Sunday afternoon, his one day off, we sat on plastic chairs in the porch of his house in Las Vueltas. He began by telling me a bit about his organizing history:

> "I joined the movement in August 1978 when I was eighteen years old. I joined FECCAS—Federación de Campesinos Cristianos Salvadoreños. FEC-CAS had strong relationships with CEBS, with Christian communities from that time. That same year I realized that FECCAS had a strong relationship with the Bloque Popular Revolucionario, but was born before BPR and was working with UTC. I was there only in 1978 and 1979. In 1980 I joined the clandestine guerrillas. But really, it was no longer clandestine because we were persecuted by the military. After that I participated in countless organizing efforts. I was never in the refugee camps. I was always a guerrilla, from being a combatant, to organizing solidarity, to working with *la base.*"

In the current postwar context, some of these genealogies of organizing have become more complicated. In many cases, narratives weave a life history with a community history and with an organizing history.

To cite another example, one day I accompanied a female resident of El Rancho back to a community near La Laguna. During the steep two-hour walk I asked Lucía to tell me a bit about where we were visiting. She embedded her own life history within the community's history. As we passed by different stretches of land, events that had occurred there were incorporated into the story. The remaining foundation of a home destroyed during the war was a site of prewar organizing and later a FPL safe house. The land is infused with meaning. As residents walk through the terrain, travel to neighboring communities, places hold local memories. Joanne Rappaport's scholarship supports this claim as she locates memory and history in geography, history encoded in physical places (1990, 10). Geography, she explains, "organizes the manner in which these facts are conceptualized, remembered, and organized into a temporal framework" (Rappaport 1990, 11). I could no longer walk to and from Las Vueltas and El Rancho without pausing for a moment on the curve of the road by the steep cliff—the site where many dead bodies were tossed.

In Lucía's history of her small *caserío's* involvement in the war, her opening words are telling. She said, "We didn't know—*no sabíamos.*" Hers is a gendered narrative where women are bystanders of an early male-led, dangerous, and divisive clandestine organizing. Her version is similar to that of Kasandra, also from the La Laguna area. Both women situated the roots of the war in a long community history of conflict that erupted and was manifested in prewar times.

Lucía explained how, indeed, she felt as though she, like so many, was caught in-between two opposed groups, the incipient Left and ORDEN. The opposition was fueled by a long history of personal antagonism at the community level, which appears to be based on differences in wealth (see also Lara Martínez 2005). She repeated, "Envy always exists, right? And it existed back then—Envidia siempre existe, y existía. ¿Verdad?" adding that she, her brothers, and her husband's family were economically much better off than her current dire conditions. They were able to buy clothes in Chalatenango back then. As we continued our walk she repeated that many residents did not know who the "*organizados*" (organized ones) or the "*subversivos*" (subversives) were.[5] She portrays the messiness and confusion of this time when alliances were not yet set and how, in fact, this produced violence. Her family was deeply affected as their commitments were in flux; her husband and his three brothers suffered these early years. She explained how originally these four brothers resisted the subversives and were thus threatened by them. The final warning was the stone-throwing attack at her brother-in-law's home. Shortly thereafter, one brother was ambushed and killed by the subversives. In the account, the newly formed Left appeared to wield a degree of community support as two women washing clothes in a nearby stream were aware of the impending attack but did not warn the young man.

In an unclear chain of events that perhaps best exemplifies the process in its lack of clarity, Lucía's story appears to collapse the transformation of her kin from resisting the Left to being incorporated into it. As an elderly Chalateco explained to me, this was a time with few options. One had two paths, the army or the FMLN, and one chose the FMLN because ultimately it granted people agency. Unlike the army, the FMLN did not order the killing of children. Perhaps this is the clarity, the moral authority. In Lucía's account, the three remaining brothers heard the gunfire and ran to the river with their knives drawn to avenge their brother's death. In fighting, the subversives were so impressed by these strong young men's ability and passion that rather than killing them, they asked them to join the struggle. And they did. Once incorporated, Lucía's extended family was no longer attacked by the Left but rather became the target of the local paramilitary forces, ORDEN, which killed another brother.

La Laguna, this remote mountain town with stories of war, found its way onto the pages of the *New York Times.* James Le Moyne, reporting on January 29, 1985, in the midst of ultimately futile discussions of peace, presented his conversation with a young *guerrillero:* "A 16-year-old guerrilla in the village of La Laguna, who said his name was Amical, carried an American-made M-16 automatic rifle with the casual confidence of a veteran. He said he had been fighting for five years. Asked what he would do if efforts to negotiate an end to war failed, the young rebel replied, 'Fight'" (1985, A2).

I think often of Lucía, painting wares in El Rancho's arts-and-crafts workshop, started not by CORDES or CCR but by two North American women volunteers who accompanied repatriating refugees back from Mesa Grande to El Rancho. Lucía is a small, thin, but strong woman in her mid to late thirties. She looked much older than that but moved up that hill so much faster than me. Lucía, whose guerrilla husband was killed in the war, is surrounded by a brood of boys. In 1997 she had three handsome teens ranging in age from sixteen to twelve, strong, lean, and hard-working that small plot of land. Then there is her blonder, curly-topped little one, her abandoned, unrecognized son. Again there are more rumors. People say that he is the progeny of married Don so-and-so with a house full of children and a wife up the dirt road. I painted many flowers on earthenwares made to order, sitting beside Lucía and her younger, rounder, quicker-to-smile friend, Chavela.

Painting a History of Violence

In El Rancho, the arts-and-crafts workshop (*taller de artesanía*) provides sporadic but essential income for six women single heads of household. The workshop was established in 1992 through solidarity sources with the aim to economically empower abandoned women and widows of war by expanding their access to resources. When there are orders for crafts, these women spend hours seated in a hot, tin-roofed room, designing and painting Chalatenango's *arte típico*—colorful flowers and birds painted in what is referred to as the La Palma style—on decorative mud earthenware and leather goods. The crafts are destined for an international solidarity-linked market. However, the international demand for these goods has decreased substantially, while supply has increased. El Rancho's *taller* is just one among hundreds of small-scale crafts projects, and like so many of them, the wages for workers' labor and products are continuously in arrears.[6]

Despite the decline in women's development projects, these remain important rebuilding sites. Indeed, one of the largest complaints at the community level is that there are not enough of these economic projects to benefit all women. And although only a portion of my fieldwork was conducted in municipal-level women's projects from 1996 to 1997 (as opposed to my work in 1993 and 1994, which was marked by almost a full-time involvement), the time I spent circulating through the various projects indicates that these continue to be sites of reflection, a safe space in which women engage in theories of explanation on the war, on the sacrifices they made, the loses they continue to mourn, as they labor arduously for truly meager amounts of payment.[7]

On a humid September day in 1997, I went for my habitual check in at the *taller*, positioned right on the main road from Chalatenango to Las Vueltas. Here I could engage in conversation with the six women, assist in painting red, yellow, purple, and blue flowers, and watch the events transpiring outside: who got off the bus, with what products to sell, who had returned from a *maquila* in San Salvador, who had returned from the United States, who was going to the hospital in Chalatenango, and so on. On this day there were only two women working in the *taller*, Lola and Chavela. Lola, Elsy's cousin and originally from a small cantón outside of Chalatenango, had raised one adult son who continued to live with her and grew a *milpa* (small cornfield) for her. She was also raising a striking adolescent boy who aspired to attend school beyond the ninth grade. He was the only fourteen-year-old male of El Rancho still successful in school. Chavela, originally from a small *caserío* of Las Vueltas, had given birth to the first freedom baby of Las Vueltas, going into labor the very day she returned with a mass of people from the Mesa Grande refugee camp in Honduras. While an abandoned young mother when the workshop was initiated, a year later she remarried to a much older man, her white-haired *viejito* (old man), and had two other children by him. Her daily struggles involved finding creative ways to have her current partner care for and support her freedom baby, her first daughter, not fathered by him.

Chavela was seated to my right and her legs were outstretched on a chair as she complained of all over body pain. Lola sat toward the back of the room and worked on a leather belt, her back to the two of us. Between painting flowers and birds and the loud hammering of belt holes, Lola and Chavela began to recount several violent experiences of the past, violence against their kin and neighbors and violence against women. They framed these narratives within present-day atrocities represented on newly acquired television sets.[8]

The conversation began with reference to the repopulation festival in Las Vueltas, which was to be held on October 10, less than a month from that time. Both women reflected that it seemed just like yesterday that they had made the long and difficult journey back to El Salvador from Mesa Grande, Honduras. From here the two women, who had experienced the war in different communities, began to exchange their recollections, finding commonalties in their stories. For Chavela, at least fifteen years younger than Lola, her narratives of the war were told from the point of view of a young child. Her stories included the horror of watching her father running from the Sumpul Massacre in May 1980 as his white shirt turned red from the loss of blood, of following this spilt blood up the hill until she and her mother finally found him, almost dead, at his sister's home. While Chavela then told of her uncles' kidnapping and of the ways in which community members organized through ORDEN to massacre their neighbors, Lola explained how the social relationships in prewar times, the antagonism and feuding between neighbors and kin, had ignited violence during the war, transforming criminals into paramilitary murderers. Chavela and Lola, though distant in years and spatially from different communities, knew the same stories. They co-constructed stories about the "Lioneses" from Las Vueltas who were the key assassins of ORDEN, waging campaigns of violence in El Rancho and other communities. Together they pieced together information on how the guerrillas finally caught one of the top ORDEN leaders and how "legend" had it, how difficult it was to kill him: "Ni se podía morir ese hombre. Tenía un contrato con el diablo." (That man just would not die. He had a pact with the devil.), said Lola.

One recollection led to another. They exchanged information on the fate of one man now living in the community of Guarjila. They sadly commented on how he had gone mad during the war as in one afternoon he went from being a husband and father of nine to a widower with no children. His entire family was marched off the local bus (along with the rest of the busload), placed face down on the road by the National Guard, and executed, down to the last two-year-old. One of Chavela's and Lola's last stories was about the torture and killing of a mother, Chavela's neighbor. I had heard this story from Kasandra and from other women in El Rancho. I include versions of this story below to place at the center the kinds of atrocities women experienced. These are stories of women raped and mutilated. In these accounts the guerrillas, men or women, are absent.

Remembering Violence against Women

When Kasandra told me this story, she embedded it within several accounts of violence. First, she talked about the rape and killing of two young sisters: "Remember where you passed with Lucía? There they killed them, supposedly buried them alive. They raped them and put them in a *tatú* and put rocks on top of it.[9] One of Lucía's aunts heard the screams but because she was sick she couldn't get up. And they were virgins. They also killed their brother. He was deaf. What can a deaf boy do? He was shy on top of it." Kasandra then talked at length about her own story of escape from ORDEN by using her wits, her young daughter by her side: "They (ORDEN) arrived and would kill you if you didn't run. For example, the woman that I told you about, the one that they raped, slit her throat, and left the blood in the bowl, well, they passed by us but didn't find us at home. But the one that killed that woman, I met him on my way out of the *finca* with my two cousins (*primas*) and daughter en route to meet the group in the mountains. We saw him and we thought, 'Hoy sí nos morimos.' (Today we are going to die.")

According to Kasandra's narrative, this known member of ORDEN asks the group of three adult women and one girl-child where they are going. Kasandra, quick on her feet, lies and explains *"a dejar almuerzo."* Women "leaving," taking lunch to their male kin in the fields, was and is a typical gendered activity. With this answer, the man asks Kasandra where her husband is working the land. She mentions a hilltop a long distance away and in the opposite direction from where they were all headed. Kasandra cannot explain why this man, who wanted to assassinate her brother, she adds, rather than kill them, warns them that the National Guard is nearby. He tells them that they should not pass by the *finca* (farm) for they would be dead for sure. She thinks God may have turned him for a moment. For, instead, he tells them to hide behind some bamboo trees. However, not trusting him, she convinces him to stay with them, which he does, hidden while the National Guard passes by.

I am confused by her story, thinking that she is going to tell me about the death of *la señora*. I ask her, "Did you know that he had killed her?" "No," she tells me. "That was at around eight thirty in the morning and at around ten he killed *la señora*." Kasandra's voice is calm on the audiocassette, but my hands start to tremble as I transcribe the one-hour-and-a-half difference between life and death. Still sounding confused on the audiocassette, I ask, "But, you knew he was ORDEN?" Patiently, Kasandra explains that she knew, but that she was confident he was not going to hurt them. He was not armed with a gun and anyway, pointing to a sharp rock on her table, she figured that if he took out his machete (*corvo*), she would smash him in the head with a similar rock she was carrying.

Kasandra asks me if she can tell me again how they killed the woman. Like Kasandra, the woman was walking through the hills on her way to join the guerrilla camp. She was captured and taken back to her home by the very man who saved Kasandra and her daughter. Slowly and softly Kasandra narrates, "He took the *petate* (mattress made from palm leaves) so he could tie her up better to the bed and so that she would suffer more against the frame. They tied her up by her feet and her arms, and then they raped her. Not one man, but the entire group." Kasandra pauses for a moment listening for the entrance of visitors. No one arrives so she continues, "After that they slit her throat, and they collected her blood in a pot and left her body in the kitchen. (Le metieron el cuchillo en la garganta y agarraron sangre en una olla.) They left a plate full of her blood with a spoon on the table. There they wrote a note, 'Aquí está la comida que les tiene su madre. Aquí está. Vengan a comer.' (Here is the food your mother left you. Come and eat.)" The note was left for her family to see, for communities to feel the repression and stop organizing.

Most of these narratives about the woman's torture are performed by speakers who did not witness the event. Kasandra was well on her way to the guerrilla encampment. However, the narrative accounts are evidence, I suggest, of how stories create and become a repertoire of collective memory that serve against forgetting. Chavela in the *taller,* however, performs a narrative from the perspective of eyewitness in the voice of a nine-year-old child who walked into the horror of that day and witnessed the results of a gendered violence. Chavela takes the floor as the key speaker as Lola serves her back channel cues and debates the date of the murder. In Chavela's account, her neighbor had been raped, crucified, and her throat and wrists slit. The blood was collected in a bucket beneath her body. The assassins were unnamed community members organized through ORDEN.

Conversational moments at the *taller,* between women, among neighbors, across genders, are common in Chalatenango and should be understood as constituting theories of explanation. As an international listener of these exchanges I believe one of my obligations is to document these stories as they carry on the sacrifices of the dead for the living. I also must theorize or interpret what these stories of past atrocities do. As Chavela told me, "Uno como ya lo vivió en carne propia, le da corazón duro. Ya lo vivió. Pero esa gente que viene, lloran cuando se cuenta eso." (Since we've lived it in our own flesh and blood, our heart gets hard. You've already lived it. But those people [internationals] that come here, they cry when we tell them this [story].) Did Kasandra, Chavela, and Lola share this among other stories more for me as audience, rather than for themselves? Were these examples of testimonial literature told for my consumption, as I fit the known category of *internacional,* like so many before me who had come to listen and document human rights abuses? For community members the *testimonio* was a vehicle in which men and women had made their voices heard during the war.[10] Indeed, in my review of the literature, I have encountered El Rancho's residents, whom I have come to know well, give their testimony, some who now work in CORDES and CCR. I wonder though, did Chavela think I should have cried?

In sum, Chavela's and Lola's narrative exchanges of past violence do three things. First, they are acts of witnessing and recollections of profound horror that create solidarity and commonality in the women's lives. Second, the stories served as a socializing practice for yet another international person. Third, I suggest Chavela and Lola engaged in what I term *memory work.* From the co-construction of shared stories of the past, the two women theorize on the present. These narratives that do memory work, like testimonial literature, are a "construct against forgetfulness" (Zimmerman 1991, 26) as in their telling emerges the political work of building a community. Leaving the past for a moment, Chavela and Lola began to speak about the increasing violence throughout the nation, the violence depicted on the nightly news that they could now watch on newly acquired television sets. Yet, the past infused this conversation. Chavela and Lola had recently watched *Rambo: First Blood,* a violent film where action star Sylvester Stallone portrays one man's "heroics" in the Vietnam War. Chavela and Lola were deeply affected by the representation of war, wondering if the movie really could be fictional. Lola described the representation as true to her life experiences. Chavela ended the exchange by describing how she had stayed up for hours later, sitting at the edge of her bed, crying.

Commemorating War Stories: The 1980s in the Present

Excerpts of interviews above and the conversation between Chavela and Lola illuminate how the postwar period is shaped by the negotiation of remembering and forgetting both personal and collective trauma and the ways this continues to socialize and structure life. In Chalatenango, as in other former conflict zones, rescuing historical memory has become a key organizing trope.[11] A past as oppositional *luchadores,* as fighters, armed and political, is called upon to rebuild not only the region but the nation. These are war stories, exchanged as men play cards in front of a *tienda,* as men and women ride the bus en route to activities, and often invoked in the context of organizing by the FMLN or grassroots organizations. I am struck that only five years into the transition to peace, the past, the war, the struggle, the suffering, the heroic agency, and so on is discursively constructed as so very far away.

In the conversations of everyday life, among neighbors or between strangers, recalling the war often opens up exchanges. I am reminded of the first time my partner visited El Rancho. As we walked to Chayo's store for my daily Coca-Cola, I introduced him to Chayo and her husband, Chico. Chico was rarely home. Typically, he was at his milpa or working as a day laborer in Chalatenango. On that day he was mending a pair of his son's pants. He had tailored quite a bit for the guerillas upon repatriation. Perhaps the sewing, or perhaps the presence of my male partner, prompted Chico to talk about his wartime experiences. He explained how in 1982, sixty guerrilla combatants managed to take out the Las Vueltas National Guard post. The National Guard was never able to regain their position. This is an act that reached an international readership. The *New York Times* reported a "flare up of rebel raids" on October 12, 1982: "Officials said the guerrillas also seized control of the nearby town of Las Vueltas, which has 5,000 people, wounding at least 15 soldiers" (1982, A5).

As we finished our drinks Chico commented that there were multiple paths to becoming a revolutionary. He uses the word "combatant" (*combatiente*). Specifically, he mentions that being a combatant did not always require a gun. Though he began our conversation with a story of success in battle, he adds that his own involvement starting in 1979 was political. He had been in charge of recruiting new members into the FPL. He sighed, "La gente era obediente." (Back then people obeyed.)

I heard this refrain often, that people, civilian supporters in particular, had been obedient. The armed struggle in this framing is predicated on the disciplined bodies of civilians. Discipline, I believe, becomes an example of an excess of war. Chayo's comments to me months later amplify Chico's nostalgia for obedient minds and bodies, but her story also illuminates the seeds of a postwar resistance to obedience. From 1987 to 1989, she explains that many residents in El Rancho sewed uniforms and knapsacks for the guerrilla soldiers, she and Chico included. Army soldiers were aware of this labor and kept a repressive presence in the area. Unsure of the year, Chayo recalls that in the late 1980s there was a military operation in and around El Rancho. Chico is alive by chance and wit. She tells me, "He was walking back from Las Vueltas, and he acted crazy like he didn't hear the soldiers calling him over. So they shouted, 'Enseña las manos.' (Show us your hands.) 'Here they are,' he said. 'Enseña la cédula.' (Show us your ID.) He didn't want to show it to them, but in the end he did. They warned him, 'You better get out of here fast or else we are going to put you in jail,' they told him. They let him go but after that he never left the house." This time Chico obeyed the Salvadoran army. Without pause, Chayo follows up with another moment where disciplined guerrillas and supporters are restrained: "Then there was the time that the soldiers came and made their camp right outside of our house. They told us not to even think about stepping out of our house, not even to urinate because they were going to place a mine right outside. Well, that was it, we couldn't have anything that showed a connection with the guerrilla or else they killed or captured you. That's how it was. We've had a lot of failures (*fracasos*) in the community." While Chico is wistful for the heights of organizing and resistance, his wife tempers his reflections. Her words are a strong indictment of the past. The repression by the Salvadoran Armed Forces is cast in the language of failure endured by the community.

Stories of the past also erupt in acts of public commemoration (Bodnar 1992) and are the clearest examples of the ways in which residents and grassroots and NGO actors invoke and contest a shared past, often times for political purposes. I turn in the next section to "commemorative ceremonies" (Connerton 1989,13), in particular, a mass commemorative celebration, the Tenth Anniversary of Repatriation. Here I am not interested in juxtaposing "official" versus "popular" versions of the past. Rather, I attempt to explode what often becomes a homogeneity of "the local." In this context, social memory as the "recollection of knowledge" (Connerton 1989, 4) is not only positioned but performative.

Repatriating Refugees:
"Recordando lo Pasado y Haciendo lo Presente"

In November 1997, there was an interdepartmental effort to celebrate the repatriation movement of the late 1980s. In my discussions with organizers, they expressed that the motivation was to celebrate historic gains and to rescue the historical memory for former participants in the struggle, for repatriated refugees, and for their children. Their aim was to help people remember why it was important to keep on struggling as they exchanged experiences of reconstruction, as the title of the celebration evidences: Recordando lo pasado y haciendo lo presente (Remembering the past and doing the present, or making it present).[12] Grassroots groups operating in former conflict zones, Chalatenango, Cabañas, Cuscatlan, San Vicente, the northern part of La Libertad, and San Salvador, spent months organizing the event with the help of the SHARE foundation.[13] After careful planning, Guarjila, Chalatenango, was selected as the site for the celebration. Guarjila is an ever-growing repopulated community with ample flat, open spaces in the middle of town to organize massive-scale festivities. A two-day, overnight celebration was planned for November 29 and 30. The event was very well organized, with posters, T-shirts and song books produced to sell during the event. Rolando, the Chalatenango CCR regional supervisor in charge of organizing the event, explained the motivation to me as follows: "There are a lot of people who lived in Mesa Grande and years have gone by and they haven't seen each other, so this is going to be a good activity. They are going to be able to talk, tell their life stories, how they are working. What they have been able to get. What they think. Why they want to keep struggling. Because there is a difference between departments. Mostly in the types of struggles and funding and in the possibilities of solidarity."

For many working on the project, the celebration was a pivotal moment for honoring people's past strengths and harnessing this commitment to social change for future battles. As human rights accounts, journalistic reporting, and oral histories demonstrate, returning to depopulated communities in the midst of war was a tremendous act of courage, a symbolic and material act of resistance. However, Rolando also framed this celebration of memory as a critical moment to break a pernicious and paralyzing "refugee mentality." Intrigued by this idea I asked him to elaborate. To do so, he contextualized his response with a history lesson about the strength of Chalatenango's guerrilla forces that placed pressure on the region and the nation:

> "The thing is that during the war the battles were constant. The guerrilla was strong and had the capacity to annihilate brigades. And part of the pressure in San Salvador was from Chalate. As a result, the army kept up constant operatives to try and hold down the guerrilla. Here in this department, from '85 on, there was not one day without combat. Because the Atlacatl Battalion now leaves through Chalatenango and today Belloso enters through La Laguna. Today Belloso leaves through here and today Bracamonte enters. It was a circle. A circle. And here the Destacamento Uno operated, the Fourth Brigade and three elite battalions trying to pressure the guerrilla."

Alongside this localized pressure, Rolando points to networks of international solidarity: "The international cooperation and, concretely, the solidarity movement also put a lot of attention on these communities that lived under this pressure of war. There was a lot of support for these communities. . . . A large part of these communities come from Mesa Grande and there they lived from the charity of the solidarity movement. They gave them from a bar of soap to the shirt they wore."

While Rolando acknowledges the critical role of the solidarity movement and the importance of refugee camps in helping people survive, or rest and reenergize, as Aquilino also asserted, he is critical about the legacies of this assistance. In part this stems from his position as an organizer who never inhabited the space of a refugee. Like many people working in grassroots and progressive politics in Chalatenango, celebrating the past is a selective and political call in order to build a community that still struggles. Many would like residents to forget or silence certain practices and perspectives, for example, to silence a vision of entitlement or expectation of indemnification born from suffering. I often heard people in local leadership positions comment about the refugee experience in language similar to Rolando's: "All those people came with many years living as refugees. They came accustomed to receiving everything and up to a certain point, they considered it a right to be given everything. So, people got used to that. We think that although that process of helping people was necessary, it also habituated them negatively and now it really hurts us to work for our own projects. It was necessary but it was damaging." To contrast, in 1983 the *New York Times* reported that USAID provided "work for more than 8,000 refugees at wages of about $2 a day" (Kinzer 1983, 12). I wonder about the damage of aid.

In any event, the Tenth Anniversary of Repatriation sought to recreate a sense of unity based on a shared past of triumphant suffering in a present that is increasingly varied. It is varied in terms of a growing social stratification that has been further solidified in the early 2000s as more and more residents from Las Vueltas migrate to the United States (UNDP 2005). During the intermediate postwar period, some residents were able to take advantage of the new economic and political openings while others were not, some because they received more postwar aid, others because they made "poor" choices with this aid. I suggest that the celebration was an attempt to recreate a homogenous community that in more recent times is heavily contested. In conversations of daily life, when people visit their neighbors and kin, ride the bus, sit at local *tiendas,* or participate in events, it is not rare to hear discussions on how they have received nothing but sadness and loss from their wartime participation. The second part of the story is that others who did not fight as hard or as long have received peace time "benefits" from an undefined system. Whether "true" or not, these conversations and rumors exemplify a postwar ideology of disillusionment and deception.

Rolando addresses and contests this much-circulated comment. His response is one that seeks to position "benefits" in a larger frame. For him the benefits are global and a result of the Left's long-term ability to organize. With the help of international actors, the negotiated peace accords and life are benefits enough:

> There are people who think that they haven't received any assistance. There are people who say, "Me molesté en esa gran lucha. (I sacrificed in that great struggle.) We lost our children, and to date they still haven't given me anything." But we've lived from the international cooperation and it would not have been possible if we had not been organized. . . . What are the benefits of the peace accords? Land, and the debt (agrarian and credit) that we still have, that they haven't paid off yet, that has not been forgiven. But we still have people who believe that they are not beneficiaries. A lot of people have houses, half of which were donated, and still they claim that they haven't received any aid. . . . A lot of people thought that because they had worked so many years in the war, they were going to receive an indemnity, that they were going to get paid. But the payment we have is our life, right, and the political spaces conquered to keep on struggling.

He is honest in his theorizing on why the past struggle is framed in light of present "rewards." He reflects that, ultimately, it is because people did not join or support an armed struggle for a negotiated peace. They participated in order to overthrow institutionalized power and put in place a socialist project. Think back to Hugo's aim to topple a fascist military dictatorship. Rolando's words suggest that today and in the future this battle must be fought without arms but rather in more abstract or removed (to most residents) official political spaces such as the legislative assembly. He tells me, "There is some reason behind this. Because what we wanted was a victory where we would be the government in power. And with that goal, we ended the war, we signed very important accords. We have access to important possibilities, including the ability to govern this country." And his political efforts have legs, as future events evidence. In March 2009 Maurcio Funes won the Salvadoran presidency, making history as the first elected FMLN presidential candidate.

The event in Guarjila was simultaneously intended to inspire a remembering and a forgetting: a remembering of an organized, heroic fighter and supporter and a forgetting of a present-day community ideology of *estamos peor que antes* (we are worse off than before). In doing so, I believe the past is invoked almost as a myth, which erases difference and is a factor in present-day contradictions of postwar lives. But Rolando always brings the issue back to what cannot be contested, that the war is over: "Hay un montón de gente, que dicen que estamos peor que antes. (There are a lot of people who say we are worse off than before.) but it just isn't so. Because before we had the National Guard that beat us and now we don't." Rolando also provided several examples to contradict people's claims. They are "facts" that "prove" how many people who had been poor(er) in prewar times have greatly increased their standards of living.

For example, he pointed to an outgoing president of El Rancho's *directiva*. In this narrative, Francisco's prewar poverty is juxtaposed with his postwar "riches" made available to him through peace-time projects. "Only to give you an example. He used to live in a shack made of wood slats, and now he lives in a tile-roofed house. He has put from his own effort here, but the [international] cooperation has also aided him. And he is one of those people who says that he hasn't gained a thing. And before, I assure you, he put on shoes made of twine because he could not buy leather."

Interestingly, in his narrative, Rolando does not mention the many accusations by El Rancho's disgruntled residents that Francisco's gains from the international development industry stem from his corrupt community politics as president of the *directiva*. Apparently, supplies would enter into El Rancho and "disappear" from his home. These accusations were a factor in his resignation from the community council. Today, Francisco lives in New Jersey. Those goods must not have provided for much. Prematurely aged in 1997, almost toothless, thin as bones, it amazes me that at the turn of the twenty-first century he made the journey to the United States rather than his strapping son Arturo. But Francisco has sacrificed and saved lives before. As his wife, Alicia, told me, the day she gave birth, the community was forced on a *guinda,* a flight up the mountains pursued by the military. With a newborn, a two-year-old and a three-year-old, she narrates how she could just not take one more step with so many children upon her back. She makes an impossible choice and leaves Arturo with his little sister resting against a rock as she walks up the mountain only with her newborn in her arms. Farther up ahead, upon noticing, Francisco drops his bundle, the precious little his family owned, retraces his steps, and scoops up his children to uncertain safety.

Ultimately, though, Rolando's point is not to chastise his neighbors but rather to instill in them the desire for organizing work, to (re)socialize them to remember "the" past, such as the everyday excesses of war indexed in Alicia's story of flight. These memories, he believes, can be deployed in the present in productive ways. However, in his reported attempts, he at times elides concrete postwar differences that have created cleavages in communities. Through a moral language that defines the war in terms of ideals that were fought for, the political economy of the present is left unaddressed. As a result, Rolando inadvertently silences people's interpretations of the past that are informed by unfolding economic injustices. He remarked, "There are painful problems. A lot of people think that the benefits of the war are those four chairs, a table, and a gas stove that they gave to demobilized combatants. But the truth is that the struggle was not worth four chairs, a table, and a stove. But a lot of people think that because they gave me four chairs and a table and you didn't get any, then I'm a beneficiary and you are not." In doing so, Rolando unintentionally minimizes the inconsistencies of the peace process and the elusive violence of neoliberal policies that penetrate El Salvador.

For example, many long-time activists of the struggle were not demobilized combatants. The reasons for this are many. Some chose not to demobilize because they were unsure of what this meant. Some feared that the encampment phase was a trap by the government. Others feared that it was an FMLN ploy to get them back onto the battleground. Some women could not demobilize because they had to take care of their children. And some combatants were kept out in order to keep doing political work.[14] Thus, while Rolando admits that many who had struggled for years were not officially demobilized, he does not acknowledge the ramifications of difference this created. Rather, he explains that this occurred for logistical reasons as people who "did not fight as much" were called upon to demobilize in order to meet the official number of combatants that the FMLN claimed to have. "It turns out that the armed troops the FMLN had was not even half of what it claimed to have. So in order to complete the number and create the battalions that were encamped, people from the population were recruited, people who had been guerrillas but who were in the communities." This comment elides differential benefits that residents in conflict zones and combatants received. Through the peace accords, former combatants were eligible for slightly more credit, fifteen thousand colones, as opposed to non-combatants who were eligible for eight thousand colones. Moreover, for some peace-time projects, a resident's status as either a former combatant or non-combatant impacts on the amount of debt forgiveness he or she is entitled to.[15]

Hugo provides a similar analysis, though his words are more tempered and allow more space for the disillusionment brought on by people's lived experience. He said,

> At the time of encampment, they didn't call me. And they called many people. They called many people who didn't fight at all, not even one day. Those people benefited. Today some of them are better off. In some cases, it was just. That's how it was. When they signed the peace accords, I understood the need to stop the bloodshed in the country, that there needed to be a negotiation. The only thing that I said was that we should have kept on fighting another six months, in order to get more out of the government. For example, the issue of land, or that there would have been an indemnity for all of the Frente, not that here we have the problem of the struggle over debt forgiveness. To win some more issues and amplify the gains.

I have provided these local theories in order to suggest that the commemorative event in Guarjila was a rallying call to suppress these differences through a language of historical memory. In a flurry of speeches, the celebrants from many different departments and communities were asked to remember the return, to *recordar* all aspects of the difficult journey in order to sustain their current activism for social change. The speakers were familiar to most of the audience. They were from regional grassroots organizations, from women's organizations, from SHARE, Salvadoran priests, Spanish priests, local residents, FMLN politicians, and long-time international residents. Microphone in hand, left fist in the air, leaders from these different spheres took the floor to proclaim past victories, present demands, and future struggles, to mobilize; they said repeatedly, "Con el puño en alto. Por las mujeres y los hombres que cayeron, seguimos luchando y trabajando." (With our fist up high. For the women and men who died, let's keep fighting and working.) It was an impassioned call, where the rhetoric of organizing was supported by the thousands of people standing, listening, and responding. *"Que vivan las comunidades organizadas"* (Long live the organized communities) was a powerful rallying cry. It ignited the speakers; it ignited the crowd; it ignited hope.

It is difficult to convey ethnographically and theoretically the sentiment or energy of "community" circulating on this day, a community not rooted in place but embodied in people sharing a living past and living memory (Sanford 2003). As people separated spatially and temporally exchanged stories, danced, listened to their historic leaders on stage, and watched a play depicting war, repatriation, and development, an ideal space and social relations were constructed. The postwar differences in everyday life were erased as a representation of the past created a deep sense of belonging, of commonality, a timeless and placeless oppositional, Chalateco citizen evidenced in what audience members talked about and their joint celebrations.

As I will further discuss in subsequent chapters, often public events and commemorations silence a polyphony of perspectives and theories behind people's life choices. Thus, the commemorative event described above constructed a meta-narrative about the strength of repatriation and the courage of refugees so often represented as agentless victims. The celebration, historic in uniting the original repopulated communities, could not include the contradictions of the journey. A month later, Hugo, however, did, enriching the stories I had gleaned from participating in everyday life in El Rancho. Folks had much to say about this period. Elsy's five-year-old daughter, born in early 1992 after the signing of peace, six years after repatriation, could talk about the journey home as if she had experienced it—it had become part of her social memory. Accounts I gathered discussed how the refugee camp was a safe haven that felt imprisoning. While benefits such as education, clothing, and food were available, the separation from kin and partners was devastating and destroyed families. Many suggested that though the camp was a refuge, it doubled as a place to move arms, medicine, material, and bodies—many teen boys and girls were forcefully conscripted by the FMLN. Kasandra's husband moved many goods during his time there. Both the literature documenting the refugee and repatriation experience, for important political reasons of the time, and present-day celebratory narratives do not voice these contradictions.

Hugo's interpretation of the camps illuminates the often-obfuscated vertical relationship between the FPL and their civilian supporters. He describes how he was granted permission to rest in Mesa Grande by the FPL but how his "rest" was limited to a few days, after which he became the second in command of organizing for the FMLN in 1986. In 1986, the call to remember was already in place. Hugo says, "They put me as second in command in the refugee camp because there were eleven thousand people. We had to orient the popular teachers. We had to orient the people working in workshops. We had to orient the lay catechists, everyone (para que no se olvidaran de lo que habían hecho) so that they would not forget what they had done. Meaning, what they had been through in the process. And from there, that they realize they could also contribute [to the struggle] in front of the eyes of the world, that the reason why they were in refugee camps was because there was a cruel enemy [in San Salvador] that persecuted everybody."

For Hugo, daily life in the camps was an ideological struggle, something that again is not discussed in the commemoration of the repatriation movement that is called upon to inspire communal solidarity. In Hugo's account, life in the camps was divided by ideological factions and sectarianism between different branches of the FMLN (FPL, RN, PC). These were wartime struggles over essential resources, both bodies and goods, as from the refugee camps material was divided and sent to El Salvador's guerilla forces. He attempts to qualify the accusations by the Honduran military that "there were only guerrillas in the camps, that there were weapons in the camps." He states, "This was not a lie, but it wasn't really like they said." This part of history, of the repatriation story, was not recollected publicly. I am not arguing that the version that remains is invalid, where civilians waged a protest movement for their human rights. Rather, I seek to foreground the messiness behind this clean and neat call of historical memory, in order to illuminate why many contest a mythic unity of the past.

Hugo's account further challenges the more "official" local history of repatriation that tends to homogenize different experiences. In his recounting, the repatriation movement originated from the top down rather than from the bottom up. It came from the FMLN. In doing so, I suggest he tells an untold story that identifies wartime practices that may be at the base of present-day processes of community disorganization and sentiments of disillusionment and betrayal. Hugo explains that as the idea of returning grew, he himself made clandestine trips six times by foot, a dangerous journey from 6:00 a.m. until 10:00 p.m. He explains the wartime tension between Chalateco civilians and the FMLN. In his version, many Chalatecos in Mesa Grande feared reprisal for desertion. He says,

We were told that we had to promote the return. So we said, "Look compañeros," because some of them there felt like deserters. Because there was this hard line that [the FMLN] didn't want people to leave ([El Salvador], because we really needed to push the struggle on. Some people left clandestinely and in the end it was right to find a refuge so that people could rest. Because the compañeros, in order to defend the people, didn't fight the enemy and that was the reality. So we told them, "Don't pay any attention to that. Those were words of just a few compañeros, but that wasn't the party line; it isn't a definitive line. The refuge was necessary. It was your initiative to find it and create it. It was our error that we did not organize a refuge. You looked for it and the Honduran Church supported you . . . and now you have the right to return. No one is going to say anything because you came here [to the camp]. Here you have also contributed to the struggle, in material that comes for you. The material that comes for you is for you, but you are sharing it with the compañeros that need it, like the shoes, leather to

make things. So, you have the right to return. You are helping. And the
fact that there is a refuge . . . is a splinter in the eye of the enemy for the
world to see. While there is no respect for human rights in El Salvador,
you will not be able to return.

It is only in this postwar juncture with new democratic spaces that narratives such as these, which portray injustices within a social movement, can be
written. Hugo's words amplify and contest the return literature that for life-and-
death reasons had to depict the repatriation movement as solely organized
within the camps and emerging from civil society groups and as the "people's"
perspective. I also invoke it to provide another reading that is silenced in the
call for historical memory. Silenced is Hugo's representation of events that indicate a more vertical line with an FMLN that, while being supported by many
Chalatecos, simultaneously instilled fear, as many, according to Hugo, fled secre-
tively and at the time were viewed as traitors, deserters, with the wartime pun-
ishment being death.

Stories such as Hugo's are not exceptional. In recollecting the past, Chalatecos
are not called upon to remember inconsistencies, different positionings, their
past fears, and unmet expectations. Rather, they are called upon to remember
and harness an idealized strength. However, people do talk about the war from
less celebratory perspectives. Mothers, for example, mourn their kin killed by
the guerillas during the extremes of war, young foot soldiers accused of desertion, spying, or stealing who were summarily executed.[16] These are less famous
than the assassinations of poet Roque Dalton or FPL comandante Mélida Anaya
Montes. But there are many stories of a brother who barely escaped assassina-
tion because he left his leadership duties and abandoned his troops during a
military operation, of a husband who was killed because he was accused of
being a spy for the government, of a guerrilla who pillaged communities and
was subsequently killed by community consent. These stories are silenced. I had
heard of other cases of guerilla justice, such as the killing of a young guerilla
after he stole some cattle. They are memories told quietly, requested not to be
shared within communities. In this silencing, they are slowly erased from the
collective imagining of rebuilding Chalatenango. Meanwhile, there is a messy
brewing of these contested paths that creates a tension in the present which is
played out in an active struggle between remembering and forgetting, between
telling and not telling. I wonder if, in the words of Daysi, a CORDES NGO director to be introduced shortly, the contradictory calls to memory unintentionally
cover things up (*tapan las cosas*) and heighten the disillusionment experienced
in postwar times.

In my exploration of social memory I do not want to engage in my own
silencing of the past or present. Clearly, peace time, with all of its inconsistencies and continued challenges, is remarkable for the hard-won battle to end the

impunity of institutionalized violence. This vision is most often articulated by the protagonist generation of the revolutionary movement, men such as Aquilino, Hugo, and Rolando, who were armed leaders and risked their lives daily. As Hugo eloquently remarks, there are many gains that were only possible because of the armed struggle:

> I don't have any regrets in participating. I'll tell you frankly, if there hadn't been a struggle in this country, there would be nothing, no political or democratic space. There would be no space to speak freely. Right? Because there have been many gains. There were people who were in bad straits before and now their lives have improved. And not only the *compañeros*, the former combatants, but rather people who were nothing in the struggle. Somehow the people have benefited from what we as the FMLN did. Now, the problems of this country have not been resolved. We are about halfway there, but the gains have been many. A new police force has been created. . . . I feel happy that those repressive forces have been eradicated, such as the National Guard that terrorized everyone and were the servants of the rich. I feel satisfied that that has been dealt with. And this not only helps El Salvador. It is an example of addressing issues of human rights, and this has penetrated into the rest of Central America.

Memories: Aphonic and Fatigued

In closing, I return to my conversation with Padre José, a vocal yet compassionate critic of campesino or communal forgetting. He eloquently locates his analysis regarding the call to memory squarely in global economic processes, in the ravages of capitalism that has infiltrated even the FMLN and NGOs and grassroots groups allied with the party. According to this local priest, the infiltration of capitalism numbs resistance, allows the dominant ideology to enter subaltern spaces, and, as a result, silences alternative versions of the past. The longer we spoke, the more impassioned he became. Toward the end of our conversation he engaged in a *compa* speech register marked by the informal use of "you" (*vos*) and a shift in intonation,[17]

> Now Lotti, the strongest point is that there is a strong machine, a strong capitalist beast, manifested in the mass media, manifested in all of the ministries that they call here Public Health, Defense, Education, et cetera. In the media they fill you with everything, but they don't give you any history. If you look over the typical educational programs that we have, like in basic education, in the very university system, you will see that we have the same framework as we did in the '70s. It's as if we are still conceiving of history in the same triumphalist perspective. For me the new educational frameworks should include Romero, also D'Aubuisson for what he

symbolized, Monterrosa should also go there, all of the *comandantes guerrilleros,* all of them, the Jesuits should be included, all of the martyred priests, everyone, the history of the Sumpul massacre, El Mozote, but you will look over . . . and nothing. And half-heartedly they talk about Maximiliano Martinez, maybe. So you feel that there is a strong machine ready to destroy, to crush what can be significant for the people.

These are persuasive words that make visible the processes of exclusion in postwar El Salvador. These are processes that entangle or silence histories with ongoing economic and political injustice. The priest's voice lowers as he shifts from speaking in the third person to speaking as a campesino, as part of the community, "Y los campesinos vamos cayendo en eso va. Nos vamos durmiendo, nos vamos durmiendo, y como nos van comiendo, nos van comiendo. (And we campesinos are falling into this. We are falling asleep, we are falling asleep, and so they are eating us, they are eating us.) Sometimes it is because the lines of organization are still too weak." Padre José's analysis is balanced; while he forwards an argument against neoliberal capitalist practices and increasingly bureaucratic NGO politics, he is hopeful and poetic in his vision of the future for Chalatecos. The practices of everyday, of war, and of peace root desperation and fatigue, but he believes they will also root future struggles:

> The people say, "Púchica, si ya me mataron a toda la gente. La guerra, la causa, la revolución, y aquí estoy más jodido que antes." (Gee, they killed all my family. The war, the cause, the revolution, and here I am more screwed than before.) Why are they going to become leaders in the community council? Postwar is new. And here the Left has been short-sighted, and they are falling into bureaucratic pits. . . . Regarding hope, I think it is important to realize that we have not lost organizing abilities. We only have to strengthen organization. Critical consciousness has not been lost. It's sort of hoarse but it has not been lost. You know that between hoarseness and losing one's voice there is a difference. The organization is half aphonic, the solidarity, the combative community. . . . I have hope that there will come a time when this fatigue will pass and the people will take over.

Throughout this chapter I have sought to provide ethnographic examples of the ways in which people in different contexts use the past to shape the present and the future. While many making policy in the Salvadoran government have attempted to build a nation on forgetting, evidenced in the widespread amnesty for human rights abusers, women and men across generations in Chalatenango use history to embrace, challenge, or redefine present-day reconstruction.[18] Their narratives mediate past histories, present practices, and a future time as they seek to make sense of an institutionalized violence whose legacies are still evolving. This is a selective process of remembering with its attendant silencing of visions of contestation, of difficult stories of political agency.

While many groundbreaking analyses have focused on the relationship between local and national stories as ways in which to analyze hegemony and explore the spaces of resistance in counter discourses (see Alonso 1995; Coronil and Skurski 1991), my work focuses on breaking apart what constitutes "local" versions. As Susan Gal (1995) cautions, I have not wanted to romanticize James Scott's (1985) useful theorizing on "hidden transcripts" of resistance. Mine has been an attempt to break apart ideas of popular versus official versions of history.[19] Through listening to how people in different contexts talk about the past, I have attempted to demonstrate the sociopolitical uses of history (see Rappaport 1994). As the book will continue to explore, whether at an NGO organized event, a CCR mobilizing rally, mass celebrations, commemorative events and their planning, or in face-to-face personal exchanges, the call to remember flows through Chalatenango in an effort to rebuild community. This memory work constructs a vision of community as both place and people, linked not only in the spatiality of everyday life, but through time's sufferings. I have attempted to ethnographically illuminate the social formation of memory, focusing on what social acts and relationships constitute social memory, which memories are dangerous, and which are silenced or mobilized for political purposes for a reconstruction that many see as spectral. As William Rowe and Vivian Schelling suggest for social memory, the question must be, "Whose memory, preserved in what way and under what circumstances?" (1991, 227). In exploding the category of "local" and grounding a definition of social memory as a political act, and thus its destruction as an act of domination (Rowe and Schelling 1991, 228), this chapter has explored the delicate balance of invoking the recent past. This is an invocation of trauma not intended to create more suffering, but to forge a struggle that leaders feel is not and cannot be over. It is a call for remembering in order to make sense of loss and seek healing. In 1997, five years after the signing of the peace accords, with a generation of adolescents becoming adults, perhaps it was time to address this call for remembrance and commemoration.[20]

NGO War Stories

On July 23, 1993, after my first long stretch in El Rancho, I met with Daysi to update her on my experiences and observations. I remember the rush of that afternoon vividly. I was in awe of the CORDES director. I wanted her input and, yes, approval. I can still feel the intimacy encircling the two of us as I sat beside Daysi watching her multitask: comment on the situation I described, tell me her narrative of survival, and edit yet another grant proposal.

I had a bit to report that afternoon. During my first stay in a repopulated community I was immediately intrigued by the less than cheerful organizing in El Rancho for this countered so much of the necessarily politicized romantic literature of resistance. Ironically, a few years later, I, along with CORDES and CCR staff, would come to mourn this 1993 period of activism. That afternoon, I latched onto Daysi's hopeful and grounded analysis. She theorized that I was witnessing a process of women's empowerment and unity. If it took women two days or a year to appoint a women's representative for CCR so be it. Though tempting to push organizing onto a faster timetable, Daysi reflected that this would just *"tapar las cosas"* (cover things up). Ultimately, women would take responsibility and would be stronger for it. Where did this analysis come from?

After sharing her insights, Daysi ended our conversation by opening a window into her war experiences. In doing so she marked her expertise, her intimate knowledge of the past as road to the future from her own suffering, a carnal suffering that was anything but atypical. Significantly, hers is a story that was often repeated among Chalatecos in NGO contexts. I cannot do justice to Daysi's penetrating persona, her voice simultaneously powerful and passionate yet fragile as it trembled with emotion. At the time, I was overwhelmed by her narrative and its weight on her postwar work. Below, I highlight the key parts of her war story. I bullet them to provide that feeling of barrage of information as I experienced it:

- Daysi witnessed and survived a massacre of eighty-seven people—she does not tell me where, and, caught in her narrative, I do not interrupt to ask in which community or when.
- The Atlacatl battalion [special forces trained by the United States] captured and tortured her. They pulled out all her fingernails and toenails. She has marks all over her chest from the beatings. She can barely see in one eye because of the damage from the *golpes* (beating).
- She was disappeared for two months.
- Her beatings were so severe that the soldiers induced an abortion, and she is still surprised that she did not die from hemorrhaging or the resulting massive infection.
- Daysi believes she was not killed, not because she was a foreign national from another Latin American country but because they thought that through torture she would provide information on guerrilla forces. Daysi specifically states that she was not a guerrilla, rather she was with "*el pueblo, con la gente*" (with the people).
- Three times she was going to be executed, but each time they (and she does not name her torturers, whether they were officers, soldiers, masked, unmasked) changed their minds, saying a single shot in the head was just too painless. She explained how she was told repeatedly that hers was going to be a slow death.
- Daysi's coda to the narrative was that her story was not exceptional. This was "*lo común*," this was common; this happened everyday.

Four years later, as I began to theorize how NGO's problematic practices can be contested and overcome by history, how places like CORDES have meaning beyond the development that they do, I witnessed many times the circulation of what I term "Daysi's capture story," outlined above. I argue that this narrative (and others) traveled as a trope of war and, in this case, legitimated CORDES's place in the institutionalizing development mapping. In these versions, speakers remark, typically collectively, about Daysi's beauty. They recount how she was young and full of life, and how during a bombing she was captured by the armed forces, accused of being a guerrilla; her dress was ripped off her body and she was walked naked (*chulona*) from community to community and finally taken prisoner to an undisclosed location. She was released during an exchange of political prisoners during President Duarte's regime. Daysi was found emaciated in a cellar in Chalatenango.

I had the opportunity to hear Daysi respond to a version of her story in 1997 as a group of women in the CORDES office asked her if the ordeal was true. She knew all of the fifteen women by name, treated them all in the familiar verb tense *vos,* and explained that she had been captured because the soldiers thought she was a guerrilla leader. She gave orders to civilians from a hilltop: "*Corran, tírense, dispérsense.*" (Run, get down on the ground, spread out.) During this exchange Daysi did not provide an elaborate narrative but rather clarified statements. First, she was not taken *chulona,* but rather *chuña* (barefoot) as her boots were taken from her. Second, rather than an old woman trying to give her a dress, she had tried to give her a sip of water, but the soldiers had pushed her away. Daysi's clarifications accentuate the Judeo-Christian martyrdom elements of the narrative.

The excesses of the everyday of war are clearly visible in this account. In each telling the aim may be different: performative for authenticity, for solidarity, for remembering, for being. In 1993 in the CORDES office Daysi was not done. Before I hitched a ride back to San Salvador, she juxtaposed her own torture story with what I now understand as the emblematic pain and life of Niña Francisca, a sacrificing wife and mother whose victimization raised her consciousness, as her womb continued to produce revolutionaries. I would meet Niña Francisca in 1996 when one of her surviving daughters was already an FMLN government official and, ironically, when Niña Francisca was coming under community attack for corrupt land purchase dealings during the land transfer process. Like Daysi, Niña Francisca's survival amidst horror is heroic, poignant, tragic, admirable, and life altering. This is her story as recounted to me by Daysi.

Early in the war, around 1975 by my calculations, Niña Francisca witnessed the torture and death of her husband and two eldest sons. The soldiers threatened to kill her two-year-old son, whom she was still nursing, if she did not stop screaming. She escaped this encounter. In 1989 one of her daughters (Daysi's close friend) who had joined the FPL was killed. Daysi graphically described the mutilation of her body in a sexualized violence. However, the tragic climax of the story is that in time, that young two-year-old boy, the one that Niña Francisca carried upon her back in flight, joined the guerillas at the age of twelve. In the late 1980s, at the young age of sixteen, he was killed. He was laid out in the Las Vueltas church for the viewing, a beautiful young boy, who appeared only to be sleeping because the bullet had penetrated his heart. Daysi explains how Niña Francisca entered the church, approached her dead son, took his head in her hands, kissed him, and made the sign of the cross, saying, "You served your country well." After which she sat down, arms crossed and stoic. One of her remaining daughters, upon seeing her dead brother, began weeping. Niña Francisca ordered her to stop crying: "Para de llorar. El no murió cobarde. Luchó para el país." (Stop crying. He did not die a coward. He fought for the nation.)

What did Daysi want to teach me with the juxtaposition of these two stories of violence? Are we to note, ultimately, the importance of masculine power (victims and victimizers) in the struggle for national liberation? From Daysi's personal experiences and the circulation of Niña Francisca's courage in the face of horror, Daysi returned to her original reflection that history has taught her that it is the women of the community that will push on. Niña Francisca kept struggling, Daysi keeps struggling, and women from the repopulated communities will keep struggling.

By 2008 much has changed. I can research Salvadoran NGOs from my home. I can find official CORDES and CRIPDES Web sites with mission statements, program areas, successful projects, and organizational history. I can also track CCR's current community activism, for example, against multinational mining efforts. With a bit more effort I can also discover the career trajectories of several NGO directors and find their statements to various national and international presses. Some, like Daysi, have left CORDES. A decade ago tracking the lives of charismatic leaders was nearly impossible. Locating information on Salvadoran organizations was garnered in person and augmented through unpublished brochures, annual reports, and access to project proposals. In the chapter that follows, I address this institutional shift in the ability of NGOs to reach out internationally through electronic media. Textual analysis of this self-representation illuminates the ongoing assessment, commitment, and historically contingent labor of grassroots efforts. Yet, my past research informs this analysis as I carry with me the ethnographic encounters and personal narratives of those who for a time were central protagonists of the very statements that are disembodied on the Web, staff and directors, for example, unnamed.

What I have come to learn about places like CORDES and CCR, if we are to theorize them as vectors of social movements, is that they are anything but depersonalized. In the 1990s, charismatic leadership predicated on a history of armed resistance or collaboration informed all aspects of NGO work: political mobilizing happened with the FMLN and wartime solidarity relationships with the European Union transitioned into development funding to support community residents as direct and indirect project beneficiaries. The past validated the future.

In the transition to democracy, reconstruction, development, and reconciliation (though note, not justice) CORDES and its "sister" affiliates CRIPDES, nationally, and CCR, regionally, are keepers of the past and gain legitimacy as a result. As we move together in the next few chapters to understand the explosion of NGOs in postwar El Salvador, and in postwar countries more generally, we need to be attentive to what the ethnographic exchange can offer, that which cannot be found and circulated in documents or interviews alone.

4

NGOs in the Postwar Period

Cattle and Chickens

The ride to El Rancho felt bumpier than usual as I held onto Walter. I was thankful for the motorcycle ride, and thankful that the bike had not broken down in the rain, forcing us to wait for the less-than-frequent sound of a pickup truck to stop and give us a ride back to the capital city. Walter dropped me off and introduced me to Rodolfo, another CORDES *técnico,* slightly older and specializing in cattle projects. While Walter headed for the women's chicken coop to organize the final leg of construction, I decided to walk with Rodolfo to one of El Rancho's *potreros* (pastures) and learn how to vaccinate cows. El Rancho was bustling with development projects that year and the energy was palpable. I traveled with Sandra along narrow paths and steep inclines to get to the pasture more than an hour's walk from the community. The day was already hot and sunny. When I got to the top of the hill, Sandra and I were the only women present, though the CORDES-funded project was conceptualized as a "women's and wounded veteran's" cattle project. The other participating women had sent their preadolescent boys for the planned training. All other participants were men, ranging in ages from early twenties to late forties. Most had degrees of motor impairment with legs, arms, hands, or feet amputated from injury in war.

The training was both a beautiful example of local development at its best and, in contradiction, a failed project. How so? The project grew out of community-articulated needs and benefited a diverse range of residents across age, gender, and household composition. However, it quickly became a problematic project because of the unintended feminization of injured male bodies. Many men felt their masculinity, already physically marked, further compromised by the very association with "a women's project." Tensions between men and women as well as shifts between communal and individual labor and ownership ultimately played a hand in the dissolution of the project. But on that day in July, petite Sandra was one of the first to volunteer. I watched with admiration as she followed through the steps of lassoing the cow's horns and then the body, and then finding the right spot in the cow's hide, somewhere in the nape of the neck or the behind, to inject the vaccine. Now, cows in El Salvador, specifically those in Chalatenango (species *Ganado Criollo* or Brown Swiss), are large, most a rusty brown color, often with enormous, slightly curved horns. They are, at first, intimidating-looking creatures—not the docile-appearing black and white–spotted Holstein breed most often depicted in children's literature. In my experience, cows tended to appear unannounced on a curve in the road, something I never quite got used to. Rodolfo was a patient and engaged instructor, not only illustrating best practices but providing information on the importance of vaccinations. He cautioned that quite often cows when released could go wild and charge directly at the vaccinator. This was verified repeatedly. The training lasted close to four hours as nearly each participant, working in teams, received hands-on training. This is strenuous, fast-paced work, often dangerous, and a physical challenge, whether people are slowed by their prosthetics or not.

Before heading back to the CORDES office, Walter and Rodolfo scheduled follow-up project meetings in a week's time. Walter left the women in charge of collecting enough bamboo to create feeding troughs for a chicken coop project, and Rodolfo planned to address a growing stress around the communal ownership of the cows. After a quick rest in Elsy's porch-side hammock, a luxury unavailable to Sandra as she returned to tend to her elderly father and three little girls, I was invited to attend a directiva meeting and, upon its conclusion, a community general assembly to be led by the directiva and visiting CCR representatives. This was an important evening as recommendations had to be made regarding anticipated development money, in this instance not from CORDES but from another international development organization, Plan Internacional. Community leaders were tasked to prioritize 400,065 colones ($45,984) of incoming aid.

THE RESEARCH DAY DESCRIBED above was typical in 1993 and served as an ideal encounter to interrogate the many emerging relationships, practices, and discourses of local development historically absent in Chalatenango. Activities such as workshops, trainings, demonstrations, meetings, and visiting delegations were constant. Two linked organizations were leaders in what can be described as an explosion of NGOs in the region—CCR and CORDES to be detailed below. This chapter describes these two organizations in the ethnographic present of the 1990s and then again at the turn of the twenty-first century. Moving back and forth in time allows me to theorize a postwar transition that troubles facile distinctions such as failure and success. These are groups with a long history in the region whose everyday labor involves reworking war skills into postwar challenges. This is no easy task and involves a material and symbolic transition from the clandestine to the public sphere.

Focusing on CCR and CORDES, while specific, highlights the politicized local development efforts that come to define former war zones. In the Salvadoran case, national and local reconstruction development in the rebuilding process with the reintegration of combatants and their civilian supporters. Roads, homes, land, and churches destroyed during the war's scorched-earth policies were clear priorities. Moreover, reintroducing official municipal government and politics was central to local restructuring. CORDES projects were critical in this reintegration of former oppositional communities into the official public sphere and productive economy. By 1996, with forty employees in the Chalatenango regional office alone, CORDES was able to give a peopled attention to community projects, something that is too often missing from development efforts. Most importantly, along with CCR's ongoing community organizing work, development in this context was deeply political and entangled with the transition to democracy. CCR's and CORDES's rebuilding projects, from cattle to mass demonstrations protesting the agrarian debt, were predicated on revolutionary subjectivities solidified in war. Development in this light is intimately linked to oppositional electoral politics (voting for the FMLN) and an everyday practice that espouses the ideals of community-led and participative democracy.[1]

It is important to contextualize NGO efforts in democratization in both the war and postwar economy. As many scholars report, for over a decade the United States bolstered the war economy through military and development aid, the United States Agency for International Development (USAID) was a key player.[2] Michael Foley, for example, aptly demonstrates the significance of U.S. government policy in El Salvador articulated through USAID. He illustrates the ways in which wartime and early postwar programs focused on "political stability and economic growth" by building upon elite privilege through the business sector and consistently "waging war" on community organizations or grassroots groups (Foley 1996, 76, 91). The European Community funded reconstruction projects differently, through a regional approach that incorporated the perspective of various actors—local organizations, many with historic affiliations with the Left (Foley 1996, 91).[3] This war and postwar economy has produced enormous political, social, and economic devastation, a deep challenge to reconstruction that is at once local, regional, national, and supranational. As Jenny Pearce cogently remarks, "In half-built nation-states on the periphery of the global economy, like those of Central America, it is international development and humanitarian agencies that are called upon to design and fund the remaining tasks and to give minimal welfare to the impoverished. And while they are engaged in this process, the international financial institutions are promoting neoliberal macro-level economic policies which may have encouraged greater macroeconomic stability but at a huge social cost for these fragile and polarized societies" (1998, 609). As I describe the transition from popular organizing to professionalizing NGO spaces the complexities are clear: How to carve out oppositional politics, create alternative productive economies, push gender equity, and struggle against an agentless-appearing global capitalism that sweeps over El Salvador with the name of poverty?

For Chalatenango, the national transition away from a historically agricultural–based economy to a service-based economy has meant opening up to multinational capital. This has produced the growth of new economic elites in financing, insecurities of labor (Brooks 2007), and increasing exploitation of the informal sector (Stephen et al. 2001). In repopulated communities these processes take on new meaning as the children of revolutionaries are *obligated* to migrate to the United States in order to remit dollars. In all of these transitions in political, social, and economic fields, from the passage of laws in the legislative assembly to individual families obligated to send their firstborn child on a prohibited migrant journey (see Coutin 2007), it is important to uncover continuities. Daysi's charismatic leadership born from struggle, as evidenced in the preceding narrative, is one such constant. For without Daysi, her war stories, and her injured body, transitions lose their anchoring. Without leaders like Daysi, postwar possibilities for new political coalitions to confront new forms of power are also more difficult. Finally, without historic leaders the global activism that characterizes globalization from below and the new media technologies that underscore it would be compromised.

The sections that follow highlight CORDES's and CCR's regional work, describing their organizations in the 1990s as well as current objectives as represented in 2008. Subsequent chapters build from this foundation in order to analyze how the transition in NGO fields impacted everyday life for men and women in repopulated communities, from grassroots efforts to reeducate fighters into oppositional citizens (chapter 5) to casting residents as what I describe as "not revolutionary enough." When I first analyzed these efforts, it was to unmask the ways in which the everyday former supporters of armed resistance remained invisible, their desires conflated into the category of "civil society" at a time where these very social actors' lack of community participation was a direct challenge to the validity of social movements and leadership in the region.

Time, however, tempers or perhaps allows for new readings. Many of these everyday supporters or low-ranking combatants, the foot soldiers of war and popular organizing, are now in the United States and speak with nostalgia about the activism of the past.[4] With distance, an analysis of the reach of CORDES and CCR across international solidarity chains shows that it is crucial to create an image of *el pueblo, la gente, la base* (the people), suffered and heroic in order to mobilize against ongoing injustice. The question becomes how to untangle the cacophony of "the people's" voices that are so often presented in the singular, not only in the Salvadoran case but in so many life-and-death movements for human rights across the world. Akhil Gupta and James Ferguson spatialize this question. They discuss groups such as NGOs as civil society that exists between the state and communities. They write, "Civil society, in this vertical topography, appears as the middle latitude, the zone of contact between the 'up there' state and the 'on the ground' people, snug in their communities" (Gupta and Ferguson 2002, 983). Their contribution is to show how this verticality is sociologically constructed, imagined, and becomes power.

CCR

Doing research in El Salvador in the 1990s involved a quick learning curve of institutions, organizations, grassroots groups, NGOs, all with acronyms and complicated histories that I was pretty certain I would just begin to understand. I was under no illusion of getting in too deep. Although my contacts on the Left were growing, my personal history did not involve rites of passage of suffering. I did not have, as a Spanish colleague explained to me, my own "*coma mierda*—eat shit stories." She did, but she was also done with her activism.[5] I was also not as intimately invested as a good friend, a former exile and son of a high-ranking FMLN *comandante* who often assessed the transition with me. As a young adult with little lived experience in El Salvador, having been exiled during the war, he observed that in the postwar period all one needed was a laptop computer and a few disabled veterans to garner a two-year cattle project and, presto, NGO. In jest, there are poignant critiques and, indeed, in chapter 7, I discuss the spaces of corruption emergent in the postwar NGO landscape. However, the folks that are the core of my analysis defy this skepticism. In 1993, through a series of introductions, I was able to meet with CCR personnel and, in retrospect, pass a series of tests of solidarity and ultimately gain entrance to their communities.

CCR was established in 1988 and grew out of a national repatriation movement organized by the now long-standing human rights organization CRIPDES (Asociación para el Desarrollo de El Salvador, Association for the Development of El Salvador).[6] With the transition to peace, CCR refocused and renamed itself Coordinadora de Comunidades en Desarrollo Chalatenango, Coordinator of Communities in Development in Chalatenango. Significantly, it is comprised of residents from *repoblaciones*. CCR is the Chalatenango regional branch of CRIPDES and concentrates on promoting community organization in order to contribute to economic, political, and social development.[7] It does so through establishing *directivas*, democratically elected community governing bodies or community councils. These are very much in the tradition of wartime *poderes populares locales* or PPLs, which were wartime organized community structures in FMLN-controlled zones (see Pearce 1986). In 1997 CCR reported serving thirty thousand people in thirteen municipalities and establishing fifty-two directivas.

Importantly, these councils charter communities, allowing residents to propose community-based development projects and garner funds.

I do not directly pursue an organizational study of CCR, its relationship with CRIPDES, or its work with CORDES. Though this is an interesting and fruitful topic, I approach an analysis of CCR through the work of its community representatives whose everyday engagement with CCR takes place in communities and within specific program areas. Gupta and Ferguson urge us to focus on these everyday articulations of "governmentality" (Foucault 1991) that illustrate the "new practices of government and new forms of 'grassroots' politics" (2002, 995). They do so to suggest the "similarities of technologies of government across domains" and how this then troubles claims over the local (Gupta and Ferguson 2002, 995, 981). This approach also supports yet amplifies David Leaman's suggestion that we consider CCR a "political NGO" that can "bridge the gap between informal local self-government and participation in municipal and national political institutions" (1998, 17). Leaman envisions CCR as a link between "unofficial" (*directiva*) and "official" municipal government politics because the same individuals move through these institutions. I argue for the importance of reading the ways in which community residents experienced CCR efforts, most clearly evidenced in attempts by CCR leadership to stimulate declining community-wide activism.

Given that postwar development efforts attempted to build from women's wartime activism and postwar needs, many organizations had programmatic areas dedicated to women. CCR's Women's Secretariat (Secretaría de la Mujer) employed women leaders from the repopulated communities to work on community organizing. During the 1990s this branch of CCR consisted of one program coordinator and seven women called regional representatives. Regional representatives are democratically elected by the women in their respective communities. Their primary task is to work at the community level with the *directivas de mujeres* (women's community councils) and help them address pressing issues and concerns as well as to continue to mobilize them and organize their activism. During the course of research, I observed many regional representatives working in various communities, holding workshops and information sessions ranging from national electoral political campaigns to reproductive rights choices. I also attended monthly CCR programmatic meetings and conducted interviews with Esperanza, the CCR Women's Secretariat program coordinator, and with her direct supervisor, Irma, the CRIPDES Women's Program director based in San Salvador.

The Everyday Women's Organizer

For Esperanza, a former armed combatant, young wife, mother of two, and CCR's coordinator of the Women's Secretariat, everyday work entails directing CCR's gender initiatives. On most days Esperanza rises early, prepares her home for her absence, secures childcare for her young ones, travels forty-five minutes to the Chalatenango office shared with CORDES, runs workshops with regional representatives, coordinates activities with CORDES teams on joint programs, and writes project evaluations and updates for sister-city organizations.[8] Very often she makes the rounds and travels to one of the eighty-three communities organized via CCR to either address areas of concern, meet with women in communities, or more generally enact CCR's mission to ground their labor in the realities of everyday life. This is physically tiring, intellectually consuming, challenging, and rewarding work. It also invokes past experiences and commitments. This is not the first time that Esperanza walked from community to community organizing degrees of opposition and action.

The regional representatives she facilitates typically do the following: attend the monthly planning meeting with Esperanza; hold a monthly meeting by region with each community *directiva de mujeres*; hold a mass assembly in each region one to two times a year; and hold special assemblies with all women in the region to celebrate important events such as International Women's Day. Activities also include visiting and checking up on women's projects, meeting with the coordinator of these community projects, meeting with community women's councils when problems arise in order to facilitate resolution, meeting as needed with community councils as a representative of women's issues, providing trainings on gender, and preparing women for elections. The salary for this work, intended to cover transport in the mid-1990s, was three hundred colones (thirty-four dollars) a month and was termed "a motivation (*un estímulo*)."

What does this organizing work feel like? Hot and dry or hot and wet, depending on the season, and full of meetings. Most community-level meetings were quite slow to start, taking as long as two hours before women arrived, at a slow trickle in from their domestic chores, many bringing their little ones along and staying on the periphery. Meetings were held in *la casa de mujeres* (a women's center) in the few communities that had them, but most often in churches, in school classrooms, on stools, on floors, on hammocks, or in open spaces within communities. I have many hours of audio recordings of these monthly meetings, some on birth control, some on safe water or latrine hygiene, and others on political campaigns, from signing on to attend mass demonstrations in San Salvador to ensuring that community members would vote FMLN in upcoming elections.

Elsy served as a regional representative for a few years before she became "*aburrida*" (bored). I happened to travel with her to a women's meeting she had convoked in a community about a pleasant hour's walk from El Rancho. Elsy was under the weather that day, but the meeting was an important one, arranged weeks before and also to be attended by Esperanza in order to address yet another community's tensions surrounding ownership of communal cattle and women's key leadership in these projects. The meeting was heated as Esperanza first chastised the men and women present for their failures in taking care of a cattle project and then for their posture of disrespect during the meeting. She closed with two penetrating critiques that I was not yet in the position to follow up on. First, she admonished the group for *burlándose* (ridiculing each other) and thus wasting her time. She analyzed in a biting way that if ARENA had convened the meeting they would be well behaved, listening and quiet. From fear? She concluded, nodding in my direction, with the comment, "What kind of image are you displaying for internationals like this young woman right here?" Why juxtapose the specter of violent ARENA with the performability of international allegiances and, ultimately, monetary support?

At the time I did not think through these comments for I was taken in by the larger narratives of war circulating in solidarity networks and that I was hearing for the first time. After this less than successful meeting, according to Esperanza, I walked with both CCR women back to a main road, through some winding small cliffs. Elsy and Esperanza chatted. I was not the direct addressee until Elsy explained: "I took Lotti here to walk and told her not to fall. But Lotti, you can't imagine how it was like. No light, in the dark, pregnant women, little children—you couldn't even see where you were going. You didn't know where you were going to end up. And the soldiers in front of you and you running away from behind, walking, urinating while you were walking because if you stopped then they would leave you behind. And the children, the young ones, how they suffered. Many died with rags stuffed down their mouths to keep them quiet." Travel constituted a significant dimension of grassroots labor. This is not "down time," as the snippet of conversation above demonstrates. In movement, through time, CCR is rooted in the past, both of community and outside of it.

This very localized work has strong global linkages in the solidarity movement. Today, following CCR and CRIPDES from a distance, though quite different, is possible. The digital age has facilitated the speed and reach of human rights and solidarity activism. It is remarkable that at the close of the first decade of the twenty-first century, international solidarity groups continue their accompaniment with El Salvador. Through the solidarity of groups such as CISPES, American Friends Service Committee, Salvaide, Sodepaz, U.S.-El Salvador Sister Cities, CCR's outspoken oppositional organizing is visible. I have found Esperanza's clear, intelligent, and impassioned statements opposing new obstacles and oppression in Chalatenango—the proposed mining in Chalatenango by Canadian corporations. I can find examples of CCR's "bridging" of oppositional former clandestine, official municipal, and national politics through these very Web sites. For example, U.S.–El Salvador Sister Cities Network has published a public statement signed by CCR, by mayors across Chalatenango, and by directors of NGOs regarding the perils of mining in the region.[9]

Revealing in the declaration of resistance is a strengthened cross-sectoral alliance (i.e., with universities and environmental organizations), a call for protests at the national level (the blocking of a planned highway), as well as an invocation of regional oppositional identities. As Paul Almeida's analysis suggests there is a surge of activism, what he terms a "mobilization by globalization" (2008), that takes off in the first years of the twenty-first century to contest, for example, the privatization of the social security health system, as Sandy Smith-Nonini documents (2010). I am curious about what has shifted in the prospects for interrupting national agendas (i.e., blocking highway construction). Evidence from the 1990s (in chapters 5 and 6) shows that efforts to disrupt national policies in the form of mass mobilizations were falling apart. Evidence from the 1990s also indicates that people experienced CCR as fundamentally a local entity, its link to CRIPDES implicit but not embodied daily. The globalization from below that erupts and creates new possibilities for solidarity, activism, and support across borders, as Almeida documents and as these Web sites suggest, can silence the very structures that give rise to social movements. For while I can find evidence of CCR's daily work in sister-city updates, CRIPDES Web sites make no mention of their regional organization.[10]

My point, however, is not intended to minimize the human rights activism of CRIPDES. Indeed, recently (July 2, 2007) CRIPDES became the target of national repression and entered the national and international headlines as the organization's president was arrested along with twelve other citizens under a new antiterrorism law, a product of the global war on terror (El Salvador's Decree 108, Special Law Against Terrorism) as they gathered with hundreds of people in the town of Suchitoto to protest the privatization of water. Nearly a year later, all charges against the thirteen protestors were dropped in no small part because of waves of activism in El Salvador and internationally that called upon past radical subjectivities. For example, in a blog dated July 31, 2007, for a solidarity group, U.S.–El Salvador Sister Cities, CCR director Isabel Membreño's words (not in the original Spanish but translated into English) are posted on the Internet: "In this most recent struggle, we have learned first and foremost who we are, that is, who we were, and who we continue to be: a strong, peaceful and revolutionary people who have proven to the world again that when we organize together we have the ability to defeat any strategy that our government chooses to employ against us."

There are many more statements circulating across solidarity networks, from the president of CRIPDES, from sister city organizations, and, most recently, from the CRIPDES official Web site, repudiating the recent assassinations of antimining activists.[11] That calls for human rights have such immediacy and possible span is extraordinary and has changed the ways in which we all experience connectedness. Yet, I still ponder the everyday of CCR, which is not about spectacle and whose pace is definitely not flurried. I wonder about our new kind of distanced witnessing.

CORDES

Donde hay CRIPDES hay CORDES–Where there is CRIPDES there is
CORDES.

Interview with Irma, CRIPDES

CRIPDES's national focus and CCR's regional focus on social and political organization is structurally complemented by its sister institution, CORDES, which focuses
on issues of economic development. CORDES is a national, legally recognized NGO.
According to its first Web site, CORDES was legally founded in April 1991 as a
public humanitarian institution, apolitical and with no religious affiliation.[12] For
more than twenty years CORDES has successfully garnered funds from international donors. Figures for 1996 for the Chalatenango office alone show a budget
of $1,040,965.39 (a decrease from the previous year of $1,380,794.24) from sources
such as Oxfam America, Paz y Tercer Mundo, and Prochalate (CORDES 1997, 19).

At the time of my original research, CORDES worked in four regions:
the departments of Chalatenango, Cuscatlán, Cabañas, San Vicente, and San
Salvador–La Libertad. In Chalatenango it worked with 110 communities and
thirty municipalities, serving 8,711 families, an estimated 52,266 people (CORDES
1997).[13] The Chalatenango office of CORDES is the largest, with a well-designed
headquarters. Staff include directors, assistants, credit technicians, agronomists,
women who comprise the Gender and Training Team, and visiting international
consultants. Like in CCR, CORDES's staff is comprised of traditionally FMLN supporters, and those with many years working at CORDES share with community
residents a history of violence, loss, struggle, and witness. As with CCR, in subsequent chapters I focus on the gendered aspects of CORDES's work and concentrate on the Gender and Training Team's events. I do so because across the
nation many NGOs funded mostly by international agencies promoted, in vary-
ing degrees, gender-specific development strategies. This is based on their
widespread beliefs that gender relations changed during the war, as women
became active participants and leaders, thereby defying traditional gender categories.[14] I also note that my relationship with this CORDES team was never quite
clear as I positioned myself liminally between community residents and CORDES
and was at times treated with suspicion about what my topic would reveal.

Though connected to the national office, CORDES in Chalatenango operates independently on a day-to-day basis. Central programs and technical
support have shifted in its twenty years of work, but a focus on agricultural
production remains a constant. In 1993, Pepe, the administrative director,
explained CORDES's role to me as one of translation for communities, putting
their needs into a language funding agencies want to hear. This is a savvy political statement and a strategy that begins, as Pepe claims, by treating communities as subjects, not objects. Yet, Pepe does not romanticize working with

communities. CORDES's accompaniment, as Daysi discussed with me as well, takes on new paths in the postwar period. Pepe termed this period one of transition, transformation, and *reconversión,* which can be translated to mean restructuring where projects, objectives, and agendas are all redefined.

Three years later, as I stepped off the number 125 bus from San Salvador and found myself in Chalatenango's new, inviting CORDES headquarters, Pepe, ever candid, commented on my interest in women's projects from years past. I was told that just the previous week a UNIFEM consultant *"vino a darnos ladrillos sobre la cabeza"* (metaphorically, hit them over the head with bricks) regarding the antiquated approach they had on women's development. They were stuck in an old model of development that created isolating women's projects rather than mainstreaming gender into all development projects. Before I headed off to El Rancho, Pepe urged me to think about the missing "interpretive aspect of development." For Pepe and Daysi, CORDES's new work had to address how to get under and alter the "return to an individualistic *campo* (rural) life." My work could then uncover the social networks needed to reignite mobilization and, in doing so, convince campesinos that the enemy was ARENA and not an intangible poverty. Follow-up research attests that CORDES has successfully made the transition from wartime popular/emergency organizing to a relatively well-funded NGO specializing in alternative development practices, including organic farming and community enterprises. While attempting to stay honest to progressive politics, CORDES negotiates a difficult positioning well.

As with CCR and CRIPDES, I do not pursue an institutional analysis. However, I am deeply interested in evolutions, in understanding how transitions get marked, particularly across time and in a field that is fickle—assistance to war-torn countries is short lived, emergencies being ever present across the globe. How long should "successful" rebuilding take? It is significant and admirable that CORDES has published and made accessible its institutional history. On a revamped Web site dated "Friday, 25 de April de 2008" (note the code-switching), CORDES periodizes its two decades of work by first producing a cogent social history and then theorizing the institution's transformations and strengthening.[15]

This intellectual history produces *"fases en la vida de CORDES"* (phases in CORDES's life) and is insightful, reflective, and informative.[16] The periodization it offers corresponds to a national context. CORDES describes its first labors as "Phase I" (1988–1992), comprised of emergency attention and coordinating with CRIPDES to meet critical needs such as food, shelter, health, popular education, community organizing, and so on.

The second phase of institutional work is periodized from 1992 to 1997, the time during my original fieldwork. Reflecting from 2008, CORDES terms this phase "Contingencia o Transición" (Contingency or Transition). Interviews with NGO leadership at the time, such as Pepe, corroborate this periodization.

The third phase spans almost a decade, from 1998 to 2006, and is described as creating the groundwork for development (*bases para el desarrollo*). Interesting is that development as a long-term process is institutionalized. During this period, CORDES also identifies itself as a national leader in rural sustainable development, helping eighteen thousand families from 300 communities in seven departments of the nation. Numbers for Chalatenango include nineteen municipalities, 106 communities, and eight thousand families.[17] Finally, CORDES describes its last phase of work, "Toward Rural, Sustainable Development," as one refocused into four programmatic areas: farming, small business, risk management, and institutional strengthening.

In this reassessment, and perhaps a revision of their labor, there are some differences, not elisions, just historically located and interesting shifts in presentation. CORDES, in its Web site dated from 2000, presents its development work through a prism that privileges its militant origins.[18] An excerpt defines the organization as *"dirigida por las comunidades rurales excluidas de los bienes y servicios del Estado"* (directed by the rural communities excluded from the state). Most interesting is the section that does not exist or perhaps gets collapsed in the newer Web site. The Web site constructed in 2000 echoes Pepe's and Daysi's legacies of wartime activism in a section entitled "Políticas" (Politics) that bullets the NGO's efforts at social, political, and economic transformations. The hierarchizing of priorities illuminates the radical social project at the root of CORDES. It supports my argument on the entanglement between transition, transformation, radical politics, and leadership. What has changed in eight years that erases this list? Daysi and Pepe no longer work at CORDES, and though I have been able to track some of their movements, their trajectories are unknown and cannot be read on any Web sites. Their charismatic leadership, particularly Daysi's, understood as the face of CORDES for so many in Chalatenango, is utterly invisible.

NGO-ization

The previous descriptions serve to contextualize the political, economic, and social landscape that Chalatecos negotiated in the early transition to democracy. But CORDES and CCR were not the only groups working in the region. As mentioned earlier, El Salvador of the 1990s is characterized by an explosion of NGOs, a phenomenon reproduced in other postwar contexts from Guatemala to Afghanistan and Iraq. Other groups included ADEL, CODDICH, and PROCHALATE, which was envisioned as "the project" and "the answer" to Chalatenango with the signing of peace accords.[19] PROCHALATE encountered obstacles, ranging from gaps in pledged funding to loss of local credibility. The parish priest of Las Vueltas renamed the NGO "PEORCHALATE"—rather than improving Chalatenango, it was making the department "worse." More successful and locally valued groups working in the region during the 1990s included Procap and Plan Internacional.[20] Yet the work of these groups was informed by CCR and CORDES history, as they tapped into the local value placed upon community organizing.[21]

I conducted a series of interviews with directors and staff of a range of these organizations. Through these meetings, a similar discourse emerged that chastised residents, the beneficiaries of their development efforts. For example, PROCHALATE's director, while explaining that they worked directly with local NGOs, for they did not want to interfere with NGO constituency—"No queremos tocar sus bases" (We don't want to touch their grassroots constituency)— simultaneously granted Chalatecos a degree of agency and then pointed to what he saw as a characteristic flaw. He said, "Only the Chalatecos will resolve their problems. We can only present our suggestions and the people will have to accept them in the best way. . . . The residents expect a prize for having survived the civil war."[22]

A representative of Plan Internacional had a similar critique, invoking a language of "relief mentality" and revolutionary ideology: "Taking infrastructure projects to these communities is very difficult because they want everything for free." He juxtaposed this claim with the comment, "No se les quita su ideología. Ya están en la jugada." (You can't get rid of their ideological positions. They are already in the game.)[23] A representative of PROCAP, working in Las Vueltas, described the NGO's position of accompaniment. He analyzed the challenges to his work: "Están cansados. (They are tired) . . . and they've started to fall asleep. It has happened in all places. The grassroots has lost its respect for their leaders."[24]

These positions are interestingly similar to the one espoused by Irma, the national women's director of CRIPDES, who has a long history of revolutionary mobilizing. Irma explained how "the long process of the organizational struggle has waned . . . and values have been lost."[25] While she understands the relaxation of postwar times, she places hope in the fact that the communities remain united, as they are almost entirely FMLN political supporters. Forcefully, she reminded me, "Quien vivió la guerra en carne propia fueron la gente civil." (Those who experienced the war in their own flesh and blood were the civilians.)

Finally, the director of CODDICH, working on concerting local development efforts, characterizes the Chalatenango reconstruction landscape as creating a tiered institutionalization that silences local development. On the bottom are the "people"; then a "popular movement" (i.e., *directivas*); followed by grassroots organizations such as CCR; followed by NGOs like CORDES, with CODDICH on top of them, and, finally, PROCHALATE. In this framing it is development money, the access and distribution of it, that moves Chalatenango.[26] It is precisely this hierarchizing within the local that Akhil Gupta and James Ferguson's work on transnational governmentality questions (2002).

By the mid 1990s scholars and policy makers were busy trying to make sense of this NGO-ization, and folks on the ground were busy trying to become NGOs. With "participation," "empowerment," "local," and "community" as key buzzwords (Fisher 1997, 442), NGOs quickly became attractive to institutions like the World Bank and USAID, *and* to critics of development practices. Why? Because NGOs negotiate neoliberal desires, on the one hand, and, on the other, oppositional struggles that seek to politicize what development depoliticizes.[27] William Fisher's call for more ethnographies of NGOs has produced a new generation of scholarship that has written against NGOs as "essentialized categories" (1997, 446) and against a romance of NGOs as beacons of civil society.[28] In chapter 6 I suggest that we need to shift the discussion away from civil society to a focus on governmentality and an attention to the practices of power across spheres that hinge on histories of organization.

Yet, following Chalatenango's story of grassroots development through time opens up windows to the unpredictable, to stories of transnationalized violence that link wartime losses with development and migration. CORDES's and CRIPDES's organizing work continues to evolve and reach across borders. Through the Internet I discover their announcement that broadcasts the death of a coworkers' brother, not in El Salvador, but in the United States in a work-related accident.[29] The announcement does not provide details on the death, though it makes clear that José Justo Mejía Mejía had been living in the United States without documents, obligated to migrate because he could not survive in El Salvador. The name "Justo Mejía" is a familiar one in the story of Salvadoran resistance. Justo Mejía was a campesino leader, one of the founders of FECCAS-UTC. He was murdered in 1977. Recall how Hugo invoked his name. Guadalupe Mejía Delgado, his widow, continues to fight for human rights in El Salvador. The announcement is a call for money, not an atypical flow of dollars from the United States to El Salvador. But this time the money is needed to bring a body back to the territory of El Salvador. It takes between six thousand and seven thousand dollars to cross into the United States, and, according to this plea, fifteen thousand dollars to bring the dead back home. The sacrifices of war and postwar for an ever elusive just and dignified life are still pending.

In these glimpses of CCR, CRIPDES, and CORDES development and activism, from the early 1990s to the first decade of the twenty-first century, new modalities of communication create networks between local and international actors in the pursuit of El Salvador's postwar stability. These modalities, like ethnography, are ever changing. As of May 2010, as this book goes to print, CRIPDES and CORDES Web sites that I have discussed have been taken down. The reasons and the larger significance of this are unclear. In the following chapters I return to the lives of residents in repopulated communities and their experiences and understanding of postwar, intimately tied to the practices of development.

Stitching Wounds and
Frying Chicken

It was supposed to snow on the evening of the thirteenth of January, and I was hoping for enough snowfall to arguably keep me home. I had that familiar eve-of-bus-ride-to-Chalatenango feeling–anxious, looking for excuses to visit NGO offices in the capital rather than travel to El Rancho and traverse the Troncal del Norte. Only this was the New Jersey Transit bus system, and I was leaving from New York City. Why the nerves? I decided upon another route and took the train instead. It was bitter cold, and Chayo was waiting for me at the station, woefully under-dressed in a light jacket and no sweater, gloves, or hat. While our first meeting in November 2007 was characterized by a rush to tell stories, this day together had a slower pace as we reflected upon El Rancho circa 1998. We shared a territorial distance from an imagined El Rancho, mine a decade old and Chayo's coming upon five years. There were many silences throughout the day.

Methodologically attentive to democratizing "anthropological findings," Chayo and I read together from a transcribed audio-taped conversation from 1997. This very document is now woven into the heart of the forthcoming argument on Chalatecos positioned as not revolutionary enough. The excavation of the past, while supporting my analysis, also raised new perspectives and recontextualized reflections. For example, Chayo had never spoken so candidly about her desertion from the FPL in 1985 because she just could not stitch one more wound of battle, place another I.V., or give another injection–and she was pregnant. Like so many Chalatecos, she lived in Mesa Grande refugee camp until she repopulated Las

Vueltas. Proudly, describing her current responsibilities as head chicken chef at a national fast-food chain where we sat together to share a meal, she places her past experiences nostalgically. "Ay, cuánto sabía Lotti–Oh, I knew so much Lotti. How I wanted to work with the women. But I had the children."

The night before our visit, in looking through my albums, I come across a picture of her eldest daughter, Victoria. She is squatting in a blue dress with a yellow slip showing slightly, barefoot, her hair up in a clip, smiling beautifully with a nine-year-old toothless grin. In the photograph, Victoria is leaning against the adobe wall of their home. The picture is either from the summer of 1993 or 1994, just when Chayo's local store was taking off. Crates of Coke bottles are on the floor, and there are no ceramic tiles, just earthen floor. Electrification had not yet come to El Rancho. Victoria is now twenty-three years old and living alone with her four-year-old son in an extraordinary red-brick and red-tiled-roof home built over the last year at a cost of thirty-five thousand dollars. This is the third home for Chayo's family built since repopulation in 1987. Over the last year, Chayo has spent hours designing the house, creating discrete rooms such as bedrooms and kitchen, incorporating features such as arched entrances and hallways. Before sitting down to watch several hours of home videos regularly sent by Victoria of local events such as the celebration of the patron saint, the building of the house, and the stuff of daily life–Chayo's grandson's first steps as he shoos chickens out of the kitchen and blows kisses to the camera to his grandparents in New Jersey–I hand Chayo the photograph of her daughter Victoria. Time, materiality, so much has changed. Chayo at first laughs and says she still has the names of people who bought groceries on credit and never paid up. Still staring at the photograph, she says about her daughter, "*Ay, pobrecita*–poor little thing," the whispered words of a mother. What exactly does that photograph conjure for Chayo? I cannot answer that. I will not ask her to reflect further. Instead, one needs to ponder the silences and the gestures (Das 2007) and query, just as in 1998, how much memory can be asked of people? Pobrecita for the poverty of wartime return? Pobrecita for the injustices of democracy that mediate paths from war to migration? To answer, let us turn to Chayo and her women neighbors' negotiation of gendered revolutionary participation and postwar development.

5

Not Revolutionary Enough?

The road was hilly and winding, and the air cool. I sat in the back of an old but cared for Nissan truck, this one with cushions and seatbelts—a luxury vehicle by El Rancho standards. Chico and Chayo were seated up front and offered to show me the landscape. I learned early that tagging along and getting a lay of the land would be a critical aspect of my fieldwork methodology. For Chalatecos war was everyday and rooted in territory. To rebuild the region involved not only the backbreaking physical labor of erecting homes, clearing land, starting anew, but the intellectual work of giving meaning to places full of stories of violent confrontations, ambivalent narratives, loss, and, yes, hope. I wasn't quite sure where we were headed, but along the way I was impressed by Chico's driving, the way he stopped at all the red lights, yielded when appropriate, used his turn signal to switch lanes, and kept to the speed limit.

At the top of the hill the view was breathtaking and expansive, a panoramic vista thirty miles wide. Chico walked me to a plaque on a rock and as I read it we both smiled: "From this rock General George Washington watched the movements of the British Forces during the anxious months of May and June 1777." In 1998 I would have never predicted this trip to New Jersey. More than fifteen years after the end of the Salvadoran civil war, how had I wound up gazing on commemorative revolutionary battles with Chalateco fighters of other wars and times? Of all locations, how did Chico find this place? Why did he take me here on our first meeting in a decade? In that smile, I thought to myself, "You just can't take the revolution out of the revolutionary." This is not an innocent comment, and one that this book seeks to question. So much of early and intermediate postwar El Salvador as it unfolded in former revolutionized spaces hinged on assumptions, positive and negative, of residents' lives in battle. For those everyday stitchers of wounds (Chayo), of cloth (Chico was a tailor for the FPL), and, more broadly, of community during the war, ascriptions were placed upon them as the nation and region moved from war to peace to democracy. What to do with revolutionaries after their demobilization, when guns are exchanged for political freedoms? How to harness their activism, build on their experiences, and reeducate them to be part of the nation rather than fighting against it?

This chapter explores a key period in Chalatenango's reconstruction and development, the mid 1990s, when postwar development projects were either well underway or, more often than not, collapsed in repopulated communities. Specifically, it addresses the entanglement of repopulated communities such as El Rancho with the grassroots organization CCR and the NGO CORDES, introduced in chapter 4. This is a focus from below that hones in on the increasing differentiation and growing unevenness between and among overlapping groups, NGOs, grassroots organizations, and women and men in communities—people who for a long while shared a life of struggle and survival. In exploring these differences, I track the ways in which historically oppositional practices and discourses are mediated in a postwar context characterized by the everyday violence of neoliberal, privatizing, and structural adjustment policies. Yes, Chalatecos continue to struggle in peace, but the meaning and practices of struggle have shifted as women, for example, begin to challenge calls for political participation because they continue to live in poverty. They challenge the national and local bargain of political participation that denies them economic empowerment.

Conflicts arise out of the very definition of the rebuilding process. These conflicts around community, individual, and larger goals of reconstruction are gendered and include a politics of memory. Women are ascribed as the guardians of community and thus become the easy targets for all (post)revolutionary "failures" in development. This targeting is an unintended outcome of NGO labors that casts women, and by extension communities, as simultaneously "too revolutionary" or "not revolutionary enough." Meaning that they are simultaneously chastised for ceasing participation in traditional wartime community organizing and for the failure of micro-enterprise development projects. My contribution is to unravel these entanglements of postwar struggles that produce a daily disillusionment, demoralization, or *decepción*—in all of its meanings from deception, to fraud, to disappointment. Disillusionment is most clearly articulated in the relationship residents in El Rancho have with their past and with historic local human rights groups turned NGOs.

Revolutionaries, Reconstruction, and Development

The 1990s was termed the "decade of reconstruction," evidenced in the pledge of more than one hundred billion dollars in aid to over thirty-five countries emerging from violent conflict. El Salvador soon became a model case. The international humanitarian intent was to create a "bridge between emergency humanitarian relief and long-term development" (Forman and Patrick 2000, 1). However, what scholars such as Jenny Pearce (1998), Michael Foley (1996), and Adán Quan (2005) demonstrate is that international assistance coupled with parameters set by neoliberal structural adjustment contributed to a shrinking state apparatus and thus an elision of state accountability in rebuilding, ultimately undermining "development." While the transition to democracy involved a great deal of internationally funded national- and local-level development projects, El Salvador's national reconstruction plan was neither predicated on cogently or detailed national development policy nor did it address socioeconomic inequalities that had generated insurgent collective action in the first place. As macro-analyses of post-conflict reconstruction in Central America (i.e., Spence et al. 1997; Spence 2004) and policy discussions on more than a decade of democracy throughout Latin America demonstrate, there is a troubling paradox: deepening social, economic, and political inequalities and exclusions despite democratization (UNDP 2004). Scholarship on El Salvador continues to illuminate how the bargain of peace, while granting political participation to the FMLN, conceded a liberalized market economy (Pearce 1998; Wood 2000) where the root causes of the war have not been addressed (Spence et al. 1997).

As outlined in previous chapters, in Chalatenango, known for its successful wartime popular organizing and revolutionary participation, a significant aspect of the transition to democracy entailed the emergence and professionalization of a postwar civil society in order to "do" development. This shift involved a sociocultural, political, and economic transformation from human-rights-oriented grassroots groups to NGOs. In many cases, grassroots groups and their constituencies had to, first, become overnight experts in unfamiliar development paradigms in order to meet the needs of new, incoming international aid and, second, work within formerly absent state parameters (Eade 1998, 93). *La base* (the grassroots) became sites to be "developed," inserted via NGOs into an increasingly uneven and imperfect globalization. This is by no means an easy, straight road to follow. As Carolyn Nordstrom reminds us, peace does not suddenly appear through the signing of accords, "habits" of war linger (2004, 141).

My original reflections on this uncharted Salvadoran and Chalateco trajectory concentrated on the remarginalization of the rank and file. This analysis is still on the mark and should raise sobering questions applicable to other post-conflict reconstruction arenas (i.e., Afghanistan). However, what happens with longitudinal depth? Borrowing from Anna Tsing (2005), I suggest that we explore the potential possibilities, the "friction" created as international agencies, state governments, and differently positioned NGOs, grassroots organizations, and residents themselves adopt, reframe, and resist practices and discourses of reconstruction and development. Tsing suggests that "cultures are continually co-produced in the interactions I call 'friction': the awkward, unequal, unstable, and creative qualities of interconnection across difference" (2005, 4). For the former rank-and-file supporters of the revolution, the uncertain transition to democracy becomes a story of development that simultaneously embraces and thwarts peoples' move from clandestine "terrorist" to oppositional citizen. A central tension is that Chalateco citizens are stuck between lowered expectations for the state yet higher expectations of rights.

How is this so? By 1997, Chalatecos, as broadly defined activists, were exhausted by both the war and the postwar. They were tired in body and spirit from a series of large and small violences and disappointments. In evidence, by 1997, a growing number of former political, military, and civilian revolutionary supporters had simply stopped. Stopped organizing; stopped going to large demonstrations held in the capital, even when free food was a possibility; stopped attending development, empowerment, training, gender, and other such workshops in the capital of Chalatenango; stopped attending community-wide assembly meetings; stopped volunteering for community leadership positions. Stopped. Exhausted. Disillusioned. Disappointed. The quiet was remarkable for an outside observer with a little bit of history. My 1993 entrance into repopulated communities, CCR, and CORDES provides a sharp contrast of constant bustle, calls for meetings, children scampering and hushed as parents participated in weekly community-wide general assemblies where there was often only standing room. Incoming pig projects, cattle projects, chicken farms, and credit programs were just getting started and women were eager. Just four years later, CCR and CORDES were stumped, particularly regarding their international, donor-driven attention to women's development. Women, in particular, the historic backbone of social movements and the present-day direct beneficiaries of development, had ceased participating in the onslaught of postwar development. Let us follow the paths of a few women from El Rancho and their engagement with NGO life. We begin with Elsy, before dawn, almost en route.

Elsy at 5:30 a.m.

On the eve before grassroots workshops, Elsy packs her small bag with essentials—lipstick, some toilet paper, a pen and calendar, and a coin purse (add a cellular phone to this list circa 2004). She also readies the adjoining kitchen. A breakfast and lunch of reheated tortillas and beans must be set for her father before his morning departure to the fields. On these days, and before her ill health, Elsy's mother, Niña Mercedes, would run the household with her charm and wit, getting Elsy's four children off to the local school or the *milpa* with their grandfather. Within fourteen months, however, Niña Mercedes' health plummeted, leaving her an invalid by the year 2000. Already in June of 1997, Elsy's fifteen-year-old daughter, Flor, had taken over a large part of domestic responsibility.

During fieldwork, for better or worse, if I was staying with Elsy and she was scheduled to attend a workshop, a meeting, an event, anywhere, I would most often go with her. I often felt like her research assistant. In this time period Elsy was busy. She served as El Rancho's women's regional representative for CCR, she was the women's representative for El Rancho's community council, and she taught a CORDES-funded adult women's literacy group. When Elsy had to travel for these activities, she was always awake, showered, and dressed, combing her long wet black hair by the time I woke up at 5:30 a.m. While El Salvador is hot for sure, mornings under a black sky and icy water are frigid. By 6:00 a.m. we were typically at the bus stop, waiting to hear the *rumbo* (rumble) of a van or larger bus picking up passengers on their way to the capital city of Chalatenango and beyond. By the time workshops were scheduled to begin, around 8:00 a.m., Elsy and her colleagues from other equally distant communities had already completed a portion of their domestic work and traveled a good hour—most without breakfast. Their triple load of reproductive, productive, and community labor was well underway.

8:00 a.m.: *Pupusas* and Coffee

Grassroots encounters in Chalatenango are expected, plentiful, and mean different things to differently positioned participants. A two-day CORDES event in early November 1997 stands out as an exemplary illustration of a "good" meeting from the perspective of women like Elsy as well as NGO staff. Why good? Women from distant communities had a space to meet, discuss common problems, exchange ideas, see old friends, and receive several well-prepared, free meals. From CORDES's and CCR's perspectives, the meeting typified bottom-up, democratic politics as key programmatic tools. As a student in the pursuit of an ethnography of reconciliation, I looked for spaces of disjuncture, overt and covert (not yet employing Anna Tsing's notion of the creative possibilities of friction: what positive production may arise from difference, from irritations), to make sense of a palpable disillusionment that in my relatively short four-year engagement with Chalatenango was both increasing and worrisome. Like on so many occasions, after inviting a few women for a breakfast of *pupusas* (stuffed tortillas, typical Salvadoran meal) and coffee at a *comedor* (small restaurant) in the center of town, I followed Elsy and other designated CCR community women's representatives with my big tape recorder in tow and pen and paper out as they entered CORDES.

10:00 a.m.: CORDES Offices

Fifty women "community leaders and representatives" (organized under CCR) participated in a two-day CORDES needs-assessment workshop designed to identify, evaluate, and address local development. Daysi, the well-liked, respected wartime survivor of torture, and charismatic regional executive director of CORDES at the time, led the workshop. Three women of the CORDES Gender and Training Team assisted, as did Carlos, the director of the organization's all-male-run credit program. The event was also supported by Irma, the national director of CRIPDES, who was spearheading new directions in women's empowerment. Finally, it was facilitated by the ongoing work of CCR—CRIPDES's regional branch. This was a smoothly run operation. Concretely, women received funds for their transportation, food was tasty and abundant, there were enough chairs to go around, the brand new CORDES offices were relatively breezy, and, critically, the bathrooms were clean and stocked with toiled paper. Women from the largest municipalities to the most rural communities attended and all were given the floor, evidenced in the six audiotapes I recorded on the first day alone.

This was an ambitious event. It was intellectually driven as an inclusive, integrated, bottom-up analysis, reaching from the home, community, municipality, and department and covering the economic, political, and social realities of women's lives. As a result, on the one hand, the evaluation meeting is a model of grassroots work. Historically marginalized peasant women, across generations, wearing aprons over their skirts and slips, flip-flops for shoes, most with only a second-grade literacy level, were empowered. Their words, written down on index cards and literally taped up like wallpaper to cover the walls, were intended to direct future grant proposals. And indeed, Elsy and her colleagues were vocal. On the other hand, we need to unpack the very definition of what constitutes grassroots, or rather, how grassroots as a process, as a practice, takes shape, how perspectives get defined, and what unintended consequences erupt. If we follow this path, then we can see that grassroots spaces for building the future are entangled in assumptions born from the past about women as warriors, as *luchadoras,* who are expected to carry forward their revolutionary perspective into development. A study of postwar illuminates the complications of this desire to empower women. Development problems get reframed into the "woman question" (*la problemática de la mujer.*) All women? Chalateca women? Revolutionary women? Eager and spent, young and old? How do development and revolution get worked out upon the backs of so many women's lives?

At this meeting, the participants, ranging in ages from twenty to fifty-five, were called upon to represent all the women from their respective communities and these women's problems. The two-day meeting ultimately served to plan CCR's and CORDES's gender strategy for the following fiscal year. Throughout the event, Daysi negotiated a difficult position of authority easily and well. She spoke from a position of common history, invoking the gendered language of *nosotras* (us) and the informal "you," *vos,* a marker of intimacy, equality, and solidarity, which women rarely use at present.

The meeting did begin through participation. Working in small groups that crisscrossed different municipalities, all present were asked to write down on index cards as many women's problems as they could think of. Daysi read each card, taped some on the wall, discarded others, redirected some, and debated the meanings of many. With pink index cards covering an entire wall after a few hours, women's multiple realities were constructed in terms of "problems" that could be intervened upon either through technology or ideology (see Ferguson 1994). These problems included illiteracy, domestic violence, crime within communities, lack of employment opportunities, lack of women's projects, and lack of credit for women. Not surprisingly, poverty came up again and again in the index cards. As CORDES and CCR staff discussed poverty, this problem was translated in a particular way that elided women's economic disempowerment through a discourse of the lack of "communal values" and "organization" that structured the remainder of the workshop. A deficit model guided the session rather than one emphasizing assets.

Importantly, Daysi qualified the role of NGOs for the participants as a way to negotiate present-day injustices. While NGOs are spaces validated by international donors, she eloquently voiced the limitations of what NGOs can do, saying that, indeed, NGOs should not exist: "We exist because the state marginalizes. We exist to support the people. We are not going to solve the problem of potable water, of orphaned children. That is a lie. NGOs cannot resolve the economic problems of all women in communities." Note Daysi's use of the word lie (*mentira*), a trope that gained currency during this postwar period. With this phrase, Daisy both marked and refuted growing complaints from residents that situated blame in local terms, on local institutions, organizations, and actors. However, this statement was followed by the familiar slippage into organizing rhetoric: "Until one day when we get power, and then we will see what we can do in the face of this terrible globalization."

As the workshop continued, "the problem" was translated into a language of crisis and placed on "women," "community," "values," "organization," and the combination of these. Indeed, Daysi, too, places blame locally. For example, during part of the session, Daysi, supported by her staff, shifted the discussion to analyzing why already existing CORDES women's projects do not work. She suggested that the (donated) projects are not appropriated by women. Carlos from Credit added that it was a problem of organization. Rosario from the gender team opined that it was, in fact, also a problem of dependence on external assistance (*asistencialismo*), where women (and men) only like to receive aid.

Isabel, an elderly resident of one of the repopulated communities, requested the floor and challenged this perspective. She offered that the projects do not work because they create difference, they cannot empower all women and this breeds envy and individualism rather than community. In this reflection Isabel elegantly identifies a key tension in the move from revolution to neoliberal

FIGURE 5. A large assembly held in the bombed-out church in a repopulated community in Chalatenanago. Meetings such as this were frequent in the early to mid 1990s and created a space to practice participatory and democratic communal decision making.

Photograph by Ralph Sprenkels.

democracy: the place of individuals in nostalgic memories of community. But Isabel's perspective was silenced as Daysi launched into "history." She began, "Recuerden Uds. vamos hacer un poquito de historia. (Now remember, we are going to review a little bit of history.) When this war started, right, remember, remember how we survived? What did we do back then? We were united. We had those Sundays, those Farabundista days. Together we would all work the *milpas* and the *frijolares*. The war united us. And the formula was: '*Dueños todos responsables todos*' (All owners, all responsible). That's how it was." Her call for women to remember their lived history, rooting it in a shared moment, continued as she walked the women through the second phase of the war, where she collapsed life in refugee camps with repatriation to bombed and destroyed communities. She focused on one element of these varied experiences, the strength of the "communal spirit." Interestingly, she located the crisis in community organizing in the peace process, in the third phase, the cease-fire. She stated, "In this phase came land transference. But we are still struggling over which piece of land belongs to who. So this brought on a crisis in communal projects. Who are the owners? Everybody *compañeras*, we are all the owners."

Can this history of communal survival carry over or perhaps even trump postwar individual and familial needs, desires, and the habits of capitalism? I think back to the anonymous NGO critic who critiqued his colleagues' inability to understand the search for happiness. Daysi ended her story in the present, by critiquing women en masse for losing this communal spirit. The fifty women representatives came to stand for all women, decontextualized, nameless, unspecified. She provided an example of how in one community no one helped two old women working in a communal store—a CORDES project. She asked, "So, when have you [and here she used the formal 'you' (*usted*), shifting away from intimacy] gone to help those poor old women carry their heavy loads? Never!" She offered her observation that the ideology has become "what can I take, not what can I give." Yet she did not address in her narrative the way in which the war destroyed families and erased the household social and economic unit, nor how this created present-day socialization challenges for a generation of wartime survivors negotiating their own transition along with that of their children. Daysi concluded by articulating for the women the key problems: loss of community practices and ideology. She linked this to how "the community needs to rethink itself, to see what it should do, should be. How it will organize." This was an attempt to harness old strategies, successful strategies of a very different context into a new terrain where the Left has no clear, easy, or cogent answer. Indeed, the conclusion articulated by Daysi is wanting. Are women to shoulder this communal task, and how?

By the end of the day the women's key problems had been identified, written in large block letters on poster paper, and tacked up on the center wall. The poster paper read, "We, as a community, are not clear about our future." The root cause was identified as "poor community organizing." Through various twists and turns, women agreed with the analysis that the current crisis in community, homogenizing and blurring differences between and among repopulated communities and women, stems from the loss of values learned during the war. This was evidenced through one of the key terms to emerge from the workshop— organization. The multiple meanings of "organization" include well-run projects, where development is seen in the repayment of small-scale loans; but organization also invokes revolutionary ideals, a cause, a common history of struggle. It is a claim of identity rooted in everyday practices. However, in the postwar context, the call to organize rings hollow at a time when socioeconomic differences are increasing. As scholarship across Latin America suggests, "democracies may be in the process of political consolidation, but they also show signs of their inability to meet basic social demands such as civil and economic rights" (Bergman and Szurmuk 2001, 386).

Leigh Binford's work is helpful here as he demonstrates how a fundamental FMLN model was participative democracy and self-management, how involvement or participation was central and reflected an "acceptance of more responsibility for one's situation and an active effort to confront and resolve difficulties rather than lament them" (1998, 16). Daysi's workshop, which focused on community organization and participation and how this is "lost" (evidenced in the failures of women's projects), was grounded in this expectation of involvement. But the call for organization is a contradictory project. It asks generations of marginalized women and men to re-educate themselves to become successful small-scale entrepreneurs and to repay their loans. Simultaneously, it critiques community members for losing their "revolutionary" ideology and practices, evidenced in their lack of mobilization. The solution to economic injustice falls upon the backs of the very poor, on women who become the embodiment of what is lacking. Economic restructuring or empowerment, key to the struggle, is elided, erased as a proscriptive to the lives of community members. Instead, the extreme poverty, sacrifice, and unity of the wartime period are held up as the model replacing a struggle against economic marginalization. Thus, NGO assertions idealize and homogenize a revolutionary past, mask difference, and mystify the challenges of reconstruction.

As raised in previous chapters, many scholars unpack this heterogeneous category of NGOs and query the theory that a strong civil society leads to democracy (Foley 1996, 69; Hemment 2004; Murdock 2003). Michael Foley highlights that democratization cannot "depend solely on the democratization of civil society: parties, state, and civil society must all be democratized together" (1996, 91). Comparative work on the transitions to democracy from communist regimes is helpful here in conceptualizing the hegemony of international models of governance. Julie Hemment, writing on processes in Russia, explores the emergence of the "third sector," a category created by international development agencies that ultimately asks NGOs to take on state responsibilities (2004, 217). Hemment's critical finding is that, in effect, the third sector has become "a professionalized realm of NGOs, inaccessible to most local groups" (Hemment 2004, 221). This echoes analyses of feminist NGOs and women's movements throughout Latin America (Alvarez 1998) and is an important reminder of civil society's constrained agency.

Like Donna Murdock (2003), who explores the work of women's NGOs in Medellín, Colombia, I am concerned with shifting the discourse away from the persistent question of whether NGOs do "good" or "bad." Importantly, Murdock unmasks the ethical and epistemological assumptions that underscore this concern and offers instead an attention to "the lived experience of NGOs, with particular attention to social actors' ongoing negotiations of meaning and practice" (2003, 508). In a postwar context lacking in human rights discourse and practice like El Salvador (Sprenkels 2005), I suggest that it is crucial to look at the negotiations between NGOs and their constituencies. Though focusing on much larger humanitarian institutions, such as Médecins sans Frontières (MSF), Peter Redfield demonstrates that the work of these types of NGOs "contributes to the greater contemporary world order, forming part of an established apparatus of crisis response" (2005, 344). While Redfield illuminates how MSF operates in the "shadow of disaster" and where a secular humanism defends both "physical existence" and "human dignity" (2005, 329, 300), my research explores the messiness of postwar when states of emergency appear to be over. The aftermath of violence, a step beyond the work of minimal existence, is harder to address. Institutionally, it brings, among other things, a classificatory liminality or slippage between categories—from relief and human rights to development work.

From NGOs to a Discourse of Lies

As evidenced in the above analysis, in Chalatenango I spent a great deal of time participating in the ebbs and flows of women's activism and listening to women's stories about the past, the present, and their occasional hopes and frequent worries for the future. Indeed, as introduced in chapter 3, Chalateco survivors negotiate the contradictions of peace-building by actively turning to their memories of the recent past, to their lived history of mobilizing, sacrifice, and loss. Often, this is a call to remember the past as one of heroic participation, a triumphant though suffered representation of Chalatecos as oppositional *luchadores,* as armed and political fighters in creating community. The recent past is called upon selectively and politically to build a community and a postwar citizen that still struggles. However, this meta-narrative is often contested in a variety of community spaces as many residents place the survival of their household economy over community politics. In the following sections, stories from three differently positioned women of El Rancho illustrate the ways in which a politics of memory confront NGO and grassroots politics of development.

Unlike her neighbor Elsy, Chayo did not travel much. Her eldest daughter, Victoria, was just a bit younger than Elsy's eldest, Flor, and could not yet run a household. However, she was just as busy. On most afternoons, I walked over to Chayo's *tienda* as it was physically a cooler space from which to gage pedestrian movements, get updated on new events, invite folks to a soda and *pan dulce* (sweet rolls), or simply sit and talk with Chayo, her husband, and her children. By 3:30 p.m. I also needed the caffeine of a *gaseosa* (soda) to keep me going. One hot, dry afternoon, several hours before an upcoming community council election where no one had presented their candidacy, Chayo and I had settled on finally tape recording a conversation together. Chayo never stopped working at her store during this conversation. Neighbors walked in and out, buying tomatoes, rice, eggs, salt, and sugar. Kids asked for homemade *charamuscas,* little baggies of frozen flavored milk, and her own children ran in and out of the house and store. On that day we began talking about El Rancho's short-lived women's group that was initiated outside of both CCR and CORDES and named itself Grupo de Animación. The group was sponsored by a long-term, faith-driven, community-based development worker who was living in El Rancho. At the time of the group's inception, I was eager to find any space of women's organizing and was particularly intrigued by activism occurring outside of CCR's or CORDES's purview.

Thirty-year-old Chayo was one of the eight participants of this group and explained the objective to "animate all the women who are depressed in order for them to defend themselves and meet their basic needs." For this group, *ánimo* was synonymous with "development," and, indeed, Chayo explained that the motivation for forming the group derived from the many failed development projects in El Rancho. She also complicated the discussion of development by referring to it as both a communal social project and an inherently personal one. With development a key discourse circulating in NGO spheres, Chayo had given much thought to the meanings of development. She explained, "To me, the meaning of development involves personal development, to have the time to devote oneself to both the family and the community." She emphasized the importance of incorporating women in community life: "I wish that all women were active in some kind of work so that they might feel alive and not feel isolated and alone, full of shyness. I want them to have personal development and participate in the different community activities. That is what I desire."

Although Chayo made the connection between development and community organizing, her analysis of the past provides an alternative reading to Daysi's uniform rendering of community organization. For Chayo, the past holds both the glories of unity and the legacy of its deceit. Her depiction of the early organizing of the struggle is one of broken promises and bankrupt dreams. Her story is one of deception, lies, and loss, as she explained, "When we first started organizing, they used to tell us, 'In twenty-four hours the country is going to be liberated.' . . . But you can see that war is quite painful and it's not an overnight matter. Many people have to struggle and die. . . . So that was a big lie, what they said about the country's liberation in twenty-four hours. And you can see it; the costs are too high to liberate a country. Right?" From these founding "lies" at the root of organizing efforts, Chayo sees the seeds of present-day community disorganization, lack of mobilizing, and community-wide lack of faith in present-day efforts. She continued, "So I thought it was a deceit . . . and that is why since that time we have this great demoralization happening. Because you could say it's been a lie since then. So now you can tell people the nicest hopeful things to lift their spirits, but no one believes it at all."

Chayo is not alone in this perspective. Recall forty-nine-year-old Kasandra, an early and longtime participant in the movement. She voiced the contradictions of the struggle by arguing that area residents were unable to take a neutral position during the war. She went further than Chayo and consciously and cautiously debunked a romantic vision of the Left. She did not deny the positive changes in postwar times but did not want to homogenize the past: "There have been a lot of things that have ruined us more. . . . There were hard times during the war, because not everything is pretty. The guerrilla was also quite cruel. It's the truth. If you didn't like me, or if you rubbed me the wrong way, I could say, 'I don't like her because of this' for whatever reason. I would go and tell a leader, 'She is an enemy, a spy.' Entire battalions died, not just a group. . . . It was hard because the government's army was as cruel as the guerrilla forces." As Philippe Bourgois poignantly shows, "the revolutionary movement in El Salvador was traumatized and distorted by the very violence it was organizing against. Through an almost mimetic process, the government's brutality was transposed into the guerillas' organizational structures and internal relations, as violence became a banal instrument of necessity" (2001, 20). Interestingly, Kasandra's critiques of the war took her to an analysis of community and its sense of unity, *unidad*. For her, unity as the basis for community was, indeed, rather characteristic of prewar social organization, kin relations, and everyday practices rather than a result or legacy of wartime organizing. This earlier sense of community characterized by strong kin ties is then broken by the war and its aftermath—the displacement of extended family, loss of kin, destruction of landscape, and an increasing socioeconomic differentiation within communities that leave many questioning their years of sacrifice. In the past, she says, "In the small communities we all lived as best we could. But we had more unity because back then when something happened to you, everybody came to help. Not now. People can see you dying and nobody does anything to help. . . . People were really united . . . before the war. If somebody was sick, everybody took turns and went to help." Kasandra critiques wartime expectations of *unidad*, which she understands as equality. This is linked to her analysis of the distribution of postwar development at the local level and continued economic injustices. She compares her present concerns to the hopes she had when she joined the struggle: "I was so sincerely happy when they said that upon taking power we would achieve unity. What one person had, all would have. For example, if somebody ate *frijoles* (beans), everybody would eat *frijoles*. If somebody ate meat, everybody would eat at least a little bit of the same. There was going to be unity. This is what the struggle was for, the search for unity."

Like Chayo, she employs a discourse of deceit and is angered by lies and disillusioned by the aftermath of organizing for social justice. Kasandra and Chayo were not alone in remarking on present-day community differences. For many, this community difference could not be reconciled with a history of loss and sacrifice. And so Chayo continued, outraged by the "success" of some who did not "really" participate in the struggle: "What I don't like in these communities is that there is always this kind of preference, I'm going to call it that. So the people who have more possibilities are those who did not necessarily work hard during the armed struggle or in community organizing, those people have benefited most."

For Chayo, the unity characteristic of community organizing is different than both Daysi's and Kasandra's. Like Daysi, she employs a discourse of community crisis located in the very emergence of postwar national reconciliation, but her focus is on the entrance of official, municipal government institutions. With the establishment of municipal government (although FMLN), community political structures are repositioned. This creates a new set of tensions as community councils struggle for autonomy and legitimacy within their communities and with official institutions. Chayo's vision of organization, community, and unity is linked to a wartime mapping; it is spatialized and, thus, recent cartographic changes are seen as critical: "The community of El Rancho was united with the community of Las Vueltas. When we arrived they formed one single community. Then, after that Las Vueltas formed a sister-city project [with a foreign country] and that relationship continues to fund projects in Las Vueltas. And now El Rancho remains alone, becoming independent from Las Vueltas."

This landscape is marked by growing differences between municipal head towns and smaller, more rural *cantones*. Unequal distribution of postwar benefits and resources aimed at rebuilding destroyed communities contributes to tense community-based politics: "And to top this, all the projects failed. Then El Rancho was left with nothing. All these things discouraged the women and men, seeing that, be it one thing or another, everything fails."

Ultimately, residents cannot forget, although Chayo hopes for new strategies and avenues to heal in order "that they lose the culture of war (que se le vaya perdiendo el sistema de guerra)." She reflects that like so many of her neighbors, she will never forget such things as "how they killed our sons, that cannot be erased. What we have suffered in our own flesh. To walk and fall through those mountains. When you had to flee pushed on by the bullets. These things one cannot erase. Some have even become wounded war veterans. This and other things makes one remember a lot. We cannot lose these traditions."

Mentiras (Lies), *Engaño* (Deceit), but Yet Revolution

A final ethnographic example provides insight into the importance of context in understanding the logic of NGO-led development and responses to it, and complicates easy moral generalizations that label women as not revolutionary enough. For this I turn again to Elsy. As evidenced in the contents of her purse in later postwar times, Elsy shifted from survival to being able to engage in conspicuous forms of consumption for the first time in a long while. And so she buys rayon in Chalatenango to make pants suits. She buys shoes with high heels and a purse to match, wearing flip-flops only inside her home. Already in 1996 she was no longer CCR's regional women's representative, held only sporadic community women's meetings, and missed many *directiva* meetings. In the early to intermediate postwar period, she would often "escape" to San Salvador on weekends to be with her partner, Avel, incorporated into the new civilian police force and taking a college course. Also, Elsy is moody—*lunática* her mother would call it. Erratic, unpredictable behavior, unfocused anger, moments of depression, incessant complaining about all things—body pain, bad tortillas, and token social services. But this behavior alternates with extreme highs and energized moments in which, for example, she tells stories that invoke her past participation in organizing for social justice. In other chapters I discuss this as her "fearless" talk.

Depending on context, Elsy constructs, frames, or positions herself differently, sometimes privileging her identity based on her history of strong grassroots activism, her face of *la mujer organizada* (organized woman). Over the course of five days, on three different occasions, Elsy narrated increasingly detailed versions of what I term her "midwife (*partera*) story." Her first account was primarily factual. Elsy had participated in a ten-day midwife training course offered by the Ministry of Health. The idea behind this workshop was to train women with past medical experiences (i.e., women with war time experiences as nurses) to become local midwives. The course received no follow-up, and in many cases practicing midwives in rural communities were not invited to participate. But the project did impact Elsy in many ways. For weeks afterwards she bought natural medicine pamphlets and began taking better care of her ill mother. Also, the workshop took over her imagination, as she repeatedly reflected on its contradictions, an example of the frustrated paths of her everyday life.

The second time Elsy talked about the workshop, she was attending to her youngest daughter's minor scrape. As asked, I passed her the first-aid kit distributed at the end of the sessions, and Elsy complained that the kit did not have the essentials, not even gloves. She explained how the training was budgeted for thirty-one thousand colones (roughly $3,560) but that clearly not all of this money was spent on the workshop. Her analysis was this: "Se lo comieron." (They ate the money.) In this telling of the story she locates the blame locally; it is not the sponsoring Ministry of Health she takes issue with, but the nurse Paty, who had led the sessions. Paty, who was not a participant in the revolutionary struggle, had denounced Elsy as a revolutionary because she contested the poor distribution and quality of supplies.

In her third recounting, Elsy embedded the *partera* story within a series of other tales, the climax of a larger conversational exchange. Elsy had just participated in a heated community general assembly, called not by the directiva but by CCR as an emergency intervention into community problems. Here, a CCR coordinator, Rolando, announced that the directiva had been defunct for over six months, and that a new one had to be elected. Residents were told that without a directiva they were going to suffer because "if you don't organize you will be a regular community, without projects." If they did not agree to hold elections and fill the vacant posts, they would be unable to propose and garner development projects. Thus, directiva-less they would be *una comunidad muerta* (a dead community). And because meaning has shifted spatially, the political landscape moving away from wartime zones of control that united communities, the CCR coordinator explained how the issue of organization and the election was a problem that El Rancho had to resolve independently because other communities would not be affected in the least, and, indeed, El Rancho would be further marginalized. This was very much a chastising session, ended only by a sudden thunderstorm.

Perhaps the rain, the electricity down, and no TV, perhaps the dark, lets people talk, because Elsy launched into a series of stories. With an increasingly agitated yet forceful voice, she moved from critiquing how she had received nothing from the peace accords, no land, no credit, simply because of bureaucratic errors, to explaining why she had ceased participating in community decision-making. She was outraged by the accusations from neighbors that those on directivas, those who worked to represent the community, actually pocketed a substantial amount of incoming aid, *"comiendo el pisto"* (eating the money). Elsy contested these claims, saying that only once had she received a personal gift from a delegation. She did not mention our personal relationship and the benefits (transportation and food contributions) most rightly perceived. Interestingly, she had to defend herself from the same accusation she had made of Paty, the midwife trainer—*comiendo el pisto.*

In these narratives, Elsy engaged in a common postwar discourse of deceit, an analysis of corruption that local people make, theories for understanding their frustrated dreams. For *engaño* (deceit), as illustrated in the section above, is used frequently to explain a range of betrayals and injustices. How else to make sense of the growing stratification within and between communities, among people whom local history constructs as arriving from refugee camps equal (meaning equally poor), *todos pelados* (all naked). Elsy's stories, like Chayo's and Kasandra's, suggest that decreasing participation, withdrawal from positions of power (like the directiva), and challenges to authority may be indicative of people's emerging resistance efforts, claims of solidarity, of the collective over the individual at odds with postwar differentiation into which NGOs are often forced.

After asserting her own incorruptibility, Elsy said that those who were truly corrupt were the NGOs working in Chalatenango. In doing so, she lumped together historically committed organizations with more recent arrivals. The problem is that international donors actually believe that Salvadoran organizations serve people like herself. Moreover, she questioned the very nature of credit as development, problematizing how NGOs that receive money as donations could turn around and charge folks like herself, yet another example of

NGOs skimming from projects (further evidenced in new cars, new offices, new staff). Then she made a powerful connection, linking present development with its contradictions, to the past, to the international solidarity movement active during the war. She explained how it was the same when internationalists arrived and sought out the most malnourished, orphaned, and injured child, took its picture and, with this, raised money in their home countries for the struggle. And that poor child received not a cent for the photograph and did not benefit from the resulting donations. Indeed, in El Rancho such a "poster child" lives up the hill from Elsy. The Save the Children print, yellowing and torn around the edges, still hangs from the façade of the girl's house.

Our conversation ended as Elsy returned to the issue of the workshop, her voice becoming more tense, louder, stronger, her speech faster. In this version, she presented herself as a leader, combating Paty, the trainer, whom Elsy described as the only one who benefited from this kind of exercise, building her career by climbing upon the backs of women like herself, *"como una escalera para hartarse"* (like a ladder to success). This time, Elsy moved from the useless first-aid kits to talking about the cloth that women received to make uniforms for themselves. All of this was a pittance, taking into account the thirty-one thousand colones budgeted. Elsy began by saying how they had all seen the three rolls of cloth in Paty's truck, but how Paty had only brought in one roll to distribute. The trainer announced that *"las gordas,"* the fat women, would receive four yards of cloth and *"las pechitas,"* the thin women, would receive three yards.

In her story, Elsy said she turned to the women and asked if they would support her in contesting this injustice. Again invoking the thirty thousand colones, the poor supplies, the lack of renumeration, unlike for the previous year's participants, Elsy challenged Paty as she argued for at least equal amounts of cloth, regardless of size, saying, "Todas gastamos y perdimos el mismo tiempo." (We all spent and wasted the same amount of time.) Elsy laughed when telling me about Paty's fury, her exclamation: "Pero Ud. es revolucionaria, se tiene que poner conforme." (But you are revolutionary; you have to conform.) At which point Elsy reclaimed her revolutionary identity by saying, "Fui, soy y seguiré siendo revolucionaria" (I was, I am, and I will continue to be a revolutionary), and added that, in fact, people should not conform but rather know their rights. Elsy ended by saying that all the participants received four yards of cloth. She never made her uniform but rather sewed a skirt for herself, one for her daughter Flor, and a pair of pants for her two boys.

This moment of victory for Elsy captured the many contradictions and irritations of postwar processes where former revolutionaries redefine and reclaim their past, the weight of their history with consumption practices. Did she wear a cloak of revolution to legitimize individual consumption? Do sites and practices of consumption, as some argue, create new ways of thinking and produce a sense of belonging that grounds cultural citizenship (Canclini 2001)? Interestingly, Elsy invoked the history of revolutionary organizing very much in the same way as Daysi of CORDES. She explained how she had mobilized the other participants by saying, "We who have organized to struggle against injustices, let's now organize for this, which is not even shit."

From Failures to Possibilities

This chapter has ethnographically detailed the contradictions of grassroots participation. CORDES's evaluation session, Chayo's and Kasandra's theories of reconstruction, and Elsy's narratives of development injustices exemplify how survivors of El Salvador's protracted civil war struggle against a series of postwar development processes. These converge on rural people's consciousness, on their "dependency" on external assistance, on their problematic organizational abilities as residents are told that they must reorganize, reanimate, and remember the past. Wartime social relations, activism, and survival are held up as the model and voiced as the ideal for community life. But an important question remains: How can the wartime sacrifice of home, family, community, and bodies be expected to move into the postwar present? How much community participation can be asked of people? Are the answers to these questions found in highlighting former participants' couched words and hushed critiques? Are they found in later undocumented migration?

Chalatenango's history of a strong social movement informs regional reconstruction expectations, assumptions, critiques, and efforts. These emphasize community organization as a key component of projects aiming to achieve sustainable local development and national reconciliation after a civil war. While it is critical to explore this legacy of organization and, by extension, the place of community as residents negotiate between performing collective, regional, oppositional identities and surviving in a rural economy where it is increasingly harder to make a living, this chapter argues for following a quieter story about what happens in the interstitial moments of daily life marked by decreasing collective action. What happens when we take this less exotic path as our point of entry for a region and people carrying the weight of a history of revolutionary consciousness? How can we talk about the shift from insurgents to citizens who move in and out of individual and collective work, keeping in mind that "it may be precisely after the revolution that the long struggle for democratization and economic justice will be waged" (Babb 2001, 15). These unfulfilled promises have created a situation in which local inhabitants place blame on local or national actors rather than more elusive global forces. The struggle is one between empowerment and alienation that may undermine the very hope for building a future collective identity. Padre José, the parish priest for El Rancho and the larger Las Vueltas municipality, spent a good deal of his labor in daily travels to communities. During his weekly sermons, he tried to make sense of the struggles ahead for campesinos like himself, too often the "spent cartridges" (Nugent 1993) of revolutions. I choose to end this chapter with his harsh indictment of postwar processes of development that he saw unfold before him. I also choose to include the original Spanish followed by my translation into English in order to privilege the urgency of Padre José's words:

> Ahora, mucho cuidado con la palabra desarrollo. No creas tú que el desarrollo ha llegado a estas comunidades. Desarrollo es la paz y en primer lugar es la justicia que corresponde a la equidad, también cementada en la solidaridad, en la organización. ¿Podemos ver que Las Vueltas está en desarrollo? ¿Sólo porque tenés casas de cemento? ¿Sólo porque mirás que hay tiendas? ¿Sólo porque mirás que las calles se pueden pasar más o menos? Cuidado, porque es el título de desarrollo capitalista, el típico barniz. Miramos que las casas son bonitas, pero através esa casa hay toda una deuda externa que no es externa si no es eterna. No es que el desarrollo ha entrado aquí ni es que la paz ha llegado. No porque hay casas bonitas podemos decir que hay desarrollo. Cuando tú te vas a las raíces profundas del pueblo, te encontrás todavía con su gran analfabetismo, de irrespeto a los derechos de la mujer, te encontrás con una mala distribución de la tierra todavía, y la mala calidad de la tierra también. Te encontrás con un problema ecológico horrible, provocado por la guerra y ahora continuada por los nuevos mecanismos neoliberales. . . . ¿Tú quieres escuchar una crítica? Creémela, las ONGs, de las que tú estás hablando, es el típico modelo del viejo mundo. En vez de fortalecer y que el pobre salga y levante su dignidad, lo que hacen las ONGs es siempre crear una dependencia tremenda de un dinero que se les da, un asistencialismo y se deja de creer en el protagonismo del pobre en la organización. Y esto es muy fuerte lo que yo voy a decir, pero a veces el nuevo nombre del capitalismo es la ONGs. Yo respeto, tú no creas, yo valoro muchas cosas de ellos, pero me parece lo que ellos manejan es una típica economía neoliberal disfrazada con el nombre de ONGs. Fuerte esto.

Now, be careful with this word "development." Don't believe that development has arrived to these communities. Development is peace, and first of all justice, which refers to equality grounded in solidarity and organization. Can we see that Las Vueltas has development? Only because it has cement block houses? Only because you see local stores? Only because you see new roads that are somewhat passable? Careful, because that is capitalist development, the typical varnish. If we look behind those pretty houses we see an external debt that is not external but eternal. Development has not entered here, nor has peace. Not because there are pretty houses can we say that there is development. When you go to the roots of the *pueblo,* you will find illiteracy, disrespect of women's rights; you will still find an unequal distribution of poor-quality land. You will find a horrible ecological problem provoked by the war and continued today by new neoliberal mechanisms. . . . Do you want to hear a critique? Believe me, the NGOs that you are talking about, they are the typical Old World model. Instead of strengthening and empowering the poor, the NGOs create dependency on the money that they get, and they stop believing in the agency of the poor, in organization. This is very strong, what I'm going to say, but sometimes the new name of capitalism is NGO. And I respect them, don't think I don't. I value many things that they do, but I think that they operate under a typical neoliberal economy masked in the name of NGOs. This is a strong critique.

Padre José articulates the search for justice that has been silenced in a national politics of rebuilding. He beckons us to look beyond new cement-block houses, beyond the "varnish" of development, a first coat that beneath is festered with the entangled roots of violence. Like other grassroots critics, he invokes *asistencialismo* (external aid) as a key problem in communities, but he blames NGOs rather than their intended beneficiaries. In the following chapters we will continue to focus on the relationship between rank-and-file former revolutionaries and NGO-led development operating in the transition to democracy. This relationship is incomplete without mention of the place of the FMLN in residents' lives.

FMLN Snapshots

Roll 1: First Sightings

It was breezy that night in Las Vueltas. The air held nostalgia. Residents from communities across the municipality, farther away than El Rancho, had arrived for FMLN municipal elections. Local party representatives were to be elected to represent the municipality at the departmental political party level.

It was also a night to remember, to see old friends, former neighbors, and kin. For the making of politics, I argue, is an embodied historic and social process. As we approached the town hall, the rich smell of coffee and tamales reached the group with whom I traveled. And there was already a crowd. Everyone knew that the FMLN had organized the cooking and distribution of food after the election—a good night of income for a few houses in Las Vueltas and a festive communal event. Like so many large meetings characterized by participatory democracy, the session was both animated and slow as all residents were given the opportunity to speak, to nominate candidates, and to reject or accept nominations.

It was a night full of political rhetoric. And it was moving and exciting despite my resistance to it. Rutilio, a longtime FMLN organizer, led the electoral process. He passionately gathered the audience with his call: "En Las Vueltas me siento realizado. Aquí está mi sangre derramada. Aquí está mi historia. Aquí puedo hablar con calzón quitado." (Here in Las Vueltas I feel realized. Here is my spilt blood. Here is my history. Here I can talk freely—literally naked/without underwear.) His very localized calling up of a painful past, his spilt blood in the heart of Las Vueltas, was followed by a larger national return to the polarized politics of the war as he asked the room of close to two hundred participants, "¿Aquí somos derechistas o somos izquierdistas?" (Here are we on the right or on the left?) The response was forceful and complete, "izquierdistas!" (Leftists!) His closing remarks, "Adelante, adelante, que la lucha es constante" (Onward, the struggle continues), passed like a wave through the room.

After months of witnessing women's staggering withdrawals from community action, from rebuilding efforts, explicitly politicized or not, that night residents were out and about, voicing their concerns, joking with each other, electing leaders, doing politics. This night was different. Well into my research, I was working hard to combat a problematic romance of "the people" that had begun to penetrate the grassroots sector as well as larger international development analyses. I was struggling against a focus on idealized revolutionary participation, ideology, and practices because these mask postwar realities that underscore former revolution-aries' disillusionment. On that night, however, the FMLN as a unifying identity as a political party, as the past of heroic opposition prevailed in the bodies of the wartime leadership.

The FMLN was the difference. Why? In part, these party leaders blur bor-ders; they inhabit the everyday of the past, present, and future as the gun-totting *comandante* who successfully ambushed a military unit in the 1980s, as a CORDES but more often CCR staff member, or as an elected municipal official. The FMLN party, embodied in its historic representatives, invokes a common past of suffer-ing, linking community with party and creating a day-to-day hegemony of the Left in the region, which continues to date.[1] This interpretation takes us beyond elec-toral politics and asks us to read the FMLN's role in the region as something more. Is this hegemony of the party powerful enough to combat organizational crises in community politics and a widespread demoralization of past participants? Can Chalatecos become FMLN citizens?

Roll 2: Leaving the Local

Dolores likes the color blue. My image of her is of a big Chalateca, always with a blue cotton dress and colorful apron wrapped across her rather large middle—that

and her loud voice and fast speech. She was CCR's women's regional representative (taking the job over from Elsy, who was "too bored" by it), and I had spent
hours with her, attending many of her meetings in El Rancho with my tape recorder
or pen and paper. These were hot, slow-going, low-participation meetings in a bat-
infested community women's house. Because of the presidential and legislative
elections in March 1997, a large portion of Dolores's work during 1996 and early
1997 converged on mobilizing Chalateca residents to define themselves through
the FMLN, to support the party, to vote FMLN, and in doing so become FMLN
citizens. Five years after the signing of peace, only five years from clandestine lives,
this combination, FMLN plus citizen, was still a rather new concept.

My recordings of Dolores's CCR meetings (note, not FMLN meetings) are
instructive and provide a gendered reading of the ways in which FMLN politics
work in the informal, in the everyday. During a reproductive health session, Dolores
switched topics, changed hats, and explained: "As women we need to insert ourselves into politics. We need to be the mouthpiece for the rest of the women.
Come on, let's go vote and, more than anything, let's think about who we are going
to vote for. And we also have to tell them that on behalf of the women, we are sure
that Chichilco is going to win [and she did]. Hopefully, we will all go vote and know
for whom we are going to vote, and let's not go and deceive ourselves (*que no nos
vayamos a engañar nosotras solas*)." "*Engañarse*," in its reflexive form, means to be
deceived, to mistake oneself, and as an active verb it means to deceive, to cheat, to
mock, to delude, to hoax, to abuse. These two meanings, I suggest, are simultaneous in this passage and in many others throughout the book. Dolores is the wife of
Hugo, a self-identified peasant communist, turned womanizer, alcoholic, and
returning repentant husband. Dolores, I suggest, beckons women to fight against
layers of despair brought on by the lies of men, by the lies of warrior-politicians, by
the misery of growing inequality in postwar neoliberal El Salvador. Yet, despite
these lies, despite being a fool of these lies, hers is a call for agency as hope resides
in the power of electoral politics outside of the imminently local.

Months after this recording, Dolores, now a FMLN municipal representative,
invited me to attend the FMLN's departmental meeting, where further party elections were to take place. The party had instructed Dolores to find more women

delegates, and so she made a quick trip to El Rancho and Elsy, always up for an excursion, was among the first to volunteer. I could tag along. Traveling to the FMLN departmental headquarters was a legitimate public and political act, taking party members outside of the municipality to engage in the everyday formation of political power. In my notes I wrote, "Finally, I made it."

Yet, recall this is neither a book about political parties at the local or national level nor about the transformation of the FMLN during the throws of the transition to democracy. Then why this entry? Why the thrill of attending another large meeting, where speeches or conversation were difficult to record or follow because of the constant overlap of voices? Why do I still have my FMLN *invitada* badge pinned on my office wall all these years later?

In part, it is because that day in November 1997 was less than ordinary. It is not often that residents across communities gather at departmental FMLN head-quarters. Though not surprisingly, things did not proceed as planned. The depart-mental elections were postponed and, instead, the FMLN leadership organized what I can only describe as an educational workshop to introduce a recently pub-lished party rulebook. Participants moved quickly with their assigned tasks to read and reflect upon the new strategic plan and discuss it in working groups. On that day, a historic female *comandante* recently elected to the Legislative Assembly, María Chichilco, directed much of the meeting and focused on the importance of maintaining loyalty to the party in order to work toward socialism, the need to fight against corruption and gain full power. Chichilco's language is one of battle in territoriality. With the FMLN gaining more municipalities and more capital cities, the language is one of war. She told the crowd that the plan was to "defend what we have already conquered, and we will conquer even more." She followed with the statement: "Nosotros estamos acostumbrados a sólo la oposición. Hoy no somos sólo la oposición. Hoy somos poder." (We are used to being the opposition. Today we are not only the opposition. Today we are/have power.) As Chichilco spoke, my eyes kept shifting to the woman to my left, to her faded yellow T-shirt. I could easily make out the image of a U.S. flag with "support our troops" emblazoned on it. Another war, another place, another time, but the legacies of U.S. military interventionist policies somehow were creeping into this oppositional space.

Roll 3: Tired but FMLN

Two weeks later the FMLN held party elections to vote on departmental *conven-cionistas* (convention participant) as well as those who would serve on the national level. The morning was chaotic. María Chichilco, present again, attempted to pacify the crowd. Anger erupted over the marginalization of municipalities. More and more representatives from the capital of Chalatenango were presented as candidates while only a handful from the outlining communities were included in the voting. The refrain from the previous meeting on the FMLN's strategic growth resounded: "Tenemos descuidada la base." (We have left the grassroots unattended.) "Hay una desvinculación con la base." (There is a disjuncture with the grassroots.) "Nos estamos distanciando." (We are distancing ourselves.) These were critiques that I had not heard in other NGO and grassroots contexts. However, the familiar observation of decreasing activism penetrated the FMLN. During the disordered election, more and more people rejected their candidacy. A man in his thirties from the repopulated community of San José Las Flores took off his hat and spoke to the crowd, "Me siento bastante cansado, no aburrido, pero cansado. Siempre soy del Frente. Siempre voy a apoyar." (I feel quite tired, not bored, but tired. I am always FMLN. I will always support the FMLN.) And with that, he recused himself. Tired, FMLN voter, but not FMLN leader.

With government institutions long absent in this former war zone, part of politics, I suggest, involves resocializing FMLN supporters to become oppositional citizens, to learn how to be part of the nation-state while fighting against it for social change. New forms of governmentality emerge, characterized by a coalescing of NGO, FMLN, and grassroots practices. In the following chapter I reflect upon what it means to maintain oppositional politics with a new politics of citizenship. How to demand rights from an ARENA nation-state, and how to demand accountability from FMLN municipalities and the broader party? How to harness the refrain I heard earlier that day from Elsy: "once FMLN, always FMLN." Over a breakfast of *pupusas* with her neighbors, she compared supporting the FMLN with her practice of Catholicism. For her, as the majority of Chalatecos socialized under liberation theology, conversion to a growing evangelical movement in the nation, as in the rest of Central America, appeared as impossible as ceasing to support the FMLN.[2]

FMLN but tired. I do not know what happened to the man who so earnestly rejected his candidacy. But I do know that Elsy is no longer "once FMLN, always FMLN." In municipal elections of January 2009, for the first time, she voted for an ARENA candidate and as a result has been publicly marginalized in El Rancho and Las Vueltas. Rumors swirl about the depth of her involvement with ARENA. These communities remain homogenously FMLN, and though the political violence of the war is over, Elsy's party positioning locates her as outside of community life and opens up many more questions that cannot yet be answered.

In the chapter that follows, I develop an argument on the period of transition as centrally about the formation of oppositional citizens. This formation takes place during a period of neoliberalism that is framed by the legacies of revolutionary agency. For revolutionary political rhetoric is not empty. The FMLN holds experiential meaning for most Chalatecos of this region. However, my research indicates that for many, this transition leaves their role unclearly defined as people are no longer either active participants as combatants or providing key logistical support within communities. Invariably, whether at a CCR-convoked, CORDES-led, or FMLN-organized meeting across the department, the same bodies circulate, depending on context, as either leaders or constituency. In a variety of grassroots spaces, residents are continually socialized into remembering and re-enacting that they "are FMLN," with the lesson being, as a FMLN representative and CCR director stated, "Aquí nadie se puede poner al centro." (Here no one can be in the center.) These politicized education efforts are also clearly gendered and often subsumed under a larger discourse and new practices of development and democracy.

These efforts also are socially reproduced. Children as young as four years of age know that they are "FMLN" and that this means they stand in opposition to the ruling government party ARENA. During the 1997 election period, ARENA's propaganda campaign included distributing free T-shirts, baseball caps, pencils, notebooks, playing cards, and so on. The FMLN pursued the same tactic but ran out of supplies early on in the region. Many parents accepted the ARENA items because of their essential utilitarian value. Some did not allow their children to wear these clothes with the bright ARENA insignia until after the elections, when a FMLN victory was assured. One parent explained that in this way, the use of the T-shirt was, in fact, a way to mock ARENA, "*burlándose de ellos*." However, some children eager to wear coveted items like baseball caps used them before the elections. Many went to great lengths to vandalize the ARENA insignia on the caps through a variety of strategies such as coloring the façade with a bright red magic marker (FMLN color) or crossing out the word "ARENA" and replacing it with "*vota FMLN*" (vote FMLN). Others chose to wear their T-shirts (adding to sparse wardrobes) inside-out as a sign of solidarity with the FMLN. Some longtime FMLN participants and supporters rejected these practices. I recall how Elsy's son Miguel, one of those boys who scratched out ARENA on a new baseball cap, also accepted a pack of cards with the ARENA label. He had very few toys. His neighbor Chico severely chastised him and tore up his cards—or so the story goes. This created a rift between Elsy's and Chayo's families for several months and impacted women's communal organizing.

A central tension or question emerges surrounding failures and aspirations of participatory democracy. In the context of postwar neoliberal democracy can former oppositional, armed, intellectual, politicized, combatant citizens be simultaneously fighting against and for the nation? Does the answer lie in Elsy's political shift? Does the answer lie in the ethnographic present of 2009 in the departing adolescent and young adult bodies of children of revolutionaries crossing borders to the United States? Does the answer lie in that 1997 departmental election with an FMLN leader's failed attempt to call order as he shouts out to a dispersing and rejecting crowd, "Compañeros, compañeras. Compañeros, compañeras . . . ya somos adultos . . . compañeros, compañeras." (Comrades. Comrades . . . we are adults . . . comrades, comrades.)

6

Cardboard Democracy

The sleight of hand is at the heart of state power, concealing domination in the discourse of "democracy."

Beth Baker-Cristales, "Magical Pursuits: Legitimacy and
Representation in a Transnational Political Field"

Imagine a typical CORDES training session funded through international development dollars. It is the dry season and thirty-five women are in a stiflingly hot room. No fan, no air circulation. Road repair noise—jackhammers, whistles, concrete cracking, shovels smacking—enters through two small windows and echoes inside, increasing the volume of women's voices and the intermittent laughter, cries, and scampering of half a dozen children. Childcare is unavailable. Bathroom facilities are "closed" (though used) due to lack of water, which happens often. The heat and stench rise as the day continues. With late afternoon approaching, the poster paper taped against the wall documenting the day's training comes undone. The women are anxious to leave, anxious to catch the last pickup truck from the capital of Chalatenango to their rural communities in time to get home, gather up children, make the tortillas, and attend to the day's missed chores. The lessons, this time on how to become a literacy educator and empower women, are on hold until next time.

Returning to El Rancho with Elsy that afternoon, too tired to engage her in conversation about the day's work, the words of an NGO director echoed in my head. Adamant about remaining anonymous, he often indicted bottom-up development schemes with this statement: "Yo no creo en capacitaciones con carteles." (I don't believe in trainings with poster board.) For this director, skills-based and empowerment training were not enough. Training was a band-aid that did nothing to heal structural wounds. Trainings, workshops, and education were no match for the absence of a long-term development plan. As many analysts note, the peace process did not elaborate a development plan to underpin the transition to democracy.

Years later, his comments foreshadow my arguments on the everyday practices of local or grassroots development that are intended to foster democracy in the context of neoliberalism. This development is the work of poster boards and flip-charts, of cardboard signs that beckon women's activism as palliative. Countless times I helped write signs that said things such as "Con la mujer en la casa la democracia se atrasa." (With women in the home, democracy is slowed.) This call is predicated on women's activism of the past and taps into an international development discourse that attempts to mainstream gender. As the anonymous director walks by these signs, he sees empty words. As I look back upon the ubiquitous *papelógrafo*, the flip-charts he challenges, I see the work of NGO and grassroots activists in terms of a metaphor: "cardboard democracy." This is a democracy that is fragile, shallow, that can be corroded, and yet not quite malleable—a Potemkin Village of sorts.[1]

Recall that in postwar Chalatenango NGOs and grassroots organizations worked diligently to bring development aid to repopulated communities. A key development strategy entailed providing educational workshops and training sessions. These ranged from organic farming technologies to women's literacy groups and workshops on gender relations and women's human rights. Indeed, the language and practices of *talleres* (workshops) and *capacitaciones* (trainings) have become increasingly popular avenues for rebuilding, as many women and men identify *capacitaciones* as a path toward national incorporation.[2] In this way development and democracy are linked at the local level. This emphasis on education technologies has come to compete with and replace a discourse circulated across social fields that emphasizes projects. However, education often times masks development's intervention that depoliticizes problems through a language and practice of technology. For education is a form of technology that invents problems that inadvertently replace underlying political, economic, and social realities. Thus, focusing on education, or rather on how residents supposedly lack particular kinds of education or knowledge, is similar to development analyses that argue for problems as being a lack of credit, of markets, of technology, and so on, which elide, for example, unemployment and continued marginalization by the nation-state (Ferguson 1994).

This chapter expands my focus on the relationship between grassroots development practices and residents of repopulated communities. It does so by theorizing educational practices as a form of governmentality (Foucault 1991). For the postwar political landscape, both government and grassroots, is characterized by what Akhil Gupta and James Ferguson (2002) and Gupta and Aradhana Sharma (2006), borrowing from Foucault (1991), place under the rubric of transnational and neoliberal governmentality, respectively. These terms are useful for explaining the ways in which postwar political subjects are regulated and disciplined in El Salvador and across its borders through NGO functions previously held by the state (Baker-Cristales 2008). As Gupta and Ferguson cogently review, an important aspect of Foucault's theorizing on governmentality focuses on "mechanisms of government that are found within state institutions and outside them, mechanisms that cut across domains that we would regard as separate: the state, civil society, the family, down to the intimate details of what we regard as personal life" (2002, 989).[3]

What is interesting about the Chalateco case is that NGO practices rub up against state structures and services that were absent during the war. After historic 1994 democratic elections, the first for the recently established FMLN political party, something new emerged. The everyday routines of state bureaucracy (and how people therefore imagine and experience the state) at the municipal level were in the hands of FMLN mayors and mayoral councils—in most cases former FMLN guerilla leaders.

Reader, let us travel back to the mid-1990s, a time, I will argue, where energies were dramatically spent on harnessing the local: local experiences, local labor, local intellectuals, and localized experiences of war in order to redefine national agendas. Though differently, this project *was* radical given that it took place within the legacies of absent official state bureaucracies and the unprecedented entrance of postwar development programs and the reintroduction of the state. Like the FMLN's attempts to create new oppositional subjects (see FMLN Snapshots), grassroots organizations worked to mold, to shape, to redefine, and, more specifically, to reeducate revolutionaries into citizens in order to create participatory democracy. For as Baker-Cristales points out, the FMLN has a history of "mimicking the official state structures and activities with the ultimate goal of becoming the state" (2008, 354).

Flip-chart Development

What happened with all that *papelógrafo?* With all the workshops, lessons, needs assessments, and best practices taped up on NGO walls documenting a day's work? My questions are not a call for a top-down approach to development and postwar reconstruction. They are rather an attempt to highlight the making of governmentality in the aftermath of violence marked by the entrance of neoliberal economics and politics. Gupta and Ferguson make clear that practices of governance have been greatly impacted or defined by the logic of the market, from the privatization of services to the very models of citizenship (2002, 989). With neoliberalism comes the shrinking of the state services and the growth of NGOs tasked with taking on the needs of civil society. Gupta and Ferguson describe this as "not less government" but "a new modality of government" (2002, 989).

A cornerstone of new modes of neoliberal governmentality across state, and what is too often conflated as "civil society," is a focus on empowerment. Gupta and Sharma cogently reason why: "It is interesting though not entirely surprising to note the rise of empowerment strategies during the era of global neoliberal governmentality. On the one hand, supranational regulatory bodies such as the World Bank are promoting empowerment as a crucial aspect of development.

On the other hand, these same institutions are asking developmentalist states to reduce interventions in the market and in welfare provisioning" (2006, 284). There is pained irony in this analysis. The international bodies that have for years enforced structural adjustment policies, which the record now shows ultimately disempowered (read further impoverished) the populations they were to aid, are now trying to talk the talk of empowerment. Gupta and Sharma continue, "Empowerment fits in with the neoliberal agenda of small government, participatory governance, and market based competitiveness. It enables developmentalist states to shift away from directly providing for the basic needs of their marginalized citizens to helping these citizens to govern themselves and take care of their own development needs" (2006, 284).

In Chalatenango, neoliberal governmentality operates. However, what distinguishes the Chalateco case is precisely the legacy of revolutionary empowerment. In the sections that follow, I ethnographically develop an argument about *talleres* and *capacitaciones* as tactics of governmentality that attempt to reeducate or resocialize the past participants of an oppositional struggle into particular kinds of postwar citizens. These are men and women who are accustomed to operating in extra-official channels, meaning against the state. My argument is this: While local development programs and policies attempt to incorporate historically marginalized peoples and places into the nation-state through a palatable program of sustainable development with practices such as microcredit and organic farming, my data suggests that residents are simultaneously targets of a socialization project that privileges oppositional politics, ultimately at odds with national incorporation. Rather than a national identity, a local Chalateco citizen is created, one that is at root fully FMLN, with electoral politics a key component of the identity. Yet, the Chalateco/a revolutionary agency produces a crisis of governmentality in response to the failures of promised participatory democracy. Residents resist structures of power—local, national, and increasingly transnational. This resistance produces often uncertain and painful consequences, the subject of the ethnographic tales below.

Legacies of Popular Education

A story about the contradictions of empowerment necessarily needs to begin with a note on popular education in Chalatenango, historically an oppositional model which neoliberalism attempts to co-opt. Throughout the rural landscape, in many communities, school-aged children from preschool to the eighth grade attend classes led by *maestros/as populares* (people's or grassroots teachers) in classrooms that until recently were named after martyred FMLN combatants. Scholars have focused on the importance of popular education in mobilizing people to participate in revolutionary social projects.[4] What developed over time was a system of popular schools built from campesino efforts that challenged the nation-state's exclusionary policies and historic marginalization by the official school system. Thematically, it challenged the meaning and practice of education (Guzmán et al. 1994, 6).[5] Today, the popular education model continues to hold local value and informs Chalatenango's socializing project that negotiates incorporation into the nation-state with oppositional political practices. As such, education remains politicized and educational encounters are sites of ongoing struggle as grassroots teachers build from their experiences.

During my time in El Rancho, I had the opportunity to visit with local teachers, attend their meetings, and visit kindergarten through third-grade classes. Miriam of El Rancho explains her involvement as a teacher upon her return from a refugee camp in Honduras:[6]

> They said they were looking for grassroots teachers from within the community. And Juana asked if I could work. I didn't know what to do because I had only studied up to the fourth grade. So she told me, "But you taught kindergarten in Mesa Grande (Honduras), they've told me. And you have experience working with children." Well, I decided to do it. I began working in '89. From that time till now, those years '89, '90, '91, '92, we worked with fear. Because when the soldiers would arrive in the community, if they found us in the schools they would get us. They threatened us because they said that we gave guerilla classes. That was a lie, you know. . . . After the peace accords, there was a change, you know. . . . Word got out that the grassroots teachers existed. Some institutions began arriving to investigate if this was true, and they started giving us trainings.

Miriam's reflections point to her wartime formation, the repression against teachers who were simultaneously educators and revolutionaries, and postwar shifts toward recognition. Indeed, after the war, educational reform came to be seen as an important vehicle toward the nation's path of democratization (Blandon Castro 1998). But how to incorporate this popular education system within a national structure?

In fact, beginning in the 1990s, popular educators struggled against the Ministry of Education (MINED) over their status and their schools. Simultaneously, in an attempt to reduce the nation's illiteracy rate and educate rural people into future participative citizens, the popular schools received Ministry of Education benefits such as Escuela Saludable (Healthy School Program),[7] and there were also evening, adult basic education programs, Programa de Educación Básica del Arzobispado de San Salvador (PAEBA).[8] Slower in coming and more contentious is the legalization or accreditation of the popular teachers. Strides have been made, however, as many teachers received the required schooling to become certified elementary school teachers.[9]

While I do not romanticize revolutionary communities, my data does indicate that these schools and teachers, though coordinated through MINED, remain popular in practice and ideology, struggling against historic exclusion. They remain a marker of community identity, socializing a new generation about the past for the future, in ultimately oppositional ways by incorporating an oppositional analysis of the past. Additionally, their pedagogy is invoked as a model for how to engage in rebuilding in other contexts. Chinda, another popular teacher explained, "We teach them topics such as history, the events that have happened, a little bit about the war and, for example, about independence. . . . We tell them about the founding fathers (of El Salvador), but we tell them that they were large landowners, and all of that because it is the reality. And like that in various topics, we always find the meaning, but differently." Miriam added, "Well, when we have to teach about the war for social studies, we teach about the massacre at the Sumpul River. The schools of the ministry don't teach about that. We also teach about Monsignor Oscar Arnulfo Romero, his life, why he died. Also about the Jesuit priests (who were killed), about the Offensive, how it was and things like that."

I suggest that the legacies of popular education are layered and often times contradictory. While grassroots teachers continue to adhere to a pedagogy of involvement, seeking to empower a new generation of Chalatecos through participative methodologies that socialize youngsters from kindergarten on to debate official versions of history, for example, teachers are simultaneously struggling for incorporation into the political economy of the nation. They are at once fighting for and against the nation. The model of popular education serves as a jumping board for current projects of social change. The model is palatable to international funders and government bodies as it falls under both the rubric of sustainable development and the logic of empowerment and yet remains faithful to the legacies of the revolution. Which meaning of empowerment wins and in which contexts?

Las Mujeres Me Desesperan—The Women Make Me Desperate

As noted, in Chalatenango many NGOs and grassroots organizations have adopted a focus on women in their development strategies and employ a discourse on gender. I suggest these efforts are a continuation of a wartime consciousness-raising project, taking place during a shifting context where women's participation, a key signifier of empowerment, has come to mean a multiplicity of things such as community leader, micro-entrepreneur, and FMLN militant. Examining targeted women's events co-sponsored by CCR's Secretaría de la Mujer and CORDES's El Equipo de Género y Capacitación yields significant insights on how governmentality is a gendered process. An ethnographic journey into these events offers a window into the making of Chalateca citizens as empowered resisters, yet not fully realized. For across NGO, grassroots, and the national sphere, the "woman question" circulates.

One day in particular resonates. I attended a CCR Women's Secretariat strategic meeting and met for the first time Sister Clara, a Spanish nun and a longtime resident of a repopulation community. Sister Clara had repatriated with Salvadoran refugees from the Mesa Grande refugee camp in Honduras. The meeting was intended to build on the CORDES gendered evaluation session from the previous month (see chapter 5) in order to draft CCR's upcoming strategic plan. My notes on the meeting are consumed by my incredulous experience of Sister Clara. With a sigh she exclaimed, "Ay, las mujeres me desesperan—Oh, the women make me desperate." She was exhausted by women's lack of participation and women's lack of solidarity. Colloquially stated, she was disappointed in their lack of organizational "umph." She followed this by discussing how the young generation of women were simply too passive. And with that, the agenda was carved. I can still feel the heat rising to my face, outraged by the critique of the everyday, rank-and-file revolutionary woman.

While arguably there is a decline in women's participation in a variety of community, grassroots, NGO, and, to a lesser degree, FMLN-sponsored events, activists' analyses of the meaning of this decline is as critical to document as the decline itself. Thus, when Sister Clara strongly suggested that CCR's strategy should be one that privileges education, the suggestion was unanimously agreed upon. Sister Clara stated, "We need workshops, workshops, workshops. Educational workshops. Not projects, projects, projects. . . . We need to begin a formative stage. The people's education system with all of its flaws continues to work. We need to launch workshops in communities and launch an educational project."

With the long-term successes of the popular education model, the focus on education seemed plausible and hopeful. And throughout the course of the rest of the day, the roots of an educational-based gendered empowerment plan emerged.[10] Sister Clara is not alone in voicing this perspective. Early into fieldwork I was introduced to this commingling of development, education, participation, and citizenship.

¡Que Viva la Mujer Salvadoreña—Que Viva!

In November 1996, shortly after my arrival, I was invited to CCR's Fifth Annual Women's Assembly. This was a two-day retreat, held at Conchalio Beach in La Libertad, three and a half hours outside of Chalatenango. The well-attended assembly was envisioned as a grassroots, participatory evaluation of the year's development program, where women's community leaders could voice their concerns to the larger CCR body. Simultaneously, the retreat rewarded women for their year-long unpaid collaboration and leadership in organizing community women to participate in CCR-sponsored events, meetings, and trainings.[11] This was also my first "big" fieldwork event and I was excited. I also expected it to yield great data. I took copious notes on those two days, between swatting flies and adjusting to the heat and communal living conditions, overused and poor-performing toilets, and lack of caffeine.

The meeting began with the arrival of the keynote speaker, historic FMLN *comandante,* Chalateca, and soon-to-be FMLN Legislative Assembly member María Chichilco. Recall her presence in the previous section. Microphone in hand, arm raised in a fist, she led the women through a volley of calls and responses. She recited, "Con la mujer en la casa" (With women in the home), and the room responded, "La democracia se atrasa" (Democracy is slowed down). This was followed by the call, "Mujeres si queremos poder" (Women, if we want power), and the response "Participadoras debemos ser" (We must participate). She ended with a series of "Que viva la mujer Salvadoreña, que viva" (Long live Salvadoran women). Chichilco's opening words were intended to ignite and inspire. Her rhetoric illuminates a continued struggle for women's empowerment, collective action, and political participation—key issues as the 1997 presidential and municipal elections were four months away. But does empowerment begin to mean something different in a postwar neoliberal context? Beth Baker-Cristales eloquently elaborates Aihwa Ong's theorizing on neoliberalism as characterized not only by the shrinking of state institutions because of the rules or logic of the market but by new technologies of governing and of disciplining, of inclusion and exclusion, of giving value or denying value to human conduct (Ong 2006, 5, in Baker-Cristales 2008, 351). During this event CCR created a governmentality that in one moment valued and in the next move denied.

Between beach breaks—for some women their first time at the ocean—participants were divided into groups along municipal lines and asked to address a series of questions. They were asked to evaluate and expand upon a needs-assessment report by CCR that elaborated "community women's" needs—a long list of what was lacking. The list included the need for more community training sessions (the topics undefined), for community daycare centers, for an increase in communal solidarity by reinstating communal work days,[12] and the need to address women's health and education needs, particularly, increasing women's literacy skills. Along with these gendered needs, the women were asked to discuss community-level problems. These ranged from lack of employment, poor transportation, unresolved land issues, abandoned children, and irresponsible fathers to increases in alcoholism, domestic violence and crime, and the "loss of values" in the communities' youth, evidenced in their lack of respect. Common to meetings of this nature, on the second day the participants were asked to develop solutions for these multiple and layered "women and community" issues. What emerged was a two-pronged attack, one which called for more women's development projects (i.e., mills, chicken farms, bread-baking projects, arts and crafts) and the other which invoked education projects under the umbrella of gender trainings (*capacitaciones de género*) with themes such as reproductive rights, the rights of the girl child, and women's rights regarding domestic violence.

However, the participating women voiced a cogent critique based on their everyday experiences. They argued that the intended recipients of these efforts, community women, increasingly resisted participating in a wide range of events. Thus, projects, trainings, workshops, or informational meetings could be offered, scheduled, and held, but a key issue remained: mobilizing women in communities to participate. One woman exclaimed to the audience, "Que no nos engañemos" (Let's not deceive ourselves), there would be no participation. She described her own experiences of attempting to mobilize women in her community and attributed the decline in organization to frustrated development projects that had not benefited the majority of women. Implicit in women's counterclaims to the need for more trainings in order to further educate women about organizing—whether for the FMLN, for communities, or for development projects—is a critique of the tactics of control and practices of regulation of governmentality. For, as scholars illustrate, a key component of governmentality is that it controls through enumerating and documenting (Baker-Cristales 2008; Gupta and Ferguson 2002; Gupta and Sharma 2006). Resistance (*que no nos engañemos*) can be read as a response to so many years of documentation, too many years of being documented, foreshadowing at the time unforeseen struggles of so many Chalatecos in the United States without documents. The legacies of wartime violence, to be without documents (subversive), haunt postwar lives.

One of the organizers for the assembly meeting, Irma, from the San Salvador CRIPDES office,[13] attempted to counter this critique by urging women to make a broader analysis of what the "real" obstacles and necessities were. Hers was an attempt to shift analyses away from the micro or community level and provide a national political context. With the elections in the near future, she attempted to unmask the facelessness of the poverty explicit in the needs and problems women identified. She challenged women to look beyond the lack of participation in the community and, indeed, beyond what CRIPDES, CCR, and CORDES could do. For Irma it was important to recognize that the key problem is that social injustice continues and that it is propelled by ARENA's neoliberal privatizing policies.

In the mid to late 1990s, analyses or critiques of neoliberalism were just emerging. Feminist scholars and policy analysts had, however, demonstrated the failures of structural adjustment policies implemented throughout the global south—indicating how these policies (reducing social services, privatizing industries in order to meet IMF stringent terms) had actually increased poverty and, more specifically, negatively impacted women, the elderly, and children. Irma, as she spoke, did not yet have the tools or the experience to make neoliberalism tangible to Chalatecas who had spent more than a decade facing a known enemy—the state in a soldier's body. Irma's discourse was one of the first indicators for me that postwar grassroots politics involves an ongoing, politicizing, consciousness-raising project aimed at incorporating women into the nation-state through oppositional practices. The trick is to redefine the struggle when the successes of the past fight are up for debate.

Thirteen months later, with funding cuts, CCR's annual evaluation could not be held at the beach. The session was held instead at a community center in a centrally located *repoblación* and was only a one-day event. Many women who had volunteered their time throughout the year articulated their resentment that they were not rewarded with a trip. Educational retreats typically involve time away from the pressures and responsibilities of running a home and create a context for women to take care of only themselves. Like the previous year, Irma's opening words reminded women of their historic and critical role in the pursuit of social change for FMLN communities, past and present. She added, however, that women are also at the heart of a contradiction. Irma elaborated that while women are critical social actors, they continue to be at the center of violence. She stated, "Que no sea la misma historia, que nos criamos para dar dar y dar y no para recibir." (Let it not be the same history, that we are raised to give, give, and give and not receive.) That year's meeting, though not taking place during an election period, was also framed by national politics and served as an ongoing site of political mobilization.

Following Irma's speech, Esperanza, the CCR coordinator of the Women's Secretariat, took the floor. Her speech, too, illustrated how these sessions doubled as rallies to remind women that they "are FMLN." She located how for CCR, like the FMLN, the "enemy" was still ARENA for many reasons, but most importantly because their policies continue to marginalize the rural sector. She pointed to ARENA's national development plan that focuses on urban-based free trade zones, or *maquilas,* a rapidly growing (and exploitative) garment industry (see Brooks 2007). She unmasked the Salvadoran government's reach into communities through the Escuela Saludable program. Esperanza characterized this program as ultimately serving ARENA's interest to create a trained workforce for their *maquilas,* as the requirement to work in one is having a sixth-grade education. The nation, thus, was only interested in creating citizens as a labor reserve.[14]

Irma called upon women to ask why the government did not support learning beyond the sixth grade. She called upon women to understand that women's projects were not the solution. She called upon women to confront the government's politics. She called upon women to confront the "capitalist system" they had all fallen into since the signing of the peace accords. And finally she called upon women to combat *"el individualismo que nos viene envolviendo"* (the individualism that is surrounding us). I suggest that these moments are key sites for educating or creating gendered FMLN citizens. The question becomes, Can the development practices heralded as bottom-up and participatory address shifting contexts and new types of battles? To answer this question, I turn to a typical NGO women's project led by CORDES.

Literacy: From Nothing to a Little Bit

From January to June 1997 I tracked CORDES's Gender and Training Team's core undertaking—a literacy project aimed at empowering women. Across CORDES-affiliated communities the project divided direct beneficiaries into two groups or literacy circles. First, Alfabetización, for those with very limited literacy skills, culturally defined as *las que no pueden nada* (those that do not know anything); and, second, Pos-alfabetización, for those with more advanced literacy skills, defined locally as *las que sí pueden, un poco* (those that can a little bit). As is often the case for literacy projects, the goals were layered. While, indeed, the primary goal was to provide women students with adult basic education, meaning to learn how to read and write at a second-grade level, the overall objective was more nuanced. It involved meeting the literacy needs of registered women students and simultaneously empowering their grassroots teachers or *promotoras* in order to create community leaders.

I attended the majority of literacy promoters' workshops. During the first introductory and ten-hour workshop, a brightly painted banner greeted the participants: "Why literacy? Why Women?" The day was a model of participatory, democratic development. All women were engaged in the task at hand and compiled answers to the above questions. They then enacted these qualities in a series of group skits or *teatrillos*—a typical popular education technique. By the end of the day, the key reasons for addressing women's literacy (both theirs and their students) included the need to develop women's potential in life, so that women are no longer deceived by men and society; to stop being ignorant; to help women know their rights; to teach their own children; to work toward women's liberation; to share what "little" they know; and to be more participative. One of the team leaders added that it was time to learn to defend ourselves, not with arms but with knowledge—something that international funders, she added, are eager to support in postwar times. The project's vocabulary is also telling. The way "*poder*" was used by both the teachers-in-training and CORDES team leaders pointed to the word's multiple meanings of power, ability, and knowledge. The literacy circles became a site of facilitating empowerment. As one teacher months later commented on the progress of her students, "Clearly, they didn't end up like they started. I along with them have learned. . . . They say, 'Ya podemos' (Now we can)."

Interestingly, during the six-month project, both the student's literacy skills and the teachers' literacy and teaching skills were not evaluated. Acknowledged, though not addressed, the literacy textbooks were the same ones used the year before. Thus, the majority of students were repeating the same material. The project's impact on teachers was tracked by monthly gatherings where each teacher participated by articulating the problems (and, to a smaller degree, the successes) encountered during the previous month's work. During these sessions, the teachers raised a series of concerns. For example, they requested additional project funding in order to supply their older students with eyeglasses, as they claimed many women complained of an inability to see the blackboard. Others requested additional funding for supplies such as light bulbs for the classrooms. And as the project reached the last months, many teachers were concerned about what gifts the project would provide for their students, and how much money they would receive to hold an end of the year party with food and drinks.

The Gender and Training Team tried to orient the literacy promoters away from these issues and focused instead on one specific area—class attendance. Here we can see that development and education are entangled within strategies of neoliberal governmentality. Recall that enumeration is a key tactic of discipline and control. The CORDES team's attention to retention and attrition speaks to project donor's need to quantify. The teachers attempted to speak outside this frame of indicators as numerically valuable. At each meeting, the team tabulated the desertion rate for each literacy circle in each community. Attendance served as an indicator of project success, critical for project evaluation and the following year's access to similar development resources.

It was in the discussion surrounding attendance that the team led the literacy teachers into an analysis of gender relations. For most of the attendance problems involved conflicts between female students and their male partners, who often times limited their participation. Teachers reported how their students stopped attending the daily classes because of childcare issues, pregnancy, family illness, or, as one woman commented, because "her man didn't like to serve his own food," as class took place in the evening—"*a él no le gusta agarrar la comida.*" The response by one of the Gender and Training Team leaders demonstrated how this should be combated and is unacceptable. She asked, ironically, "*¿Es cuto?*" (Is he an amputee?) In a region characterized by a high proportion of male wounded war veterans, men who are, indeed, missing limbs and struggle against a feminization of their masculinity, this comment, while ringing true, received quite a bit of laughter.

The last literacy workshop, held in the Chalatenango FMLN party offices, served as the project's final evaluation. Flip-charts were everywhere. Women were placed in groups in order to answer questions on large sheets of paper. "Officially," in the teachers' public presentations, only positive comments were voiced. However, Rebecca, one of the team leaders, circulated through the room and listened to women's musings. She happened by the group Elsy was in and overheard a critique of the CORDES team. The group questioned the very term "training" or *capacitación,* asking if they really had been trained. Rebecca brought this query to the public floor. Critically aware, she in fact agreed that literacy teachers were not monitored or evaluated and that the pedagogical material was ineffectual. However, Rebecca added that the women themselves needed to take responsibility, for they were more concerned with arriving to receive their monthly *estímulo* (a token payment of three hundred colones per month) than with addressing their training needs. The critique on both ends is poignant and addresses the limitations of these types of projects.

Can we interpret this encounter differently? When I first analyzed the meanings of literacy as development and democracy, I ended with a sense of failure. Now I wonder if the Chalateco case illuminates the productive postwar fissures of governmentality. In CORDES's everyday acts of development, it falls short of the instruments of control documented in so many cases across the global south. In falling short, in not enumerating or documenting well, disciplined, regulated bodies are freed. In a comparative case, Gupta and Ferguson aptly document the ways in which development workers in India engage in practices of surveillance and regulation (2002, 985) and how these actions constitute the majority of their supervisory labor (2002, 987). In their case, development workers do not fall short, but community residents resist. Are there layers of resistance in postwar Chalatenango able to combat the emerging forms of control within, across, or among grassroots, NGO, and community borders? The answer is a qualified yes. Resistance shifts and is seen best in the phrase *dando paja,* used to underscore the lies of postwar, the lies people tell themselves and others.

Dando Paja: Resisting Micro-Credit

While some development efforts in Chalatenango are explicitly gendered, as evidenced in the work of CCR's Women's Secretariat and in CORDES's literacy circles, other projects receive little in terms of a gendered perspective. Micro-enterprise projects are one example.[15] As in much of the global south, Chalatenango has participated in sustainable development models that foreground the making of locally based entrepreneurs. Micro-credit models attempt to create small-scale capitalists out of, and in opposition to, people's longtime experience and commitment to a social project that at base and in practice is founded on communal solidarity, not individual labor and profit. Women, in particular, reject this model. In doing so, they are critiqued for misunderstanding the meaning of credit and mismanaging the practice of credit. Simultaneously, residents are reproached for placing their individual needs over "community." Once again, residents are either too revolutionary or not revolutionary enough.[16]

I tracked women's experiences with credit in El Rancho. By 1997, of the fifty-two loans from a CORDES credit program, eleven were distributed to poor women. In 1992, each woman had received a loan of one thousand colones ($115), totaling eleven thousand colones ($1,265). Five years later, the loan remained unpaid. Though CORDES acknowledged that in 1992 the credit program was not well defined, and further muddled with confusion as the staff member responsible for administering the project was summarily fired due to corrupt project administration (he stole the money), the recipients were routinely convoked to address repayment.

I observed one such meeting in October 1997. A credit trainer, frustrated by the stalemate in repayment, once again convoked the eleven women, along with over twenty community men who had received loans that year for fertilizer and related agricultural products. He critiqued the community men and women for having a misguided notion of credit, stating, "Aquí en El Rancho, hay la mala propaganda que créditos vienen regalados. Se interpretó mal, de ese momento. Crédito es crédito, la misma palabra se lo dice." (Here in El Rancho, there is the misunderstanding that the credits are free. It was interpreted incorrectly from the beginning. Credit is credit; the very word says it.) He addressed the hostility that the credit program had created for some. He requested to be seen as someone in solidarity: "No vengo aquí que me vean como enemigo." (I don't come here to be seen as the enemy.) He also agreed that (donated) projects are easier to work with than credit because they are, indeed, free. He reiterated that he received no direct benefit from credit projects: "No es de quitarles dinero. Yo no me echo ni cinco en la bolsa." (It's not about taking your money. I don't put a dime in my pockets.) It is clear that here the CORDES *técnico* must negotiate his credibility, his positioning, and his privilege. For though while he, indeed, is not making a direct profit from credit programs, visible is his postwar professionalization and status as a member of the NGO field. To the women, he heeded them to finally come to a decision, to pay the loan bit by bit or collectively or individually decide not to pay the loan. His last words were, "Yo no voy a meter presas a once mujeres." (I'm not going to jail eleven women.)

The eleven women decided to meet in order to arrive at a collective decision regarding the individual loans. Sections of a transcript below illustrate how, although credit is seen as a development tool to chart a path of women's empowerment, on the ground this credit is resisted for economic and ideological reasons. Elsy, the president of the women's community council at the time, began the meeting and established her positioning regarding the loan. While simultaneously refusing to take responsibility for the non-recuperation, she posited a critique of the very meaning of "credit," as CORDES received the money as a project and has never had to repay the loans to the international funders. As Elsy spoke she was both oppositional and defensive in her stance, "Look, *fulana* says, 'You are to blame' because, well, because I told you all, 'Don't pay.' I didn't tell anybody that. Let Pancha or Niña Marta tell me that, 'No, you don't pay.'

I didn't say that to anybody. What I said is, 'Well, although that was a loan, that money arrived there [CORDES] as donation.' That is what I said."

Following this comment, debate ensued regarding what had transpired during the past five years. How in 1995 they had originally resolved to not pay back the loan, but how this unity was undermined by some women who decided to pay back the loan bit by bit, evidenced in two women making a few payments each of twenty-five colones ($2.90). Ultimately, no payments had been made since 1995. Sandra, one of the poorest women in the community (her aging and sickly father unable to work the land to provide subsistence, her four daughters under the age of ten, each fathered by a different man who abandoned them), voiced a critique based on women's realities. This led the group to decide once and for all to not repay the loan.

> No, look women. I'm going to tell you something. I haven't studied. I'm nobody. I cannot pay back the loan. It's been a long time that we've spent in meeting after meeting, and for something as trivial as this loan they keep coming. Come on, let's all of us decide that we are not going to pay and that's it. Let these meetings end. Let's send a signed paper ... and stop lying to those men that one day we are going to pay, that I have faith to pay and I don't know what else. No one has a job to be able to save one colon; what's this about paying twenty-five colones a month. Let's take this into account as women. Because the debt has fallen upon single women. Nobody here has a man who is earning even one thousand colones a month. That is what we have to think as women. We don't have a job that gives us twenty-five colones a month; what is this that we would pay back the loan. Let it be clearly known that I am not committed to pay. That is to lie to them and to lie to oneself. (Es darle paja a ellos y darle paja a uno.)

Sandra's statement is powerful on many levels. First, with "I haven't studied. I'm nobody," Sandra gives great pause to the success of a wartime consciousness-raising project underscored by the pursuit of equality and justice, whether gendered or not. Elsewhere I discuss at length (Silber 2004a) Sandra's vocal critiques of postwar *engaño* juxtaposed against wartime unity. Second, in this passage, we can further see the impact of war on women and how in postwar, neoliberal El Salvador a traditional gendered division of labor still resonates. Third, for Sandra, credit did not empower; it did not create local sustainable development achieved through small-scale entrepreneurial status. The pigs she bought with the one thousand colones so many years back are long gone. The "benefit" long spent on survival, from purchasing milk to make cheese to buying medicine for her daughters. Note her focus; her anger is directed at the barrage of meetings that consume time and energies, time away from cultivating, time away from domestic chores and the larger structures that constrain women's economic empowerment. Thus, Sandra's pained, honest response illustrates yet another dimension of postwar governmentality—the control of time, the pressure of time, the calling for more and more meetings to assess, to enumerate problems, to enumerate solutions, and that, ultimately, as I heard repeatedly, lead nowhere. As she concluded, one is left with the circulation of lies, the lies that one tells oneself and others and that fall within the larger discourse of disillusionment as inequality cannot be resolved through a politics of solidarity and struggle.

For the next few hours the group debated what to do and agreed to compose an official letter of intent directed to CORDES. To date the women have not returned the funds. I translate and reproduce the letter:

> On Sunday at five in the afternoon, the eleven beneficiaries of the one thousand colones per person given in 1992 met at the house of Maria, in the community of El Rancho. In this document we would like to explain to you why we cannot pay back the credit. The eleven of us have decided not to pay back the loan because we don't have the means to do so. For example, many of us do not have a job, a salary, or an income. So, for these reasons, men and women of CORDES, we hope that you will take our petition into account and forgive our debt. We would also like to thank you for your good intentions in facilitating this credit for us. Cordially, [all from the group signed].

By sending this letter to CORDES, the women, acting as a group, a difficult feat to achieve in itself as the credits were individual in name, contested the practices and meaning of a minimalist credit program. In doing so, they negotiated their oppositional identities, garnered through years of struggle, with a compliance of sorts as the letter serves as a statement and apology. This is a difficult balance that characterizes the region's political economy of development.

In Chalatenango, postwar reconstruction and development have focused on rebuilding wartime-destroyed infrastructure and depopulated communities. As documented in the repatriation literature and early postwar chronicling, the transition from war to peace was characterized by a strong community-based grassroots social movement that was able to enlist the support of international donors. While arguably, as we approach two decades after the signing of peace accords, the period of transition to democracy may be over, yet the question of the meaning of democracy, the practices of democracy, the everydayness of democracy in the lives of those who fought for it is clearly not over. There are several ways to read this moment. Ellen Moodie cogently suggests that the "democratic disenchantment" of postwar El Salvador is wrapped up in an unrealized belonging, a loss of a "community of care." She writes, "In El Salvador, most people I know had yearned for something less than utopia. Rather, they had, for a moment, hoped for a liberal democracy" (Moodie 2010, 168). In part, this chapter suggests that we understand democratization as a time of multiple tensions between inclusion and exclusion, between past and present and the unknowable future, between nation and region, between Salvadoran and Chalateco, and, increasingly, between rooted citizens and those who are "mobile citizens" living outside of El Salvador (Baker-Cristales 2008; see also Coutin 2007; Menjívar 2000). These are critical pressures that involve the reeducation of survivors and illuminate the struggles in creating participative, contentious citizens (of old) in new clothes. This is a difficult struggle in Chalatenango, particularly for women who negotiate a series of new relationships and spheres in their attempts to procure their human rights as citizens of a nation in the throes of an uneven reconstruction.

Aftermaths of Solidarity

The earthen wares lay discarded.
I have kept them in the same green plastic bag
disintegrating with time.

Miniature *cántaros,* cups and plates
for my daughter now
who knows of El Salvador
who knows of Chalatenango
through the young people she meets
in Los Angeles
in New Jersey
in Virginia.

Obediente hands
sweep and haul wood
wash clothes, dishes, and children,
start fires and grind corn over stone
to slap out tortillas for guerillas of the past.

And with shame
I cannot remember who walked far

to just that right spot,

who dug deep into the fresh red mud

to make those miniature wares

meant to travel back with me.

The ones my daughter refuses to hold.

7

Conning Revolutionaries

> By definition, corruption is a violation of norms and standards of conduct.
> The other face of a discourse of corruption, therefore, is a discourse of
> accountability.
>
> Akhil Gupta, "Blurred Boundaries"

In December 1996, bus number 125 travels on the Troncal del Norte, the "high-way" from San Salvador to Chalatenango. Along the way, the landscape is densely populated, with house after house lining the road and very little green in between. The bus passes by key cities and towns such as Apopa, Guazapa, Aguilares, and El Paraíso. At each stop, lasting about one minute, venders sell their wares, sodas, *pupusas, pastelitos* (popovers), and ice cream, through the open windows. Two *cobradores* (conductors) always work the bus, helping people on and off and loading the heaviest of supplies onto the roof. One *cobrador* stands at the front; the other dangles from the back door. Both push through the packed aisle between stops, asking for fares, giving change, and, for many months, yelling, "Avisa, avisa niño, kilómetro veintiocho, kilómetro veintiocho" (Attention, attention, kilometer twenty-eight). They announce this spot, twenty-eight kilometers from San Salvador, to the large groups of women traveling daily to the site of a new "women's organization" founded in August 1996.

The first time I heard these young men make the announcement I was perplexed and began to research the organization, first by asking women in Chalatenango that I knew, then by approaching CCR and CORDES leadership, and finally by tapping into larger NGO women's networks. My curiosity stemmed from a seeming contradiction: As we have seen, while historically located groups like CCR and CORDES were losing women's participation, even getting women to attend meetings within their own communities nearing impossible, an unknown group was pulling women into their organization by the dozens.

For months I observed women mobilize energetically, individually, and independently to this *"kilómetro veintiocho,"* and I heard them talk about two new figures, the Ingeniero and Patricia.[1] Women from the repopulated communities in Chalatenango were among the travelers who paid initiation fees, weekly dues, and needs-assessment fees to participate in kilómetro veintiocho (KM28 here on). Why did women race here? Why did many sell their last chicken, borrow money, go hungry, and resign from community work in order to afford the weekly trips, dues, and make time for meetings? According to many accounts, the Ingeniero and Patricia promised their members a significant amount of money (fifteen thousand colones, or $1,715)—the line between credit and donation was a hazy one, as evidenced from the previous chapter. By January 1997, when the promised money did not arrive, rumors, concern, frustration, and division grew among women in the repopulated communities. CCR and CORDES maintained their position and admonished women for participating with an unknown group (not affiliated with the FMLN) and indicated that they neither supported nor took responsibility for the consequences of this mobilization. Over time, however, CCR leadership began to notice a disturbing pattern. Within communities, women were becoming divided into two camps: those that supported MOLID and those that questioned MOLID. Quickly, a split emerged where "CCR women" and "MOLID women" were at odds.

A decade later, when I reflect further upon this story, I cannot get past the cobradores, young, transient men, living en route, dirty from the diesel buses, quick thinking, constantly jostling coins in sacks, loud, brusque, helpful, and sometimes high. As I sit and write in New York, these young men in their late teens and early twenties have become for me Wilfredo, Elsy's eldest boy, a cobrador at seventeen. At eleven he was already a young man, fatherless, slight, capable with the machete, and so sweet. In searching amidst my photographs, searching for the man he has become, I realize that of Elsy's family he is the least photographed. In pictures, he is always in the background, shadowed by Miguel's presence, his charismatic younger brother. Yet, the images capture his tenderness. But Wilfredo is no longer a cobrador. He reached Virginia in the summer of 2008, the third of Elsy's children to make the journey successfully, meaning alive. Why can't I shake Wilfredo—a cobrador turned migrant—from this story on the limits of NGOs? How is his path from child of revolutionaries, abandoned son of a peasant farmer, to informal laborer and, most recently, unauthorized migrant and fast-food worker linked to this story I want to tell about women's organizing, corruption, and NGOs? Wilfredo, living in transit, whether on the highways of Chalatenango or the highway across the Americas, is symptomatic of the generation that democracy and development failed. MOLID, too, stands as a metaphor for the injustices that crop up through democratization processes, what Philippe Bourgois would perhaps identify as simultaneously structural, gendered, and everyday violences that unravel the "global lie of democracy and neoliberal prosperity" (2006, ix).

This chapter tells the story of "KM 28," which soon became known by its official name of MOLID, Movimiento de Liberación y Desarrollo (Movement of Liberation and Development), and the small movement that grew to contest its hold over women in the *repoblaciones*. In doing so, I explore emerging forms of activism within the backdrop of waning social movements. Theoretically and politically, it is an important story because it illuminates the spaces of corruption that emerge in the political openings of El Salvador's transition to democracy. As Akhil Gupta reflects above, "The other face of a discourse of corruption, therefore, is a discourse of accountability" (1995, 388). In El Salvador a discourse of accountability has not erupted (Sprenkels 2005; Viterna and Fallon 2008). This is in stark contrast to the Guatemalan case, for example, where the local and indigenous claiming of universal human rights discourses and practices has been central in the search for justice and truth, for transparency and accountability (Sanford 2003). In both cases, however, impunity prevails. In El Salvador, I argue that the struggle for economic justice that framed pre-war and wartime organizing, though marginalized in the postwar period, trumps human rights practices, discourses, and the use of legal mechanisms at the grassroots level.

MOLID is also a story that I promised to tell when back in the United States even though for many of the NGOs that comprise the Salvadoran women's movement, MOLID never even registered as a concern. Who remembers MOLID now, and the unintended consequences of my sideline, engaged practice? The story has been forgotten, become invisible, like the earthenwares innocently brushed aside by the small hand of a three-year-old girl. When Elsy and I speak, linked by cell phones, MOLID is old trouble. There are other pains: the pain of a hysterectomy, the pain of separation and of growing into middle age without her children. There are new worries about old lovers, new lovers, and what this means for her remittances. And there are new suspicions that I learn only from others about her shifting political inclinations and resulting social ostracism. In writing about MOLID, my aim is, first, to work through Nancy Scheper-Hughes and Philippe Bourgois's theorizing on the continuum of "violence in war and peace" (2003) that marks the everyday in Chalatenango and, second, to address the role of engaged anthropology, of witnessing and beyond.

Perhaps it is the banality of this story of poor revolutionaries fooled, like the much-circulated stories of immigrants swindled at borders. Yes, it is the everydayness of it all, of the money that never arrives, and of the long-awaited promises for change. A change that might be on the horizon with the first FMLN-elected president, Mauricio Funes, on March 15, 2009. But, this fact is hindsight. The question remains: How could a group of savvy former activists get caught up in an increasingly obvious economic fraud masked under the legitimizing rubric of "women's movement"? Why would this create such strife within politically homogenous communities? I am reminded of Michael Taussig's similar questions in *My Cocaine Museum* (2004), where he weaves a narrative of the legacies of gold and the violent introduction of coca in the Pacific Coast of Colombia. In this marginalized space, where descendents of slaves toil for kernels of gold and where the state, paramilitaries, guerrillas, and smugglers intersect, Taussig tells the story of "daring scam artists," supposed guerrillas who promise residents, mostly women, many riches for their labor. These riches never appear, and the "fake guerrillas" abscond with women's last nuggets of gold. Taussig writes, "The fake guerrilla . . . entered as saviors and left as thieves, and what is most surprising to me, and hence salutary, is that without so much as a blinking an eyelid, the villagers believed them. How could such cautious people be so naive as to think that the guerrilla would act this way *and* be willing to pay to join them to the extent of the women parting with their jewelry?" A local friend of Taussig responds, "'Their poverty!'" prompting Taussig to ponder, "But surely poverty makes you suspicious?" (2004, 142, emphasis in original). MOLID is the story of so many women in Chalatenango, moving in and out of cautious belief, eyes wide open.

This is a complicated story to unravel for it was and still is to me shrouded in mystery. Because of the volatile and secretive nature of unfolding events, I chose not to tape record the process. In part, I followed the advice of the remarkable Father Jon Cortina, Jesuit priest and scholar of the Universidad Centroamericana José Simeón Cañas (UCA), who spent much of his life's work based in the repopulated community of Guarjila. He too was very concerned about the presence of MOLID. When I discussed the situation with him, he advised to tread with care, for the group had potentially dangerous connections. How to take care and whom to take care of? In response to his words, I decided that it was pivotal to record events as they developed and to attempt to subvert power inequalities through questions of representation and a feminist politics of location.

Women's Movements in the Transition to Democracy

Before turning to this story, I begin by highlighting salient findings from the significant surge of social science research on women's social movements in El Salvador. Much of this work has been comparative and predicated on rich interviews with differently positioned social actors who reflect on their wartime and postwar activism (see DIGNAS 1993; Fundación 16 de Enero 1993; Luciak 2001; Moreno 1995; Rivera et al. 1995; Vázquez et al. 1996). This work, along with previous chapters' attention to unmasking the postwar demoralization of women's participation, provides the larger context for interpreting the crisis that became, for a while, MOLID, and the experimentation with human-rights framing that in the postwar period was subordinated by the hegemonic call for reconstruction.

The literature on women's popular organizing and militant revolutionary participation during the Salvadoran civil war has been pivotal in locating the gendered nature of the revolution and enters into larger scholarly conversations on women's social movements under authoritarian regimes. In doing so, it has detailed the opportunities and constraints women have faced from prewar organizing to postwar reintegration processes. Early work documents the explosion of women's participation in social movements, within labor unions, in peasant land-rights organizing, in the teachings of liberation theology, and in women-specific organizations. CO-MADRES (Committee of the Mothers of the Disappeared) is an important example of this type of women's human rights group; it organized publicly under the rubric of culturally salient definitions of motherhood in their search for their disappeared kin. Like other human rights organizations, such as CRIPDES, CO-MADRES's search for justice to end human rights abuses was met by violent state-sanctioned repression.

Early texts also document women's active participation in the armed resistance. They illustrate how women were critical actors in various capacities and joined the revolutionary movement in more "traditional" gender roles, such as nurses, cooks, and community collaborators, to more gender-bending roles as military commanders, and also engaged in the dangerous political work of consciousness raising (Montgomery 1995). Most often these accounts follow the genre of the *testimonio* that serves in part as a vehicle to make public a struggle for human rights and social justice. *Testimonios* provide narratively driven accounts of women's stories that stand for and bear witness to the collective struggle of the time (see, for example, Alegría 1987; Rivera et al. 1995; Tula 1994).

In the emergent postwar period, scholars and activists have sought to deepen their understanding of the many contributions of women's activism. For example, scholarship foregrounds how of the thirteen thousand FMLN militants, nearly one-third were women, with a significant proportion of these representing the political cadre (Luciak 2001, Vázquez et al. 1996). Scholars also began to reinterpret the motivations behind women's wartime activism and to analyze the legacies of collective action in the transition to democracy. Julie Shayne for instance asks, "What do women do for revolutions and how does revolution relate to feminism?" (2004, 3). She is careful to not overdraw the category of feminist, and to do so she develops the concept of "revolutionary feminism."[2] Significantly, research such as Shayne's has been critical in demonstrating the ways in which women's roles have been undervalued and the importance of the everyday ways in which, as women, they were able to "win over the people" and engage in high-risk mobilizations precisely because of gendered assumptions about what women can or cannot do (2004, 38). This research provides specific yet comparative data for theorizing women's social movements in the context of war, peace-building, and democratization.[3]

Karen Kampwirth also discusses the impact of larger structural forces such as the explosion of agrarian capitalism by the late 1960s. With men migrating to work, she details how women in the countryside become single heads of households, creating the context for the deployment of multiple roles within the home and community. Women, too, increased their labor migration and entered the informal economy during this period and, as a result, gained organizational experience (Kampwirth 2002, 7–8). As Kampwirth notes, "the experience of organizing in an unarmed capacity both pushed and pulled women into the guerilla struggle; they were pushed by the governments' escalated violence, they were pulled by their own growing political skills and consciousness" (2002, 8). Indeed, Kampwirth defines women's activism beyond armed combatant and theorizes gendered political identities into three categories: "high prestige revolutionaries," defined as women in leadership positions, "low prestige revolutionaries," such as cooks, and "mid prestige revolutionaries," who had some degree of leadership in the revolutionary movement but, like low-prestige women, suffered the sexism of the guerilla structures (2002, 13).

In her subsequent work Kampwirth (2004) further details how "mid prestige revolutionaries" in the postwar period redefine their activism with an emerging feminist perspective, one that pushes their former revolutionary activism. An important contribution of this work is the focus on the individual within the collectivity and an attention to the "personal roots of revolutionary activism" via "transformative events" (Kampwirth 2002, 59). Kampwirth focuses on those mid-prestige women who often become leaders in women's NGOs and within the women's movement because they are closed off from positions of political power in the postwar period *and* because of their wartime experiences, feel that they cannot go back to the space of the home (2004, 10). This is an important sociological contribution. Similarly, Shayne offers the concept of "gendered revolutionary bridge": "Gendered refers to femininity, revolutionary to the type of social movement of which the women are a part, and bridges implies the strategic connections women make as a result and subversion of femininity within such a context" (2004, 43).

However, my work troubles the category of "low prestige" woman and the impact of gendered revolutionary bridges for the majority of Salvadoran women with whom I worked. I agree with Kampwirth's depiction that the international leftist and women's movements did not penetrate so deeply at this level, that women were indeed impacted by what is broadly defined as a guerrilla sexism. Yet, building from Leigh Binford's ethnographic work, it is important to recall that it is precisely the ways in which the revolution did not ask culturally very much of rural peoples that marks its success so to speak (Binford 1998). This book takes up the postwar circulations of what I bracket as "rank-and-file" men and women. In doing so, I attempt to write their intellectual agency back in.

In all of this work, scholars highlight how state and parastate violence is a key factor in rural women's revolutionary activism (Viterna 2006) and in the formation of radical subjectivities and political identities that become entangled in the aftermaths of war (Shayne 2004; Silber 2004a). It is in the postwar period that feminists begin to recount and reinterpret the ways in which the revolutionary process subordinated the struggle for gendered justice and, indeed, how the revolution itself reproduced gender discrimination (Kampwirth 2002; Molyneux 1985; Vázquez et al. 1996). Feminists also begin to highlight the repercussions of a peace process without an intentional gendered perspective (Kampwirth 2004; Pampell Conaway and Martínez 2004) and without a development plan. These findings engage a larger conversation on the ways in which democratization negatively impacts women's mobilizations across cases, such as historically in Venezuela, where political parties win out (Friedman 2000), and more recently in Chile, where women's community groups, organized around topics such as healthcare, lose their footing (Paley 2001). Christine Keating, demonstrates how globalization produces a democracy at once market centered and participatory (2003, 419), which produces a new "mode of political regulation" (Keating 2003, 421).

Tracy Fitzsimmons synthesizes the trajectory of Latin American women's movements in the 1990s. She summarizes, "Under democracy, oppression now looks different, as do the oppressors and circumstances in which women might win or lose. Similarly, the reasons why women mobilize, how various women's groups interrelate, and how women and the state interact have also changed" (Fitzsimmons 2000, 216). More recent work continues with a comparative scope in an attempt to determine the range of factors that are needed to produce more "women-friendly" states and reassess how women's movements fair under democratization (Viterna and Fallon 2008). Viterna and Fallon's findings suggest that women fair best in countries where there has been "a complete transition, a cohesive coalition within the women's movement, a transitional ideology that aligns easily with feminist frames, and a legacy of women's activism that legitimates present-day feminist demands" (Viterna and Fallon 2008, 669). Their review of the literature reveals important patterns about how women's movements operate in a transition to democracy and speaks directly to the Salvadoran case. They discuss how most women's movements begin by building coalitions, preparing platforms, and pushing political parties to adopt them. Most women's movements also focus on increasing women's political participation and push for female candidates (Viterna and Fallon 2008, 672). They uncover how in the Salvadoran case, from 1995 to 2005, a decrease in women parliamentarians places El Salvador from "9th to 16th out of 21 Latin American countries" (Viterna and Fallon 2008, 673).

They conclude that "in El Salvador, women were mobilized at the moment of transition, but they did not use the transitional ideology of peace to forward their goals, perhaps because women's earlier participation in the rebel army would make attempts to appropriate the language of 'peace' difficult" (Viterna and Fallon 2008, 682). This is an interesting point that could explain the marginalization of human rights discourse after the war. Among their cases, the Salvadoran example—with no real structural changes to the state, a history of women working in mixed-gender protest movements only divorcing themselves from the FMLN verticalism after the war, and saddled with new donor calls for measurable objectives—echoes Fitzsimmons's assessment that "democratization often brings popular disillusionment, changes in funding availability for non-governmental organizations (NGOs), a rise in partisan politics and the emergence of new arenas of participation. All these outcomes present obstacles for women's continued mobilization" (2000, 221).

Finally, in a recent review of the status of women in El Salvador, Jocelyn Viterna and I (Silber and Viterna 2009) provide a comprehensive view of the gains and obstacles for women's activism. The international women's movement, specifically, the 1995 Fourth World Conference on Women, impacted El Salvador. This event prompted the Salvadoran State to create ISDEMU (Instituto Salvadoreño para el Desarrollo de la Mujer, the Salvadoran Institute for Women's Development), an official government institute devoted to opening up access to resources for women in areas such as health, education, and politics. However, time has shown that ISDEMU's positioning reflects ARENA's neoliberal policies, which highlight family values and places solutions to gendered issues on women's backs rather than on the state (Silber and Viterna 2009). And while women's coalitions surge in spurts, for example, around the creation of a political platform in 1994 and 1997, Viterna's research suggests how leaders "lamented the absence of a true women's movement in El Salvador" (Silber and Viterna 2009, 344).[4] While spoken from the perspective of leaders of women's NGOs, this lament mirrors the ethnographic findings of this book. Where is the women's movement? We need to ask this question not only at the national level or even regional level; we need to travel farther afield, beyond even Las Vueltas, to the smaller communities that make up the municipality. How do we define mobilization from these spaces? Below, I ethnographically detail how MOLID entered into these community spaces, the activism that developed, and the unintended consequences of this collective action that attempted to use new human rights discourse and avenues for redress.

Conning Revolutionaries

As NGOs and international agencies privilege women in their postwar reconstruction plans, and the nation nods on (creating ISDEMU) and off (constitutionally outlawing abortion even in cases of rape, incest, or where the life of the mother may be at risk),[5] and place women's rights on the agenda of democratization, it is perhaps not surprising to hear about new women's organizing. In Chalatenango from October 1996 to December 1997, I traced a series of events relating to MOLID, attentive to the diverse social actors, their version of events, and the social relationships involved. Methodologically, I borrowed from the Manchester School's extended case study or situational analysis (Van

Velsen 1967).[6] The situation is complicated in Chalatenango, where the violence of the recent past informs the social interactions of everyday life.[7] When conflicts arise, how they emerge, who the social actors involved are, and how or whether the conflict is resolved are matters that are inherently political and point to the ramifications of the war in the present transition to democracy.

Specifically, I followed a heterogeneous grouping of women and men. They include the following:

1. women representatives of the Secretaría de la Mujer of CCR;
2. several women from the municipality of Las Vueltas and neighboring municipalities, such as Guarjila, that organized to contest MOLID's practices;
3. women from Las Vueltas who chose to support MOLID;
4. two leaders from MOLID, the Ingeniero and Patricia;
5. Jennifer, a solidarity and development worker of faith and four-year resident in El Rancho;
6. Virgilio, a human rights lawyer based in a San Salvador legal advocacy group, FESPAD (Fundación de Estudios para la Aplicación del Derecho, Foundation for the Study of the Application of the Law); and
7. myself.[8]

During one of the first encounters I witnessed between MOLID leadership and several Chalatecas, I jotted down and translated MOLID's mission statement, handwritten on a flip-chart. It borrowed the language in circulation at the time, defining its movement as follows: "MOLID is a civil society organization, for non-profit, apolitical, without creed or religion, composed of women from the countryside and the city, affected by the war."[9] There is nothing suspicious or surprising about this statement. The definition could apply to a wide array of women's organizations operating in the nation. However, unlike most women's organizations, to join this one women were required to pay a sixty-five colones ($7.50) initiation fee, present their identity card number and two photos for a membership card, pay membership dues of five colones at meetings held every fifteen days, and cover additional costs such as surveys for a needs-assessment study. Payment for development appeared, to many staff at CCR and CORDES, peculiar, to say the least. Over time, CCR as well as a few women's organizations (i.e., MAM, Mélida Anaya Montes) working in Chalatenango began to exhibit concern for the personal information MOLID had been accruing and that it could be abused during the upcoming election.[10]

Recall that, as established in previous chapters, *repoblaciones* received emergency relief projects both during the war and continuing afterward as development aid. These were for the most part organized, solicited, initiated, and managed by CCR and CORDES and placed in particular communities. This was a politicized arrangement that rooted development and reconstruction efforts within the discourse and practices of the FMLN. Thus, for many working in the region, the entrance of a politically and historically unknown "women's move-ment" was problematic. In a region that operates out of historically grounded relationships and knowledge, the entrance of difference, of an unknown group, politically not FMLN and religiously not Catholic, immediately raised eyebrows.

By November 1997, the Secretaría de la Mujer of CCR publicly announced at its yearly evaluation that it did not support MOLID. While its members did not tell women to cease participating, they voiced their skepticism and warned women that if they continued participating in the group, CCR would not take responsibility for their actions. With time, it became clear that a crisis was occur-ring between CCR and many women in the communities. While CCR struggled to keep women interested in their organization, many were choosing to attend MOLID meetings, despite the sacrifices this entailed. Almost a year after the establishment of MOLID, its presence had spawned divisiveness among women within repopulated communities. Women were split into groups, MOLID sup-porters versus CCR supporters.

Elsy's practices (she was president of the directiva de mujeres from El Rancho at the time) epitomize Chalatecas' frustration yet participation in MOLID "devel-opment." There is a schizophrenia in this, a chaos and decision making not easily mapped. For close to one year, Elsy, from one week to the next, shifted her stance on MOLID. After publicly calling all women to stop traveling to KM 28 during CCR's evaluation meeting in November 1996 (note this is one year before CCR's similar statement), within two weeks Elsy resumed traveling to KM 28. At the time I was perplexed. Indeed, Elsy used her literacy skills one long evening to help her neighbors fill out a MOLID document. Word spread quickly that once this survey was filled, the money would arrive for the Christmas holidays. Elsy offered her services because many women had filled the forms out "incorrectly" and had to resubmit the paperwork with an additional ten colones as pay-ment. Women throughout the communities told of the violent way in which the Ingeniero had ripped up a series of these questionnaires, angered by women's incorrect answers. Despite the insult that women felt, and the need to pay another ten colones to resubmit the document, they continued participating.

On this night, Elsy helped seven women fill out the complicated, six-page questionnaire, for some the second time around. I engaged in the discussion, but I did not fill out the forms for women. Why? At the time I felt that in refus-ing to fill out the forms for or with women, I was taking a stand against MOLID. The literature on activist anthropology (i.e., Hale 2006, Scheper-Hughes and Bourgois 2004) and engaged practice (i.e., Sanford and Angel-Ajani 2006) was not yet in circulation, and I was working out my positioning vis-à-vis the 1990s cultural critique at the time (i.e., Marcus and Fischer 1986). I am not sure if I would do the same now. My notes from that evening indicate that many of the women's responses were political. They were asked, "What is the root of your problems?" Most women answered in terms of sociopolitical and economic injustice—that only a few are wealthy, whereas most people are poor. Questions ranged from what women felt they needed to develop to whom they had lost in the war and what they most wanted to accomplish. I remember Doña Marta, age forty-five, answering in the plural: "Que nadie nos engañe y poder defendernos." (That no one trick us and that we be able to defend ourselves.) This sentiment soon led to an investigation and small mobilization "against" MOLID.

In El Rancho many women had grown frustrated by MOLID's practices and turned to Jennifer, an international development worker in religious solidarity who had lived in the community for over four years. In her work throughout the municipality, she had encountered many women who voiced their concern over the money that never materialized. At each MOLID meeting, the date of arrival for the international funds was postponed. Upon the request of many community members, Jennifer began to investigate MOLID.[11] I was not approached because my position was much hazier. I did not locate my work in religious practice; I was not affiliated with a recognized faith-based, solidarity organization; I did not have a vehicle (Jennifer did); and I was an international student-researcher, a category with not much history in the region.

Jennifer began her research in order to facilitate women's options for redress, pathways not quite clear in the postwar period. Soon her information prompted a few women to mobilize for their legal rights and work through a post-war, restructured legal system (Popkin 2000). Jennifer, with Elsy and Margarita (presidents of two community directivas de mujeres organized through CCR), began by going to an office of the Procuraduría de Derechos Humanos (Human Rights Ombudsman) in Chalatenango. From here they were sent to the Fiscalía (public prosecutor's office) in San Salvador and from there to the Ministerio del Interior (Department of the Interior) in San Salvador as well. These inquiries took several weeks. It was here that they discovered that MOLID was not a legal NGO—it did not have a *personería jurídica* (legal status).[12] The next step involved verifying MOLID's claim that it was supported and affiliated with two important institutions, receiving "trainings" (recall chapter 6) from one and funding from the latter: CEMUJER, a longtime leading women's NGO in San Salvador, and Oxfam America. Jennifer used her international status, connections, and resources to explore these claims. Ultimately, her questions to these reputable organizations were a factor in both groups' disassociation with MOLID.

By April 1997, Jennifer offered her information to several directiva de mujeres in the communities in which she worked. Elsy and Margarita continued to "represent" the women in their communities and agreed with Jennifer's suggestion to meet with a human rights lawyer in San Salvador working in FESPAD on legal advocacy issues. I question the idea of representation as it is precisely Elsy's and Margarita's global claim to speak for "the women" in their communities that became problematic. For example, Margarita appeared to represent the women from her community as she stated, "Las mujeres se cansaron, quieren que se ponga en claro la situación." (The women are tired; they want the situation clarified.) However, over the course of the next few months it became clear that Margarita's activism stemmed from a particularly heated crisis within her community that pitted the directiva de mujeres supported by the Secretaría de la Mujer of CCR against a newly formed MOLID directiva. While Margarita was the president of the CCR group in her community, she had never participated in MOLID. This fact ultimately compromised her leadership. In fact, she had attempted to dissuade women in her community from participating from the onset. By the time of this first meeting with FESPAD, community divisiveness was peaking, positioning woman against woman, neighbor against neighbor, survivor against survivor, and sometimes husband against wife.

In early April, I traveled with Jennifer, Elsy, and Margarita to San Salvador to meet a FESPAD lawyer, whom I will call Virgilio. After months of watching Elsy cease participation at the community level, I felt a wave of nostalgia, problematic as it was, as Elsy broke into a well-rehearsed speech register of resistance and empowerment that I first encountered in the early 1990s. It was a performative moment. Elsy and Margarita articulated a powerful political critique grounded in their transformative experiences of the past. They recounted the course of events from August 1996, beginning with the radio announcements that called women to KM 28. Elsy and Margarita impressed upon the lawyer that this was a trick and a trap (una estafa, una trampa), a congame, a scam, with "seven thousand women fooled (siete mil mujeres engañadas)," indicating that the crisis was larger than their communities, larger than their department. They explained how they had been unable to get answers from MOLID directly, and that local NGOs were not involved in helping them.

Elsy and Margarita delineated for the lawyer what sacrifices women made in order to participate in MOLID. They also repeatedly invoked MOLID's characteristic mistreatment of its female members. This was a central concern for many as their wartime experiences and participation in local development projects was grounded in discourse and practices that intended to cultivate solidarity and respect. Narratives recounting the degrading of women were as prominent as those about when and where the money would arrive. Margarita, invoking the Ingeniero's discursive violence, reported his speech about the botched surveys: "No sé por que son tan tercas, pidiendo proyecto de ganado si ni tienen pa' donde vivir." (I don't know why you are all so stubborn, asking for cattle projects when you don't even have a place to live.)

This first meeting with the lawyer was inspired as Margarita and Elsy framed the matter in terms of injustice, though not within a human rights paradigm. Margarita felt that the poverty of postwar times had made former activist women vulnerable to this fraudulent group. The injustice for her was rooted in long-standing economic concerns: that the poorest women were becoming even poorer. She lamented, "Me da lástima esas mujeres bajando con su tercio de leña por esas gran barrancas." (I feel for those women who work so hard getting wood to sell, going down those huge cliffs.) Second, she feared that if by some slim chance the MOLID money were to arrive, the funds would not be distributed through the community, as the dissent between groups of women had heightened. Third, she indicated how the crisis had become personal. She herself had come under attack from MOLID, something that would shortly come to take hold of Elsy's life as well. Word had gotten to Margarita that she had been accused of *"desanimando las mujeres"* (discouraging women), of telling them to cease their participation with MOLID. The message from MOLID was this, "Del pelo tráiganme esas personas que las están desanimando." (Bring me those people by their hair who are trying to discourage you.) For Elsy this, too, was a social injustice. While not the violent human rights abuses of the past, where lives were lost, the injustice was unacceptable. She framed MOLID's "lies" in terms of the extremes of the past and stated, "Mucho más perdimos en la guerra," (We lost much more in the war). The history of violence and collective action gave her firsthand experience and socialized her toward combating injustices. They embraced this opportunity for redress and placed their activism in a historically ineffectual and oppressive justice system.

After their eloquent and passionate presentation, the lawyer agreed to pursue the case. From the beginning Virgilio presented himself as a facilitator. He provided legal guidelines for how to pursue the case, from how to inquire about the group's legal status to how to mobilize in order to file an official complaint against the organization in San Salvador.[13] The question became how to pursue redress, not whether to pursue it or not. What was it that women from the communities wanted? Was it the credit? Did women want the money they had spent in membership dues returned? How to get redress for vulnerabilities? What kind of justice? Ultimately, this small group decided to pursue the return of membership dues, and from here onward an incipient collective action was forged, though the first steps were done "covertly" in an attempt to not cause further tension between the groups of women—at least until more information was gathered.

Patience and Faith versus Fearless Talk

One week later, Virgilio organized a meeting with the MOLID leadership. The Ingeniero and Patricia were present. Margarita and Elsy introduced themselves as CCR women leaders from their respective communities—individuals whom local women came to for guidance. The meeting began with the two MOLID leaders introducing themselves and with Virgilo invoking Elsy and Margarita as *"la portavoz de la comunidad"* (the voices of the community). He explained that he was at the meeting to represent them. Virgilio took the floor and expressed that the reason for the meeting was to clarify MOLID's activities for women in the communities. Specifically, was the pending money donation or credit? When would it arrive? The Ingeniero responded by evading the questions and giving a brief history of the group, how it branched away from another NGO because of its gender focus. He also claimed to be working with the prestigious Fundación Arias in Costa Rica.

For most of the three-hour session, the Ingeniero and Patricia were evasive, circling around specificities of credit and repeating that they had never forced women to join: "Nunca se dijo vénganse a afiliar." (We never said come and join.) Furthermore, they blamed women for being "ignorant" and affiliating without knowing. When they alluded to the credit, they blamed women for the delay. The Ingeniero pointed to a pile of paperwork on his desk. Exasperated, he indicated that the women had filled out the survey information incorrectly, and it was the women who did not "understand."[14] Moreover, they presented themselves as victims of violence by residents of the repopulated communities in Chalatenango. In Patricia's account, disgruntled members' male kin had attempted to physically attack her. In her analysis, Chalatecos did not understand how development worked. As my data reveals, residents have years of experience with development projects, which in many cases has made them development experts in their own right.

This first attempt to find redress was challenging as MOLID's position during the three-hour session remained vague. Both leaders changed their stories several times and were creatively selective in their sequencing of events. For example, first they stated that the membership fees had covered administrative costs. Then they suggested that the membership fees had created a rotating credit fund. According to this scenario, women from unspecified communities had defaulted on their loans.[15] Margarita and Elsy were far from silent during this event. Margarita confronted the two leaders' evasiveness in search of some concrete answers. She did offer specificities, such as that since December 22, 1996, the women in her community had been waiting for the promised MOLID credit. Patricia responded with, "Tengamos fe y paciencia. . . . Los Salvadoreños lo queremos para ayer" (Let's have faith and be patient. . . . We Salvadorans want everything yesterday).[16] But Margarita persisted and asked about a supposed raffle for thirty thousand colones. Rumor had it that two directivas were going to receive these funds. Margarita also wanted to know what about the gossip that two groups of women were traveling to Mexico and Guatemala in a development exchange project. These inquiries were never adequately answered. The Ingeniero and Patricia indicated that their MOLID supporters knew the answers to these questions. Finally, with more pressure, the two did provide a crude summary of MOLID's projected programs, but gave no timeline for their implementation. The projects included training, credit, commercialization of products, land, and gender, borrowing the development discourse circulating at that time.

As the meeting concluded, the lawyer, Virgilio, reviewed the situation. He accused MOLID of being poorly structured, unorganized, and lacking clarity in project design and implementation. Furthermore, he critiqued them for not understanding their target population. He asserted that while the two women present were literate with a long history of activism and empowerment, most rural women were not. MOLID had not employed the right language or vision. In Virgilio's attempts to address this problem, his representation of rural Chalatecas as illiterate and thus having diminished intellectual capacities reproduces the very structures of power that Elsy and Margarita work hard to shatter. MOLID's leaders responded to his criticisms by stating that women could simply stop participating. For Elsy, this was not a valid response. At this point she confronted the MOLID leaders, stated that this was unacceptable, that she would not back down, for she like Margarita was empowered, "Nosotras no tenemos miedo porque ya podemos hablar." (We are not afraid because we can already speak.)

Through talk Elsy articulated her ethics in words (Keane 2002). Elsy, herself having spent hundreds of colones in membership fees, transport, filling out surveys, and so on, asked the critical question, How could they get their money back? Note that to Elsy economic justice constitutes a form of redress. Accountability is rooted in colones, and the truth on the status of the organization is on hold. Finally, both the Ingeniero and Patricia suggested that each woman personally deliver a letter of resignation with receipts for each weekly quota paid. Receipts had never been given with payment. MOLID would then return an undisclosed percentage of their costs. This concession was seen as a first step toward redress. All agreed to a second meeting to further elaborate these points. The meeting was scheduled in one month's time, to be held in Margarita's community in order to reduce women's travel costs and to physically and symbolically bring MOLID to Chalatenango.

Making of Lists

MOLID canceled the meeting in Chalatenango. After a series of Jennifer's phone calls, the Ingeniero agreed to reschedule and to travel to the larger municipal seat of Las Vueltas at the end of the month. The meeting was to be held in the church, the site for many large community assemblies. It was the last week in May and a group of more than seventy women arrived at ten in the morning to the church—still in disrepair from wartime destruction. Women came from Las Vueltas and neighboring smaller communities. Many of these women were CCR supporters, still participating in a limited fashion in their events. Many also had a personal relationship with Jennifer through her church activities. Present also was a group of women from these same communities who were MOLID supporters. Spatially, these women stood off to the side and made critical comments as

different people took the floor to voice their opposition to MOLID. Given per-
ceptions regarding my stance against MOLID, this group of women would not
talk to me about MOLID.

When Virgilio arrived, the meeting began. It was coordinated by Dolores,
the CCR regional representative for the region, who happened to live in Las
Vueltas, and by Lilian, the community's president of the directiva de las
mujeres. As time passed, it became clear that neither the Ingeniero nor Patricia
was coming. Virgilio took the opportunity to update the women on the course
of events and presented the legal options available to them. He expressed that
ultimately it was their decision; he could not tell them (directly) what to do. His
language exemplifies what I found to be a common practice in El Salvador in
dealing with conflict and its resolution. He negotiated a stance between giving
advice, speaking for others, and taking responsibility for actions. He bracketed
his opinion by placing responsibility on women with the phrase "*ahí vean,*"
which roughly translates as "you will have to see about that." I include an excerpt
from his speech in Spanish followed by a translation into English:

> Ahí vean Uds. . . . Por lo menos yo no confiaría pero eso es algo muy
> mío. . . . Si Uds. aguantan, si Uds. soportan esas movidas de aquí para
> allá, ahí vean. . . . Mejor compren las dos libras de frijol y arroz pa' sus
> hijos. . . . No anden sacrificando por algo que no va dar.
>
> You will have to see about that . . . but I wouldn't trust them, but
> that's my opinion. If you can bear it, if you can endure those trips back
> and forth, you'll have to see about that. . . . Better to buy two pounds of
> beans and rice for your children. . . . Don't keep sacrificing for something
> that will not give you anything.

Virgilio informed the women that from his professional experience, as a
human rights lawyer, he could not confirm that MOLID was a legitimate organization. His status lent an authority to his remarks, as women asked him about
the pending credit and the reimbursement of membership fees.[17] An elderly
woman from El Rancho, a woman who had lost all seven of her children during
the war and in the postwar juncture barely subsisted on a small plot of land
donated by the community, sadly responded to the lawyer's explanations through
the discursive critique of the time: "Es un engaño que nos hemos hecho nosotras misma por la mismas pobreza." (We have deceived ourselves because of our
poverty.) Hers were not the only words of disillusionment, a disenchantment
born from structural forces and in oneself.

The meeting became a space for the exchange of stories and gossip, to air
frustrations born from the unmet hope that finally an organization could solve
the economic injustices of war and postwar. Some of the anger was voiced
through humor. One woman commented that Patricia was always lying—"Ella
siempre sale con una nueva payasada" (She always ends up clowning)—this time

missing the meeting because fuel was too expensive. In spaces of corruption, the everyday lack of justice shines in stark relief.

After several hours with many women taking the floor and expressing their worries and opinions, a consensus was reached. Women concluded that the issue could be resolved if they were returned their membership dues. With consent in the air, the lawyer suggested compiling a list of names with MOLID identity numbers followed by women's signatures and each individual's amount of money requested. Once this was completed he would set up another meeting with MOLID on their behalf. Dolores then took over the pragmatics of registering these names, and she offered that those women who wanted to end their participation with MOLID register with their local CCR directiva de mujeres. From these community lists she would compose a master list for the municipality and then hand it over to Jennifer, who would then give it to the lawyer. The idea was for it to be a movement of redress from the bottom up.

Gringas and Garlic

During the next few weeks, the lists were compiled in each community. Sixty women voluntarily registered with the hopes of having their money returned to them. Interestingly, when the master list was given to Jennifer and subsequently handed over to the lawyer to initiate proceedings, several women began regretting their petition. Word spread through the communities that MOLID had new housing projects for its members. As a result, many women arrived at Jennifer's doorstep requesting that their names be removed from the list. Once the list was finalized, what the lawyer would do with it became a critical question. The crisis in communities was peaking, the attempted efforts at redress had failed, and the weight of what to do with the list of names became a greater concern as division within communities became more and more apparent. Should Chalatecas use the spaces opened up in the new postwar period and pursue MOLID through the court system under the rubric of human rights? Should they employ their legal rights and resources and follow through with a *denuncia* (formal complaint) of the organization, now based out of Guazapa? Ultimately, the list was turned over to MOLID; and, as was expected, they gave no response.

The "leaders" of the mobilization for redress against MOLID did not take action until September of 1997, when they decided to go to Guazapa and make an official *denuncia* through the office of the Juzgado de Paz (municipal court). By this point Margarita was replaced with her neighbor Beatrice on the CCR directiva de mujeres; Beatrice could claim personal engagement with MOLID. En route to the local Juzgado de Paz, the group (myself included) decided to try and resolve the matter outside of the court system and headed unannounced to the new MOLID office. Here we were met by an armed security guard who eventually let us in. While Patricia accepted the visit, she called her lawyer before speaking with us. She explained that the Ingeniero no longer worked with MOLID and pointed to the current development project MOLID had initiated: four women receiving a sewing workshop in a backroom. With the MOLID lawyer present, Patricia explained that the crisis situation was a creation of the mobilization against her, of the mobilization in Las Vueltas. Patricia was quick to contest FESPAD's involvement, adding that legally MOLID did not have to attend any of the meetings that had been scheduled during the past months.

As Patricia's lawyer positioned MOLID as an organization working toward women's rights and the importance of civil society, latching on to the discourse of the time, the meeting took a turn for the worse. Elsy became the center of attention. She was repeatedly attacked, maligned, and threatened by Patricia, who accused Elsy of forcing women to sign their names on the list and blamed her for the crisis in MOLID. Jennifer contested this by explaining that the mobilization—first, to find answers and, second, to have women's money returned—emerged at the community level out of the dissatisfaction with MOLID's practices. Jennifer reiterated that she never had dissuaded women from participating in MOLID. She did not want to create camps of women against each other. Negotiating an insider-outsider position, she presented her involvement as a facilitator, attempting to help women with whom she lived and worked and who had come to her for assistance.

Despite the attempt to take the focus away from Elsy, the personal damage to her was great and circulated alongside the spreading gossip about Jennifer, myself, and the lawyer. Jennifer and I were often referred to as *"las dos cheles que huelen a ajo"* (the two white women who smell of garlic). This was clearly an insult. We were never quite sure why we were referred to as such, a reference that was sometimes made of internationals as a marker of difference. Patricia also claimed she had known Virgilio in the past and called him *"el abogado mañoso"* (the lawyer thief) because he had stolen people's money.

The meeting was a failure. Patricia denied that MOLID had ever promised credit and, most importantly, stated that they had never agreed to return the women's membership fees. As Elsy, Beatrice, another woman representing a neighboring community, the human rights lawyer, and the development-religious activist and anthropologist left the MOLID office, the level of hostility and increasing community divisions clearly indicated that the crisis was heightening rather than resolving. The consequences of pursuing a denuncia seemed increasingly volatile, creating more tension within the communities and possible physical harm against Elsy. Elsy articulated her fear that the denuncia would bring even more women to mobilize against "us" rather than MOLID. Despite Jennifer's (and my) attempts to play a facilitating role rather than a leading one in a search for truth, for justice, and for transparency, the collective action was characterized by our international presence. It discredited the movement, erasing its local and grassroots origins.

For many women who had first approached Jennifer for advice on pursuing redress, they suffered the negative ramifications of the mobilization in a very personal way. Tainted by their association, they were easy targets for counter accusations, safer than directing threats against the two foreign women. The women who had been most active in this mobilization became victims. And so Elsy, one of the strongest critics, one of the first to make the trek to the lawyers' office, to walk from house to house collecting women's names, became the target of abuse by MOLID in its threatening discourse. To make matters worse, at the time, I was residing in Elsy's newly built second room, and Jennifer lived in El Rancho. Patricia sent verbal messages to be delivered to Elsy that were meant to discredit and terrorize her. With threats to personal safety happening all too frequently as Elsy made weekly trips down to Chalatenango to purchase goods, everyday life became stressful. Women from other communities who had not seen her in months would come up to her and pass on an "indirect" message from Patricia: "Que ni se asome por aquí." (She shouldn't even think of coming by here.) Why? Because Elsy would not leave with a breath in her.

In a nation healing from the horrors of war, and Elsy herself living with the trauma of her past—the murder of her best friend, the disappearance of her FMLN-incorporated though disabled brother, the death of at least three partners and a premature baby—these postwar death threats compounded her suffering. After the meeting in September, Elsy stopped participating. The threats from MOLID, psychologically violent, disrupted her sleep and caused her a great deal of anxiety each time she left El Rancho. Ultimately, MOLID was able to blame their delay in project implementation on two gringas, a few disgruntled women, and *"un abogado mañoso"* (a lawyer thief).

Going Back to the Grassroots

After this last meeting with MOLID, Jennifer reflected on the mobilization process, asking why it had been such a slow-paced confrontation ending with an unforeseen crescendo. Was it our fault? Today, I think back to Daysi's cautionary war stories first told to me in 1993. Was my presence a critical factor that actually pushed collective action too quickly and that ultimately covered things up— *¿tapando las cosas?* With tension mounting at the local level, Jennifer wondered what the agenda should be. With the next step unclear, the decision was made to present the situation to the Secretaría de la Mujer of CCR, who had during the past year remained uninvolved in the situation.

In early October, Jennifer was invited by CCR to explain the movement of women with whom she was working.[18] Eight regional women representatives were present, as was a member of the CORDES Gender and Training Team and Irma, the director of women's projects of the San Salvador headquarters of CRIPDES. During the four-hour meeting, it became clear that communities throughout the region were experiencing similar internal divisive crises whether they had participated with Jennifer or not. One regional representative recounted how she could no longer visit a CCR-affiliated community because the women were now organized through MOLID. She explained how these were longtime participants in the war who felt abandoned, who felt that they had not received postwar reconstruction benefits (i.e., roads, schools), and who felt that CCR had not come through for them. As in much of the reconstruction and development that happens in the repopulated communities, people conflate the practices and expectations they have of the FMLN, grassroots organizations, and NGO development projects. The representative countered that these communities had received development projects, such as a woman's store and bakery project; but, as in so many other communities, these projects had faltered. She wondered aloud how women were so easily fooled, "Hemos pasado tanta guerra, con tantos engaños dentro de la guerra." (We have had so much war, with so much deceit in the war) that we should know that legal projects come organized, first through CRIPDES, then CORDES, and then CCR."

For CCR and CORDES, as previous chapters argue, their critique of women's declining participation was further complicated. They were witnessing a women's mobilization aimed not at the local level and not following in the long history of pursuing social justice, but rather women were mobilizing for individual gain and with an unknown organization based outside of historic FMLN territory. Irma, articulated her concern as follows: "That's the worry. There are women who believe it [MOLID] entirely . . . and they are willing to participate no matter if they get anything or not. But there are a number of women that have said no, because we understand that this is a scam and we can't go on with this." Note how Irma moves in and out of speaking about women in the third person, distancing herself and CCR from this group of women. In a turn of the phrase, she aligns herself with "a number of women that have said no." Implicit in this critique is the question of political representation. Will these women continue to vote FMLN? Irma follows up with the comment, "It's strange because they were women of the war, women fighters. It's odd for us that they have become involved with another ideology. Why are we like this now, if before everything was different? There was solidarity. Why is this happening to us? We want to recuperate our values." She added that CCR must find a method or mechanism to alert women that MOLID was "politically dangerous." She suggested that CCR return to the work of consciousness raising, walking from house to house to talk to women about unity, solidarity, and mutual respect in order to convince them that divisions between women generate even more problems.

As Jennifer recounted the work of five months of investigation, she and I were met with criticism from CORDES and CRIPDES, who accused us of leading the movement. We were told to cease. Rebecca from CORDES argued that the focus of these efforts was problematic. She suggested shifting attention back to the community in order to minimize the ongoing internal divisions. For Rebecca, who had not addressed this issue previously, it was more important to hold a large assembly of women and present the "facts" of MOLID in order to let people decide what they wanted to do. Her goal was to end the dynamic of CCR "against" MOLID. She said, "We have to clarify to women that the Secretaría de las Mujeres is not opposed to them, but here is the information, and those that are interested in recovering their money, here is the path to take. I think in that way we don't create more contradiction nor are we confronting the women."

While Rebecca did not hesitate to oppose the process initiated against MOLID, rightly concerned not only about community life but about the implications for future CCR and CORDES collective action, Irma tempered the critique by situating the lack of CCR resources that had made facilitating a mobilization against MOLID impossible. She stated, "It is important that we keep this up . . . that we confront MOLID ourselves, not them [meaning Jennifer and myself], . . . but the problem that we have is that mobilizing requires a great deal of expenses, like transport. The Secretariat has zero funds, but we can find a way."

When Jennifer took the floor, she did so for an extended period of time. I appear silent in comparison. She presented MOLID, rather than the movement she helped blossom, as the creator of community crises. She reiterated that her aim had always been to help women contest MOLID's practices and the spins Patricia had put on these:

> She is trying to create a great deal of division within the communities, between the people who do not want to keep participating and want to get their money back and those who are really involved in the organization. And for me, that is the worst thing. The lawyer wants us to pursue the official complaint. But there are still a lot of questions, and I would like to inform you of the process but also ask for your advice about what can be done. I see, like I have said, the risk of creating even more division between women who live in the same communities. I do not want to participate in that. But I also do not want her [Patricia] to keep going because she will keep up with the division. I have always said, if some women want to keep going [to MOLID] they can, that is not a problem. It's not that we don't want the women to go. But knowing that there are so many women that are dissatisfied, something has to be done. Because if it is a scam, the women do not have to stay with their arms crossed. So here we are; we haven't decided what the next step should be, or if there will be a next step.

With Jennifer's portrayal of the last five months, the regional representatives agreed to continue the efforts started in El Rancho. After much deliberation, they decided to schedule another meeting with MOLID in ten days. The participants would be eight women of the CCR Women's Secretariat, a representative from

CORDES's Gender and Training Team, a representative from CCR's organizing branch (the only male of the group), the women from Las Vueltas who had been involved in the investigation from the beginning, Jennifer, and myself. CCR's idea was to make this a national campaign by taking the information garnered at the departmental level to CRIPDES's next national level meeting, because the same process was occurring throughout the regions affiliated with CRIPDES where MOLID was also developing a high profile (i.e., San Vicente, La Libertad, Suchitoto). The idea was to wage a larger and more concerted effort for redress.

Ten days later, the agreed upon group traveled to Guazapa and arrived at the MOLID offices. Patricia was not present. Her daughter, the secretary, spoke with the group and provided information. The meeting began with Esperanza and Rolando, both CCR leaders, introducing CCR and the reason for the meeting. Over the course of the meeting, Rolando actively voiced his critique of MOLID, from its organizational chart that the young woman supplied to the unspecified and date-less projects it claimed to be working on. For example, Patricia's daughter explained that a "limited" credit project had been initiated with a few hundred colones given. Regarding membership dues and recuperation of these expenditures, the answers remained vague. Once again, the young woman explained that each member had to write a letter of resignation and again personally deliver it to the Guazapa office. In the exchange, CCR presented itself as the voice of the communities, as simultaneously the experts in the region and the voice of people themselves. Rolando, himself a resident of Las Vueltas and longtime activist, stated: "Para nosotros nos interesa que no nos engañen. (We don't want to be fooled.) We are not opposed to you helping our communities. . . . We already know these communities . . . when something is promised and then not met, you'll see. . . . We, as CCR and CORDES, have never charged them a cent."

After one hour the meeting ended. Over lunch in the plaza in Guazapa, the CCR members discussed the next step, as this meeting had not resolved much. They decided to meet again with the MOLID directiva on a subsequent Saturday. This was the last meeting I attended. One week later I ended my fieldwork and returned to New York City. I do not know if a follow-up meeting with MOLID was held as the end of the year was a hectic time for CCR with a historic ten-year celebration of repatriation. After this meeting Jennifer stepped away from the mobilization as CCR took over. And after four years of solidarity work, Jennifer left El Salvador in April 1998. The lawyer from FESPAD was not contacted again. According to communications with women from Las Vueltas, the issue was never resolved and the mobilization for legal redress halted.

(Im)mobilizing Postwar Justice and Engaged Practice

During a recent lecture, Webb Keane reminded us that the anthropological mandate is to locate our study in the midst of things.[19] It is precisely from this positioning that the task to unravel begins, in this case to disentangle the perplexing stories of corruption and the everyday of postwar injustice where the implementation of reforms to the legal system lag far behind. This task is always already positioned. My own position in the early to mid 1990s, as a young "South American gringa"—Argentine-born and raised in the United States by immigrant parents, anthropologist in training—brought with it implicit and explicit ethical commitments. But being in the midst of things is ever changing, as is our positioning—from grinding corn in a hand mill under the tin roof of Elsy's home to making *pupusas* with Elsy's daughter Flor in Los Angeles, California, with my own daughter standing on a stool beside me patting out two-inch wide tortillas while Flor's newborn slept in my arms.

When I first left the field, despite the surge of literature that cogently critiqued notions of "the field" and "community" as bounded, I felt El Salvador as, indeed, very far away and bracketed. Leaving felt like a loss. How to translate the contradictions of postwar into something tangible to act on and theorize? An international aid worker, and close friend at the time, articulated well the weight of the project because of the entanglements of my own subject position and expectations of solidarity that are complicated in aftermaths of war. She offered, "There is no denying that this experience will have a profound effect on our lives when we leave. . . . You have the double pressure of being reminded of your time here constantly with the writing up of your doctoral thesis. Most of us can forget about it slowly as the memories fade. It's bloody hard, this experience: before, during, and after. Remind me again why we do this to ourselves?" (personal communication, April 1998).

For my friend, the balance of remembering and forgetting is simultaneously about the violences of postwar El Salvador and the struggles of doing community-based, non-imperial development work that takes place within a framework of intercultural exchange (Silber 2007). Hers was an explicit mandate from her national volunteer agency. Mine departed from a position of solidarity at once personal and academic. As I hope this book makes clear, this is an attempt to elaborate the practices, theorizing, and representation of an activist-inspired anthropology rooted in the *everyday* nature of witnessing, of being present to testimony, of engaged listening. As Victoria Sanford eloquently explains, "the seemingly inexplicable and yet mundane everyday life is what draws us into these zones where 'no one goes' but where real people actually make and remake their everyday lives as best they can" (2006, 1).

In recent years anthropologists have entered into both a theoretical and methodological conversation on activist practice. Charles Hale, for example, exposes the limitations of cultural critique by privileging methodology. He defines activist research as "a method through which we affirm a political alignment with an organized group of people in struggle and allow dialogue with them to shape each phase of the process, from conception of the research topic to data collection to verification and dissemination of the results" (2006, 97). In my case the difficulty arises in defining what constitutes the "organized group." Is it CCR, CORDES, the women who attempt to find justice against MOLID, Las Vueltas, El Rancho? Beyond this question, perhaps most vexing is how am I to be a collaborative activist while a social movement is falling apart? Yet, Hale is right to state that "scholars who practice activist research have dual loyalties—to academia and to a political struggle that often encompasses, but always reaches beyond the university setting" (2006, 100). This I too believe is the mandate of anthropology. It is a complicated professional ethics, as Sally Engle Merry makes clear. Merry illustrates the divergent approaches that activists and researchers take in the production of knowledge. Building from her ethnography of gender and human rights workers, she writes, "Activists worked with notions of outrage and urgency. . . . A successful NGO is one that builds an issue that has a name, evokes sympathy, defines a villain, and compels a form of action" (2005, 251). In contradistinction, she posits that "academics, however, focus on shades of gray, on context and structure" (Merry 2005, 252).

This story of MOLID and my place within it thus takes place at a time when social movements dressed in new NGO frocks come to be asked to do too much under neoliberalism, to organize urgently, with moral outrage against a too often elusive villain of globalization. For while CCR and CORDES worked diligently to mobilize community leaders to work on the land-transfer program and benefits for wounded veterans, other programs made available through the peace accords simply could not receive much organizational attention, let alone a scam aimed at former rank-and file-supporters of the armed struggle.

These benefits included funds for orphans and the elderly who lost children during the war. The collection of these benefits was bureaucratic and fell upon individuals. Elsy's experience is typical enough, though Elsy's abilities to negotiate travel and understand bureaucracies are not. Recall her fearless talk. In 1993, she began advocating for Flor to receive funds as an orphaned child of war because her father, a guerilla platoon leader, had been killed in an ambush. To do so, Elsy needed to attain Flor's father's death certificate (a cost of three hundred colones), three "originals" of her daughter's birth certificate, again more money, and the father's birth certificate. Flor's father was born in the department of San Vicente, quite a distance from Chalatenango. Elsy made several long trips to the mayor's office there, always leaving her children in her own mother's care. Elsy explained to me that she also needed two witnesses and, lastly, twelve copies of the entire application. In December 1997, with Flor fifteen and only eligible for three more years of payment, the case was still not legally recognized. Like benefits for the elderly, Tercera Edad, receiving allocated funds took years and for others the benefits never materialized.

The incipient movement for redress against MOLID can be theorized as a form of social protest that occurs in the spaces "in between," what Richard Fox and Orin Starn discuss as the "terrain in between mass revolution and small scale resistance, an intermediate zone of what can be labeled 'dissent' and 'direct action'" (1997, 2).[20] During the 1960s and 1970s scholars focused on revolution, and the 1980s saw a shift to an analysis of the everyday forms of resistance, to what James Scott (1985) coined the "weapons of the weak," evidenced in the hidden transcripts of compliance that mask opposition to state and power. I borrow from Fox and Starn's conceptualization that much happens in between these two extremes and that it is critical to examine the "midways of mobilization" (1997, 3). This chapter has provided a narrative of the relationship or trajectory of the ways in which women's dissent becomes a grassroots action and how the legacies of a past of collective action frame the present. It also provides an ethnographic analysis of the limitations to these types of mobilizations in transitions to democracy. Ultimately, this action is not transformative, engaged practice is unclear, and redress unmet.

The role of an anthropologist dancing the line between participant, observer, witness, and coded as international, with all the access to resources that this implies, must also be addressed. Did my initial romance of a past of resistance color my ethnographic interests and help facilitate a movement? As I traveled from El Rancho to San Salvador with a group of women, it felt like the kind of research I should be doing. Had I finally found some action, some opposition, a search for justice? My participation in this attempt for redress highlights the political repercussions and tenuous effects and unintended consequences of the role of the anthropologist. Merely being present and read by others as an *internacional* affected people's lives in ways out of my control. This chapter has been my attempt to repair these contradictions, to portray as honestly as I can the spaces and times of the ordinary, everyday violence that damages without spectacle. In this way I seek to take responsibility for the stories I collected and observations I was invited (or not) to witness.

I close by returning to Wilfredo, who very well may have been calling out a new version of KM 28 up and down the Troncal del Norte up until the summer of 2008. He departed for the United States to join his brother and his stepfather in Virginia. When I first learned of his pending travels, it was through Miguel and Elsy each deploying narratives of economic success in the United States in comparison to the grinding poverty in El Salvador, where making a *milpa* just could never pay off. A year later the rumor circulated, through one of my few international contacts that still remain in El Salvador, that Wilfredo left, disillusioned not only by the poverty of postwar, but by the postwar sexuality of his mother, happy to accept remittances from her partner in Virginia while taking on new loves in El Rancho. The story goes that Wilfredo beat his mother's lover, a picture I cannot make out as my image of Wilfredo is of a small, thin, and speedy boy of eleven. Wilfredo is not an activist. He is also not a gang member. He is a young man who felt no alternative but to leave the hopelessness of democracy and development that fed him crumbs from the jangling coin purse, that left him a mother whose arguably empowered sexuality flies in the face of cultural expectations of femininity and migration. Wilfredo's hope traverses the highways. It is the same hope that carried women up and down the Troncal del Norte on the back of pickups, jammed into sweaty and smelly buses in search of that elusive escape out of poverty on the postwar highway.

Postwar Dance

Eva is twelve or thirteen years old. That is what the mothers say.
No one can really place her though she has been among them for the last ten years
as she crossed the border on her mother's breast now dead five.

In her *guaro* intoxication by the river
orphaned daughter calls upon her mother
as she dances naked in the stream
falling into the laughter of boys surrounding her.

Eva who does not like to work. That is what the women say.
That is what Elsy says with tears in her memory
of how she tried to bring the child into her new cement-block house.

Girl-child slips through the window
with her electric blue unitard she wears for a dress
the color of my dance uniform when I felt thin enough.
But her budding little body erupts into womanhood
created by the hands of boys by the trees with their pants pulled down,
her panties by her ankles as they pass her in the night.

Eva returns as quietly as she leaves,

early morning with fire to start, corn to grind, plastic dishes to wash

and still with the imprint of the hands of boys

with machete grips for the *milpa*.

So she glides out the window.

Es que no le gusta trabajar. That is what the mothers say.

Several took her in for a day, a week

clothed her, sewed her skirts

the *campesina* kind, tight to hold the body in.

She exchanges this binding, mother's cloth, for the freedom of that unitard.

Eva should be doing *grand jetés* down the one paved road.

I could teach her how to leap into safe men's bodies

hands opening her legs only to move her through the air.

Eva in the air.

Eva falling from the mango tree.

Hips inverted, body bruised, a child one afternoon.

No more slipping through windows from mothers to boys.

8

The Postwar Highway

I was in the struggle. Not with a rifle on my back but for three years. No three years and nine months I was in solidarity. Because when you are in your mother's womb you feel the suffering, the falls, the hunger, the pain of war.

Miguel, author interview in December 2007

Seven-year-old Miguel with his broad grin and electrified blond hair was the first person I saw through the bus window as I approached the rural community of El Rancho on a hot, late morning in November 1996.[1] He was racing along the cracked cement road, dragging a deflated red balloon on a string, hoping to catch some air. Miguel was dangerously and nearly underfoot of the aging, unsteady, local bus making its second trip from the rural capital city of Chalatenango to El Rancho. Despite what at the time I understood as so many "lacks," he wore an everyday exterior that I can now only describe as "little kid happy."[2] In the time it took me to step off the bus and unload my knapsack, laden with what I hoped were useful gifts, T-shirts, pants, skirts, batteries, the basics, Miguel was skipping back from announcing my arrival to his mother, Elsy, a central protagonist in this ethnography whose trajectory illuminates the arcs of inhabiting the public role of "women's community leader." Within minutes, Miguel walked me down a less muddied path to his home, a new cement-block structure, twice the size of the one I had seen two years before and made possible by postwar benefits and international development projects.[3]

Fast-forward to November 2007, Virginia and New York. It is Sunday, late morning, and, as I've come to expect, the phone rings. Miguel is eighteen years old now and on weekends as he rides the bus in Virginia to his day job he calls. When he phones, we talk about his mother, Elsy, in El Rancho, raising a seven-year-old grandson, her daughter's child. Miguel tells me how he is befriending the *internacionales* at a national food chain where he works double shifts with *papeles chuecos* (false social security papers). They are trying to fatten him up. A wiry adolescent to begin with, he made the near month-long journey crossing borders in June 2007. Interestingly, he uses the word *internacionales* as a gloss for the white folks who are the store managers, putting them in the same category as foreign aid workers, solidarity activists, and, to a lesser extent, researchers like myself that he saw float in and out of Chalatenango. He has followed his mother's partner Avel, who emigrated three years ago, and his sister Flor, who took the lead in 2003 and now lives in Los Angeles. Miguel and I met for the first time in a decade in December 2007 and his weekly check-ins continue. While this book opens with his tears, during most of his calls he celebrates his ambitions. He is working toward promotion to *supervisor,* to "kitchen manager."[4]

Throughout the book, I have presented the perspectives of those who lived the war in Chalatenango, a former war zone, beginning when the transition was unfolding, alive with expectation, when wounds of war were raw and guiding and when political alternatives to historic state repression were opened. I have done so to show how peace and democracy in these postwar times are, at best, shallow. This chapter explores a central paradox of El Salvador's democratization: the ongoing emigration, mostly to the United States, of generations of former revolutionary Salvadorans whose labor outside the borders of El Salvador, I argue, maintains the nation's fragile democracy, 2009 FMLN victory and all. For the Chalatecos at the heart of this ethnographic journey, this movement is a different migratory project than the one taken up by thousands of Salvadorans during the war. While many Salvadorans ultimately fled to the United States in search of political asylum during the 1980s, the Chalatecos at the heart of this study either stayed in their communities to fight the Salvadoran armed forces or retreated to refugee camps mostly in Honduras. Migrating to the United States at the turn of the twenty-first century involves negotiating a different set of ideological borders along with geopolitical borders. For despite waning activism in the 1990s, described throughout the book, the heroic call, the oppositional metanarrative of *"adelante, adelante, la lucha es constante,"* meaning the struggle must continue, along with a spectral national policy of reconstruction and reintegration of civil society, was hegemonic. Men and women reduced their activism in community politics and allied less with the FMLN, but they still voted for the party. Residents in my analysis of the 1990s were struggling to learn how to become oppositional citizens and fight in new ways for sociopolitical and economic justice.

The ethnography that follows highlights how Chalateco and Chalateca migration evidences the entangled aftermaths and lies of revolution and democracy. As men and women from El Rancho travel across borders and, for some, frontiers, their trajectories are not linear, their movements tack back and forth, directions are unclear, and lives get knotted under new forms of governance.[5] The challenge is to unravel, to find that right string that when pulled releases tension rather than ensnares more. What are the entanglements then of war, of postwar, of shattered dreams of revolution and democracy, of losses and perhaps possibilities? What can following paths such as those of Miguel, his kin, and neighbors tell us about the failures of a transition to peace and about a revolution that was negotiated in a postwar context lacking in human rights discourse and practices (Sprenkels 2005)? What are the avenues of socioeconomic and political justice for the everyday revolutionaries turned undocumented migrants? Are there possibilities emerging when we put, as Anna Tsing offers in her analysis of globalization, "the question of distress center stage rather than trying to avoid it" (2005, xi)? This chapter will follow several Chalatecos to see if, indeed, tangles come undone in "transnational life" (R. Smith 2006).

Migrants and Methodology in the "Middle of Things"

For fifteen years, I have been tracing the lives of the rank-and-file members of social movements for justice along their passage from broadly defined revolutionary activists to postwar development recipients and ambivalent grassroots actors to, in many cases now, undocumented migrants. In juxtaposing these cartographic shifts, I render more visible the gendered vulnerabilities and possibilities for the everyday participants who moved both in and out of armed and political combat, and in and out of postwar development and nation-building projects, often to the chagrin of those in various levels of command. Like the very social movements Chalatecos dropped out of, my study has also ebbed and flowed for a variety of reasons such as the demands of the university and the time needed to reflect upon the overwhelming sense of loss in writing up Chalateco disillusionment in neoliberal times.[6] This temporality has been productive, as I believe the project opens up larger disciplinary questions about methodology, the importance of time, and the rhythms of longitudinal studies on the aftermath of violence.[7]

Debates shift, interests transform, and original interlocutors keep talking, doing, and thinking about their lives in a changing world. Children become adults and offer new points of view on the sacrifices of the past. Susan Bibler Coutin (2005) in her work on Salvadoran transnational belonging writes about how anthropologists revisit "the field" as we write.[8] Borrowing from Bruno Latour (1999), Coutin suggests that "data" becomes "excerpted," meaning that talk, events, moments, interviews begin to stand in for larger processes. Indeed, "the field" did, as Coutin suggests, "rematerialize" (2005, 203) around me as an ethnographer, first in my research writing, then in my articles and in my classroom lectures. In time though, this *version* of the field was jolted as "the field came to my door" through the phone calls announcing unexpected arrivals and the emotional (at least for me) meetings with Chalatecos.[9] These were *reencuentros* that I did not predict would happen first, if ever, in the United States. Analyzing this migration rematerializes the field of this study and suggests a reconceputalization that deterritorializes the possibility of democracy in former revolutionized spaces.

This project has evolved over time then, and, as the data below illustrates, its temporality is its strength as I weave together "pieces of truth" (Biehl 2005) that Chalatecos carry with them and that sometimes I bring up for them.[10] Together, in the United States as I meet with newly arrived Chalatecos from Las Vueltas and El Rancho, specifically, reflecting back upon the mid-1990s, the time of my research, invokes new interpretations of the past. I am reminded of Monique Skidmore's work in Burma on fear. Skidmore (2003) posits "violence as a temporal marker" and explores how survivors search for meaning in histories of violence. She suggests that survivors live through "pools" of time and in essence become a "population in waiting" for democracy, freedom, employment, and so on (2003, 8). It seems to me that in acts of Chalateco migration, there is a different form of heroism; the waiting has stopped. Like Skidmore, Veena Das (2007) seeks to understand how people comprehend and inhabit violence and its aftermath through the category of time. She juxtaposes and reflects upon two different ethnographic projects on violence, first, the recollections and silences surrounding India's partition in 1947 and, second, the immediacy of erupting ethnic massacres of Sikhs in 1984 where her methodology involved urgent human rights work. She raises a series of questions intended to theorize violent events and everyday life, the "ordinary" and the "eventful" (Das 2007, 7). She writes, "My interest in this book is not in describing these moments of horror but rather in describing what happens to the subject and world when the memory of such events is folded into ongoing relationships" (Das 2007, 7–8).[11] She asks, for example, "What is it to inhabit a world? How does one make the world one's own? . . . What is it to lose one's world?" (Das 2007, 2). It is precisely this entanglement, Das's "folding" into sociality where the eventful and the ordinary intertwine, that I believe Chalateco migrants carve out their pasts and present and hopes for the future. This is the entanglement of Miguel's youthful echoes of revolution, emergent even in a mother's womb.

In this move across time and space, I also build upon recent work by Coutin on deportees and unauthorized migrants. She suggests that we take on "an ethnography of motion" that follows "people . . . along paths that end abruptly, double back, and begin again in a new spot" (Coutin 2007, 16).[12] These are arcs that suggest an "ethnography of global connection" and that beg for becoming "embroiled in specific situations. And thus it is necessary to begin again, and again, in the middle of things" (Tsing 2005, 2).[13] For the study of El Salvador has taught me that if anything we need to be attentive to the particular, to the specifics of regional formations, to the stories that belie our assumptions about the workings of capitalism, the legacy of revolutionary participation, and now migration.[14] By doing so, we can examine the analytically expected structural traumas. Scholars have pinpointed these structural traumas well: we know so much about the ravages of uneven global capital that we can write eloquently about the challenges, gendered no less, of rebuilding and reconciling war-torn societies.[15] However, coupled with Anna Tsing's provocative analysis of "constructive possibilities" emerging through globalization, it is important to give voice to the unexpected joys, those unexpected productive frictions that come about as Chalateco migrants recreate their past and present and earn their always not enough dollars. Recall Miguel's pleasure of owning a new car, his goal of becoming kitchen manager, and, as we will see shortly, his sister Flor's new life in Los Angeles.

Salvadoran Border Crossings and the Words of a Father

Since Linda was a minor, we paid more, seven thousand dollars. I didn't want her to suffer. And she rode right in the front seat with the driver. She didn't suffer anything.

Do you remember, Lotti, I told you in 1997, marry me and take me North? No, you don't remember? Well, I came in 2000, after Hurricane Mitch. And I'm the oldest brother. They all said that I was too old, that the youngest should go. But I told them, "You think I don't have the courage to migrate? I was in the war! This is nothing."

Chico, author interview in 2008

Labor migration as an economic strategy is nothing new to many Chalatecos like Chico.[16] Historically, men and women have pursued seasonal wage labor within El Salvador and in neighboring Honduras.[17] One could argue that Chalatenango has been of value to the nation in its constant supply of cheap labor. On a national scale, Beth Baker-Cristales remarks, "The Salvadoran economy has been transformed from one that traditionally relied upon the export of a few agricultural products to one that relies upon the 'export' of cheap labor" (2004, 136). However, it is only during the later postwar period that Chalatecos begin to flee en masse, this time not to the hills, not propelled by bullets, but to the United States, pushed by the socioeconomic processes of aftermaths of war, the structural violence of uneven globalization that creates what some celebrate as "Salvadoran adventurers" (UNDP 2005, 5).[18] Chico's words above temper any hint of romantic celebration as with fear he brings his daughter across borders, attempting to garner safe passage with dollars. For the political economy of late capitalism, as Lynn Stephen so cogently articulates, is predicated on cheap labor, the regulating, policing, disciplining, monitoring of borders, rather than their closings (2007, 27–28). Moreover, border policies post-9/11 (September 11, 2001) have "formed part of a larger discourse and policy centered on homeland security that is supposed to keep out terrorists and keep American citizens safe" (Stephen 2007, xiv). Coutin further argues that the immigration system "*creates the very disjunctures that seem to undermine it*" and that ultimately ground system coherence—the unauthorized territorial "disruptions" produce the myth of national "integrity" (2007, 4, emphasis in original).[19] As traditional areas of crossings become "secure," emigrants are pushed into new paths. Many now navigate the vast desert, where trafficked bodies commingle with drugs and guns, where many die and are becoming a new generation of the disappeared, resignifying the Latin American "*desaparecido*" (Stephen 2007, xv). This is the violence Chico compares his war experiences against. I do not remember his claim that he suggested we marry in the late 1990s so that I could bring him to the United States. He laughs as he reminds me. His wife, Chayo, is by his side. They were married at the time and they are married today. I am uncomfortable by his joke in part because I know that Chayo is in the United States to keep her husband. She made the difficult choice of following her husband and leaving her three children in El Rancho, the youngest, a boy of thirteen struggling with his mother's departure. She cries at the mention of his name. Linda, the middle child, a bright, successful high school graduate, joined her mother several years later to work and send money back home to help school the youngest. The work ended a little after a year. Linda is a new mother to a healthy baby girl.

Despite the insecurity of borders and the unexpected turns of life in the United States, migration is an ongoing force. Open leading Salvadoran newspapers such as *El Diario de Hoy* and *La Prensa Gráfica* and one will find entire sections devoted to the "15th department," which refers to the Salvadoran diaspora residing in the United States.[20] Open leading U.S. newspapers, the *Washington Post,* the *New York Times,* and one will also find a series of articles on Salvadoran migrants, their electoral political pull from the United States, the lives of wartime kidnapped children adopted in the United States, and the economic role of migrants for their kin and nation.[21] As highlighted in the book's introduction, a significant body of literature has addressed transnational, diasporic communities, Salvadoran and beyond. Scholars have examined the particulars of Salvadoran immigrant experiences, for example, the obstacles faced through fragmented social networks (Menjívar 2000), the demoralization migrants encounter as realities jut up against the mystifications of the pursuit of the American dream, a pursuit that opens frontiers in its process of personal transformation (Mahler 1995), and the bidirectional flows of globalization and capitalism from the United States into rural towns in El Salvador (Pederson 2002). Others have theorized the relationship between legal and political clandestinity (Coutin 1999), the negotiation of belonging (Coutin 2003a, 2003b, 2005), and the impact of transnational feminist and rights discourse to women's mobilizing (Burton 2004), and queried the very politics of transnational protest movements in the garment industry (Brooks 2007). James Quesada eloquently explains the aftermath of Central American wars as one that has produced "a weary and wary people," migrants embodying suffering and exhaustion (1999, 166). Again, note Chico's attempts to allay his daughter's suffering.

Salvadoran migration has also entered policy discussions. As the most recent Human Development Report by the United Nations Development Programme (2005) argues, El Salvador's human development indicators must include Salvadorans building communities in the United States.[22] The authors write that "migration has contributed to create a yet unknown El Salvador. Meanwhile, people still carry out assessments and make plans for a country that has ceased to exist" with more than 20 percent of El Salvador's population living outside of El Salvador (UNDP 2005, 9). This is supported by Baker-Cristales's point that Los Angles can be considered the second largest Salvadoran city (2004). Coutin theorizes that El Salvador, like the United States, has become a nation of emigrants with one out of every four Salvadorans living abroad, 2.3 million in the United States (Coutin 2007, 7). These analyses of migration are significant in that 22 percent of local Salvadoran households receive remittances from abroad. These remittances total more than two and a half billion dollars and constitute more than 16 percent of the gross domestic product and an astounding 655 percent of foreign direct investment (UNDP 2005, 7–8). Estimates suggest that remittances from abroad have lowered the national poverty level in El Salvador by 7 percent, providing temporary relief to the problems of un- and under-employment and poverty without actually addressing their structural causes or creating "more dynamic local economies" (UNDP 2005, 16, 22). Locating these experiences in particular contexts is critical as

FIGURE 6. Photograph taken inside of a Chalateco's home in the United States. One half of this is a U.S. flag and the other half is the Salvadoran flag. Below the flags are photographs of children still living in Chalatenango.

Photograph by author.

there are regional differences (UNDP 2005).[23] For example, as productive community members leave, community organizing is challenged, families are fragmented, demographics shift, the rural landscapes' urbanization accelerates, and agriculture is further marginalized and replaced by the service sector (UNDP 2005, 10).

Next, I focus on two portraits as a way to hone in on these complex processes in what I theorize as a reluctant, clearly precarious and violent, yet ironically productive migration, articulated through what I term *narratives of obligation* and the continuity of a discourse of lies, traced through the book. I begin with Avel, political prisoner, national police officer, and reluctant migrant, and then shift to Flor, guerrilla daughter and migrant mother. In both cases, the ethnographic encounter creates a space for disruptions. Both Avel and Flor end our conversations with nuanced stories that reflect the entanglements of postwar violences.

Avel: Political Prisoner, National Civilian Police Officer, and Reluctant Migrant

I met with Avel in Virginia in October 2006, after close to a year of phone communication.[24] He is Elsy's partner and an interesting, soft-spoken, yet forthcoming man. During the 1990s, we had talked about his life many times, informally, when he passed through El Rancho on his days off. Speaking with him again, close to a decade later, I was struck by the consistency of his narratives of the past, his search for meaning amidst a history of marginalization. Avel's narratives echo João Biehl's recent ethnography *Vita* and Biehl's analysis of what he terms the "life codes" of the socially abandoned in Brazil, narratives that "maintained an impressive steadiness and contextuality." He comes to understand these narratives as "pieces of truth . . . through which the abandoned person attempted to hold onto the real. . . . These accounts were spaces in which destinies were rethought and desires reframed" (2005, 88).

In 2006, Avel, as in the past, describes his life, his losses, and his successes through a labor and education history framed by violence. In wanting to tell me about his employment experiences in the United States, he begins with his father, who instilled in him a strong work ethic. Invoking his father leads us to the war. However, unlike the accounts I collected in Chalatenango in the mid to late 1990s, where I, like several scholars, noted the emergence of a valued hierarchy of suffering, what Quesada describes in the diasporic context as a chronic "contest of suffering" (1999, 170), Avel's stories do not apologize for deaths that were not "directly" related to battle or that do not support romantic depictions of FMLN identities.[25] His narratives emphasize what Paul Farmer (2001) would define as structural violence and what Philippe Bourgois persuasively theorizes as a continuum of violence. Avel's narratives of migration combine astute political analysis of the ravages of globalization as experienced by even the most successful peasant activists such as himself as well as the personal unfortunate turn of events that are seemingly disconnected.

My audio-taped interview begins with Avel describing a typical flight in the middle of the night during a military attack in a small village in Chalatenango. He explains:

> There were only three of us in the cave. We got up at six in the morning and my father said that at around 2:00 a.m. he had felt a hot air enter his body and then later a cold air. It was really hard [meaning dangerous], but I went with the other *señor* and we got some pills (*pastillas*) and made a lemonade. Until 4:00 p.m. my father could speak. But then he lost the ability to talk (Perdió la palabra.) Then his body was covered with bruises. At 6:30 p.m. he was dying. That was in March of 1981. I was barely eleven years old. Then he died and we continued with the problem of the war, sleeping in the hills, and all of that, and then it got worse. But, yes, my father, and I thank him for it, taught me the importance of work.

Avel's phrase, "continued with the problem of the war," semantically situates him already outside of larger processes, reluctantly entangled, yet, as further described below, aware. Avel then reminds me that he moved to another community where he was able to participate in an adult literacy project. Avel is sharp. And he does really well. Within a few months he moves through first and second grade—until he is imprisoned:

> On May 14, 1988, the soldiers got me. There was a small confrontation with a group of guerrillas where I was working the land. Back then *agarraban a medio mundo* (they caught anybody and everybody—literally, half the world). They took me to prison. I ended up in a prison in Santa Ana, which at the time was a maximum security prison. They said I was very dangerous. They accused me of being a guerrilla and I wasn't. They accused you in order to keep you accused. (Lo acusaban para poder tenerlo acusado.) But thank God, the church was always involved, the Red Cross, Doctors Without Borders, and so we started to get some lawyers.

Unfortunately, though typical for the war period, Avel's case turned out to be complicated, his rights were oppressed, and a series of lawyers attempted to handle his case. As Avel remembers, it is not until "*una chamaca de CRIPDES que era la Mirtala,*" a well-known human rights activist, Mirtala López, who is now a FMLN congresswoman, gets involved, bringing her own lawyer on board, that Avel's case moves forward. While incarcerated, Avel kept studying, passing through the sixth grade. Through persistent legal work, Avel and two other prisoners are released on December 22, 1989. And from here, Avel begins to work full time in CRIPDES, one of the leading human rights organizations during the war. It is here that he meets Elsy, and through Elsy that I meet him.

In the postwar context, the work of human rights organizations dramatically shifted, in no small part because of greatly reduced international funding and a national and oppositional political focus away from human rights to reconstruction and development (Sprenkels 2005). Avel, positioned at the bottom tier of the human rights community, characterizes this period as dedicated to the reintegration into civilian life—the very process described as spectral from so many Rancheros in previous chapters. Avel describes the early 1990s then as full of "many different obstacles such as lack of employment, lack of technological training. We at CRIPDES had to think about training teachers. And CRIPDES itself was also changing, losing its international funding (*ayudas*) with the end of the war." As a result, Avel explains that, encouraged by CRIPDES, he saw only one option; to take part in the restructuring of the national police system, an important component of the peace accords. Because of his commitment to education, Avel is able to meet the requirements for joining the PNC, the Policía Nacional Civil (the National Civilian Police). This is a major accomplishment given his adolescent development of literacy skills. He explains that this new police force was intended to be "*un amigo de todo el mundo*" (a friend to the world). Not like the National Guard, where first they hit you and then they asked your name. First they hit you and then they asked for your papers."

In this chronological unfolding, Avel theorizes his own trajectory. Throughout our conversation, multiple times, he returns to the phrase *estábamos obligados* (we were obligated).[26] And this has struck me as something of importance. What does Avel say about his role as a police officer in the postwar incorporation of survivors into civil society? "We were obligated to make this change happen. And the only way to do it was by entering the process. . . . But then with the political processes and the economic changes brought on by globalization that enters all of Central America, things get even more difficult." Why did he feel obligated to join the police force? As Avel explains it, and as my research in the mid-1990s elaborates, the idea was that by incorporating FMLN sympathizers, the force could not so easily become a corrupt, violent, state tool. Indeed, through the course of my research, I encountered several former FMLN commanders who joined the PNC in various levels of regional command. Recent scholarship, however, continues to illuminate the ongoing corruption and human rights abuses by this very postwar institution (Enzinna 2008).

From feeling obligated to help restructure and rebuild a war-torn society, it is compelling that a decade later Avel feels obligated again, this time to leave. He tells me, speaking in the voice of the collectivity:

So, the pressure gets closer and obligates us to migrate to the United States. I'm telling you, when you go visit the communities, you won't see old, familiar faces. They've all come here. José came; Francisco came, and he was already quite elderly, Margarita's husband. You remember them?

Tulio came, Facundo's son. Oh, William also. Why did they come? Because you can't find work. And everything is expensive. Se obliga. Uno se siente obligado. (One feels obligated.) You say, "I don't have any options; I don't have any opportunities." So the only option, the only dream that awakens is to come to the United States.

Obligated, yet dreaming. With the broken promises and bankrupt dreams of revolution and postwar, new constrained dreams emerge. What Avel says is a lived reality. Recent scholarship, such as Coutin's *Nations of Emigrants,* Baker-Cristales's *Salvadoran Migration to Southern California,* Sarah Mahler's *American Dreaming,* and the UNDP Human Development Report (2005), points to the workings of the neoliberal state and the everyday economic insecurity produced by dollarization in El Salvador in 2001.

The contradictions are significant as "migration has become the main way El Salvador takes part in globalization" (UNDP 2005, 7). There are many Salvadorans living in poverty in the United States. Some figures suggest that the poverty rate for Salvadorans residing in the United States is "7 percentage points higher than for U.S. citizens. . . . However calculations also show that in 2004 the income of Salvadorans living in the US was equivalent to 127% of El Salvador's GDP for the same year" (UNDP 2005, 11).[27] The question lived across borders is how to make sense of this disparity. Avel is able to articulate a cogent critique of globalization that has produced a return to clandestinity in new borders. Yet, as Baker-Cristales finds, he like "many Salvadoran migrants perceive their exploitation in the United States as being a result of their lack of legal status in the United States rather than as a result of their position as workers within a global capitalist system" (2004, 97). This is what Avel says about his work in the United States: "We aren't taking jobs from people. We are doing legal work. . . . I'm not involved in anything illegal. I pay taxes. I'm following the norms here. . . . If I don't, well, then they are obligated to get me and put me in prison, pay a fine and even deport me. So our hope is that Congress will give us our papers. . . . Meanwhile, we keep working, sending money to our families and friends. . . . While we can do it, we have to do it." Like Salvadoran migrants before him, Avel's analysis of hard work, paying taxes, and so on follows findings suggesting that migrants define themselves via "economic roles rather than their legal status in the United States" (Baker-Cristales 2004, 123). In the familiar language of struggle I heard countless times in NGO meetings and in party meetings, Avel summarizes, "We have to do it to, *seguir adelante*"—*adelante* here meaning moving forward, but also moving forward in struggle.

However, Avel's relationship to the legal and the illegal has been always already a contentious site, one characterized in struggle where ascriptions are placed upon him, categories are conflated or entangled—political prisoner, armed combatant, human rights activist, unauthorized migrant. As Coutin elaborates, "clandestinity positions its subjects in a non-space, where actions are denied, relationships are discounted, identities are assumed, and events do not officially happen . . . yet those who are clandestine understand how they are positioned in relation to others, are aware of their own presence, and can experience their lives as normal" (1999, 54).[28] The historic and contemporary clandestine moves of Avel's neighbors, friends, colleagues, and kin are placed within a fluid notion of the legal precisely because of their "normal" subjectivities. For example, reflecting upon Flor's difficult journey, Avel explains that he never trusted her coyote, adding that the young man is currently imprisoned for rapes. Avel juxtaposes the corruption and violence surrounding this type of human courier with the responsible, "good" entrepreneurs who transport Salvadorans across three borders. For instance, he describes a young man who led his brothers to the United States: "El chamaco era bastante responsable. (The guy was quite responsible.) He knew that I was in the police and that he would lose out if there was any foul play. But he died later. I told Elsy that Flor shouldn't travel with that coyote, but the money was paid. She suffered too much (*sufrió demasiado*)." Wartime, post–peace accords economy, a shrinking neoliberal state, and the limits of kinship become entangled in migration that has become an individual and national strategy (Coutin 2007, 8). Recall that Avel is Elsy's partner and only the father of her youngest child. He is not Flor's father and did not, unlike Chico above, garner Flor safe passage. As an informal economy grows, so does human insecurity.

In pondering over Avel's theory of postwar as a series of obligations, reluctant though agentive moves amidst constrained options, I end with one of his narratives of migration that jostles the picture a bit. During much of our exchange, Avel constructs a linear narrative, one that is consistent in its tellings through time, a trajectory from an eleven-year-old witness to war, to political prisoner, to human rights worker, and then to police officer "to the world." But then he provides another version, a slice, or moment of reflection. After explaining larger forces, processes, and experiences that compel, that obligate Salvadorans in their often reluctant postwar journeys, he tells me an interesting and still unclear aspect of his crossing-the-border story, one that illustrates the complicated webs of postwar violence.

Violent Trails

Much is currently being written about rampant violence in El Salvador, how everyday life is marked by fear, with increasing "random" violence and crime and delinquency (*ladronismo* or *delincuencia*) in both urban and rural places. Scholars note that "defining violence as criminal rather than political in nature legitimizes state security measures and suggests that perpetrators deserved to be repressed" (Coutin 2007, 151–152). Statistics indicate that violence is as high as during the height of the war (Moodie 2006). Figures place El Salvador as the unfortunate Latin American leader in homicide rates with the figure of fifty-four murders per one hundred thousand people (Henriquez 2006). In 2005, data suggests that fifteen people were murdered daily (Enzinna 2008, 11). By 1996 World Bank statistics indicated that El Salvador was the most dangerous country in the Americas (Coutin 2007, 162). In her most recent and comprehensive study of Salvadoran migratory processes, Coutin takes on analyses of national and transborder violence and how they underscore the national strategy of emigration. She writes, "Violence is generally considered to be destructive. Violence wounds bodies, kills people, tears apart families, destroys buildings, annihilates social orders, and in some instances, makes nations something of a fiction. What does it mean, then to be *produced* by a *destructive* force (Feldman 1991)? And how do *traces* of violence remain within its products?" (Coutin 2007, 149, emphasis in original). For Miguel, whose words I intend to echo through this chapter, these questions are more than theoretical. Reproduced in violence and raised through the economic marginalization produced by late capitalism's neoliberal project, he discursively becomes yet one more emigrant, both "product and cause" of the shifting nature of violence in El Salvador (Coutin 2007, 161). It is imperative to unmask the mystifications articulated in this shift. Was the war a "safer" time? How different is present-day violence? Ultimately, while scholarship may differ in theoretical orientation, research in El Salvador demonstrates that contemporary violence is underscored by ongoing (gendered) inequalities and institutional structures that foster social and economic exclusions. These factors penetrate the realm of the political and can be understood through a human rights lens (see Bourgois 2002; Coutin 2007; and Moodie 2006). Avel's interpretation of postwar violence elegantly addresses the state's political project, simultaneously locating violence on mostly marginalized male bodies through anti-gang measures while creating the seeds for this violence through macro-level socioeconomic exclusions: "What does the government of El Salvador do? Super Mano Dura [Super Iron Fist—a zero tolerance to violence agenda]. That doesn't work. The government is pursuing a politics of free trade, dollarization, and I personally believe, and what I think most people believe, is that they have suffered; they have lost so much. Our economic models can't work. There just isn't any space."

Avel's perspective comes from his two-year PNC rotation on anti-gang violence in the capital of Chalatenango. This was no desk job. While trying to complete arrests, he was involved in a series of gun battles. In these assigned missions he killed several people and, as he narrates, ended up in court at least twice. On the second occasion, Avel explains that he was warned by the proceeding judge that he would more than likely go to jail in the event of further altercations resulting in death. It is unclear if Avel fled the court. He does not want to elaborate and I do not push. Pursuing this line of research could help illuminate the ongoing challenges to building a rule of law in El Salvador (see Popkin 2000). However, I suggest we listen a little differently, and in doing so we can hear the legacy of his father's socialization to work, which Avel presents as a duty to rebuild the nation—only in peacetime with a gun. Avel continues, "Since I went to court for that case, I told Elsy, 'Look, I just don't have any options. Because when I'm called and they say there is a problem somewhere, I go. That's my job. And either I will end up dead or the delinquent is dead.' Thank God, I always come out OK." Avel is clearly entangled as a police officer in the gang- and non-gang-related violence in his everyday labor. Inadequate training? Corruption through the ranks? Resistance to an increasingly well documented corruption in the police force? The answers are unclear. Significantly, Avel seeks an out to this complicated situation, intending to work out democracy through flight: "I told Elsy, 'Look, I'll just go and work for six years and then we'll see how things are going. Flor is here; Miguel may be here; maybe there will be options for you to travel; maybe you can get a visa. Meanwhile, we have to keep struggling here, until we can.'" This phrase, the call for ongoing struggle, reveals Avel's constrained structural position, which is clearly in tension with a wartime discourse of collective agency, of a common struggle. There are further discursive continuities recontextualized by Chalatecos in their migration. While Avel's narratives emphasize obligation, Flor's reflections play with the discourse of deceit, *engaño,* and lies that she was well socialized into as a child of war.

Flor: Guerilla Daughter, Migrant Mother

Los Angeles is sprawling, and weaving through traffic is something that Flor has learned to do well since she arrived in 2003. Flor's confident driving is just one of the many things that I have come to admire as a pedestrian New Yorker. We arranged our first visit in early 2007 as a reunion of sorts. I traveled with my husband and young son and daughter to Los Angeles to meet Flor's newborn daughter and her partner. Motherhood and fieldwork commingled as my son fell into the fieldwork context along with the other boys and men in the room watching a professional basketball game. Video shows my daughter making inadequate *pupusas* beside Flor while her baby rests in my arms.[29] Baby Jennifer is Flor's third child at twenty-four; her second, a boy, is in El Rancho with Elsy. Flor's partner Raul is also Salvadoran, but not from the countryside and not from a former conflict zone. He completed several years of university studies in El Salvador before emigrating to the United States, also in 2003. He is currently a mechanic and a handsome, warm, and quick young man. His English, self-taught these last years, is excellent. Their apartment, which they share with another Salvadoran couple, is modest but a good size, two bedroom, two bath, in a safe neighborhood. Architecturally, the apartment complex feels like San Salvador— white cement structure, three stories high, with exterior corridors, and a broad, open courtyard. The baby has so many things, diapers, car seat, developmentally appropriate toys, all a sharp contrast with Flor's first experiences of motherhood in El Rancho at fifteen.

This is not the first time that I have written about Flor and the generation of young girls turned women in the postwar period. They were ten-year-old *bichas*, barefoot or in flip-flops, with slips under knee-length skirts in 1993, now sporting tight jeans and T-shirts, often with children on their hips.[30] I have done so as a way to understand gendered socialization in the aftermath of violence, specifically, as a way to think about the making and unmaking of radical subjectivities and as a way to build upon the literature on the legacies of "gendered revolutionary bridges" in El Salvador (Shayne 2004). I ask, How do gendered ideologies, wartime experiences, expectations, memories, and skills translate in postwar and across generations? "What stories get told or forgotten? How are they circulated? How will community structures born from the organizing of the past take shape in the future?" (Silber 2004a, 577). When I have written about Flor, then, it is always in light of what she represents for the protagonist generation of the revolution. She is always, first, Elsy's daughter, whose story of waxing and waning organizing frames the analysis. While I reflect upon Flor's trajectory, her own recollections are sobering. She tells me, "Sólo me acuerdo que llegabas a dormir a la casa." (I only remember that you would come and sleep at our house.)

I capture a version of Flor in the ethnographic present of 1998 (Silber 2004a). I compare Elsy's wartime trauma, the horrific losses she suffered of *compañeras,* of partners, of babies, of brothers, which leave her with the analysis that after all of this, "Quedé con las manos buenas y los pies buenos." (I have both my hands and my feet.) I concentrate on Flor's childhood trauma, the death of her father, an FMLN platoon leader, and her postwar cargo. For it is Flor's labor that maintains her mother's home. She makes the fire, *tortillas,* wakes early to cook for her grandfather, takes care of her siblings and her aging and increasingly invalid grandmother. Meanwhile, Elsy takes to the street, so to speak, from *reunión* to *reunión,* from grassroots meeting to meeting, happy to attend training sessions in the capital as life in El Rancho has Elsy bored (*aburrida*). At the time, Flor was a real beauty with thick, curly black hair, a heart-shaped face, and full lips that would break into a quiet, timid yet warm smile. And the rumors are true; at fifteen she moved into her lover's house and shortly thereafter had a baby—only later I found out he died.

In 2006 for a chapter in *Engaged Observer,* an edited volume that embraces the challenges of public anthropology, I also conclude with Flor, capturing another moment in her life cycle, an account that I gleaned from cross-border conversations with her mother, Elsy. I wrote, "Today, Flor is a young adult living in Los Angeles. She is learning how to speak English, like so many Salvadorans she sends money home to her close kin, and she has bought a car. Her experiences inspired her stepfather, Elsy's partner, and he too migrated to the United

States, though to the East Coast. I have not seen her though pictures show a beautiful, healthy and happy young person. I am left wondering about the meaning of her trajectory" (Silber 2006, 205). In these instances, Flor has come to stand for something: for loss, for the lies of gendered consciousness-raising, and for the "lies of democracy" (Bourgois 2006, xi) masked in the everyday violence that runs through El Salvador. The poem that precedes this chapter, written during fieldwork, is for this generation.

Significant scholarship has theorized migration through a gendered lens, exploring, for example, questions of shifting gender relations and power, redefinitions of masculinity and femininity, the importance of kinship, and the structural forces that push and pull men, women, and children across borders.[31] In the Salvadoran case, the literature has addressed these common themes and consistently analyzed Salvadoran displacement within the context of wartime violence, the importance of the solidarity movement, and how people seek to make meaning and transform their "social worlds" (Menjívar 2000, 9). While data indicates that historically women were the first to migrate, from the 1950s to the 1970s as domestic workers, for example, during the civil war and continuing into the contemporary period, men migrated in larger numbers (UNDP 2005, 334–335).[32] Men and women are also structured differently into the labor economy with men earning more for their labor though women gaining access to more labor (UNDP 2005, 340). With the passage of a 1986 immigration reform, IRCA (Immigration Reform and Control Act), employers are accountable for the legal status of their workers and, as a result, migrants are pushed further out of the formal economy.[33] As a result, like her brothers Miguel and, more recently, Wilfredo, Flor has worked double shifts in the service economy, paying off her debt within a six-month period. With pregnancy and motherhood in the United States, Flor did stop working for a time but returned to work when her daughter turned three months.

On her day off, I tagged along with Flor and her roommate Zoyla as they took baby Jennifer for her three-month vaccinations at a local Medicaid clinic, and then to the mall to buy her some educational toys, and to finish off, a meal at Pollo Campero.[34] Though housemate Zoyla was Jennifer's temporary childcare provider while Flor returned to work, I assisted the baby-well-care visit. The waiting room, though well organized, was overflowing with patients, mostly Spanish-speaking women and children. There was a wait, but not inordinate. The front desk staff was comprised of bilingual Spanish speakers, efficient, professional, and seasoned. At first, the lead receptionist explained that Flor had not filed her paperwork correctly and Jennifer could not be seen. Flor, keeping her emotions in check, insisted that she had indeed completed all appropriate paperwork. A phone call to a proper agency confirmed the visit. I was impressed by the oiled bureaucracy that could so quickly catch an error. The physician was a foreign national pediatrician who did not speak Spanish, though the nurse did.

Jennifer had been in the week before because of a bout of diarrhea. There was no follow-up to this episode. Jennifer was weighed fully dressed in a diaper, heart listened to, and the pediatrician directed her questions to me. Significantly, my position of white privilege, assumptions about my relationship with Flor, but, importantly, my own expectations of what infant well-care visits should be like, based on my own experiences, colored and shaped this exchange. Though Flor was not rattled, I was. For me, the visit was too quick, the baby not looked over enough, and developmental milestones were unaddressed, to name a few issues. My children, with unionized, private health insurance, in a private practice, had received less hurried infant care. The nurse explained the follow-up pain and fever medication for the vaccinations and we were on our way in less than two hours.

Back at her home, Flor and I began to talk explicitly about the day and about the journey that brought her to Los Angeles. Like Avel, she emphasized her work history, how she left her partner in El Rancho who had limited employment opportunities but who also was spending too much time drinking with his friends. Flor is quick to add that she was never physically mistreated by her partner. She left her second son, Robertillo, when he was one year old in her mother's care and went to work in San Salvador as a domestic worker. Her day began by working at her employer's downtown market *comedor* (small restaurant). By the early afternoon she picked up the employer's children from school, attended to them, cleaned the house, and cooked dinner. Flor received one day off a month. Again, like Avel, almost immediately her story turns to suffering, the ordinary suffering made of structural violence. Her account of working in San Salvador is refracted through her memory of her son Robertillo's near death: "Look, Lotti, with God as my witness, when I left Robertillo at home he was fat, that child was fat [meaning full and healthy]. I said to my mother, '¿Ese es el niño?' (Is that the boy?) His neck was skinny, skinny. He was dehydrated. They were getting ready to do a wake. That's how sick Chepito, no, I mean Robertillo was. And so I asked my mom, 'Is that the child?' And she said yes. He got well, but I was scared because of what happened to Chepito, my first baby that died." With Flor, I experienced the familiar postwar rush to tell a story. She asks if I had ever heard about what happened to Chepito. I explained that I only knew that he had died as an infant. Quietly, while patting Jennifer on the back she begins the story.

She and her mother were on their way to take Chepito to the public hospital in Chalatenango because he was suffering from a persistent and congested cough. On the road from El Rancho to Chalatenango, ten masked men assaulted the local *microbús*.[35] Flor explains that it was the same "*muchachos* from El Rancho that typically robbed vehicles up by the brook, and others from Las Vueltas, and others from Chalate too." Is she too young to recall that *muchachos* is also what folks called young men who joined the FMLN? Elana Zilberg has written eloquently on the mimesis of gang youth and FMLN transnationally—"gangsters in guerrilla face" (2007).

Traveling in El Salvador is precarious, vehicles are in various states of disrepair, and seating is flexibly defined if there are seats. Indeed, Ellen Moodie (2006) suggests vehicular homicide be framed as a human rights issue. On this occasion, Elsy asked the driver's assistant to hold Chepito on his lap in the vehicle's cabin. And he did. Tragically, in the assault, this young man was shot and a bullet hit Chepito. Flor tells me that this degree of violence was rare.

> Chepito was full of blood. We ran back to El Rancho and then up to the clinic. They gave him oxygen; the baby was desperate from fear and from the bullet. But then he calmed down and then the police came and asked if we wanted a ride. But my mother said no. She was scared he would be shot again. We got on the one o'clock bus and went to the hospital in Chalatenango. All the doctors were amazed that Chepito was alive. I was with Chepito at the hospital for seven days. On the seventh day he got really sick. The medicine was making him sick and my mother said, 'We are taking him out of here; he is getting worse. . . . If he dies here, they won't release him without a coffin, and we don't have a coffin.' . . . So, we took him home at noon and he died at midnight.[36]

Flor's voice is so soft, sad, and old beyond her years in this exchange: "And we buried him next to my *abuelita* (grandmother)." Across borders, Flor's infants have such different trajectories and contexts of security and insecurity. But the story does not end here, and opens yet more questions. Unexpectedly for me, Flor introduces Chepitos's hydrocephalus. In the picture of Chepito, one of the last ones taken at six months, and that rests prominently on the mantle in California between pictures of Robertillo and Jennifer, I can see the signs of hydrocephalus—the enlarged infant skull. According to Flor, it is only when she arrives with her son near death at the hospital that she discovers that he has this condition. She narrates, "When I got there they asked me, 'Miss, are you bringing the child because of his hydrocephalus?' I said no. I had no idea. And I had given birth to him there. He had been getting his shots at the clinic [in Las Vueltas]." An odd question. I am left with the image of the infant shot, bleeding, struggling to live in his mother's arms, and Flor shocked by new medical information. What are the entanglements here? Local adolescents, sons of revolutionaries, stray bullets, poorly operated and funded public health facilities, illness, and trauma. How do these entanglements shed light on the failures of participatory democracy? As Flor narrates more postwar deaths, we can see that the entanglements are in the closed off lives of youth.

Collectivities and Naming the Dead

In that afternoon, death surrounds us while baby Jennifer gets patted, nursed, cooed, and loved. In a transnational social field of loss and memory, Flor reproduces a list of the postwar dead. Naming the dead is something that Flor has been socialized into since she was born in a Honduran refugee camp. Indeed, her mother was involved in creating a commemorative site naming the dead in El Rancho. She begins,

> You know that they killed Paco? He was the tall and white one? They say he was one of the crime leaders. They killed him in his home. And you remember Juan, Luz and Pedro's son? [no longer together, Pedro is a wounded FMLN soldier and an off and on community council member]. Well, do you know what he was going to do in San Salvador with a few friends? They were going to kidnap a kid from Las Vueltas living in San Salvador. But just as they got into the house, the old man woke up and shot them to bits. And Juan had been studying up to the eighth grade. He left a letter for Pedro saying, "Papi, I'm going to work because here I don't do anything. I'll be back in a few days."

Her analysis, "La vida está tremenda en El Rancho." (Life is tremendous in El Rancho.) Indeed, for adolescent boys to reach the eighth grade is a tremendous achievement in these communities.

And, as in other cases of transnational migration, a young woman leads the way across borders and frontiers. Flor left El Rancho one seventh of June and arrived in Arizona on the twenty-fifth of July. It took her forty-eight days and nine attempts to cross the U.S. border. Like Avel, her migration story reflects the narrative practices of testimony as she frames her own trials in a larger collective process. Her account is peopled with those who traveled with her, suffered alongside her, and made it across the last border. These stories are not exceptional; they match up with so many migrants' experiences of crossing borders. However, the collective concern is significant—an entanglement of the past.

With a last good-bye from her mother at the bus stop in El Rancho, she begins, "There were thirty-five of us when we started. We partnered up in the bus to Guatemala. In Guatemala I left everything, my knapsack with my shirt. We were in Hidalgo and they fed us, then it was time to get in the van. And there were a lot of young people." Traveling in airless, hot vans is an enormous risk and a common theme of suffering in narratives. Flor explains that in her first van ride, there was air-conditioning and the group made it through two checkpoints. However, "at the third checkpoint, they hit the van to see if anyone would answer. But nobody, nobody said anything. They hit the van saying, 'Does someone want water?' But no one, no one, no one made a sound. But they kept pounding the car, they got on top of the cabin and broke the metal and they saw us all." The Mexican officials were bribed by the coyotes, however, and the group was allowed to run off: "We threw ourselves out of the van and had to jump over barbed wire, through enormous puddles of mud. And they kept screaming, 'Run, run, run, the helicopters are coming.' And I cut myself up to here on the wire [indicates mid-thigh]. But we got to a ranch and we stayed there eleven days."

In this long exchange, Flor provides rich detail on the process of crossing borders, alone, with new companions, and with those who may want to do her harm. Quick on her feet, for example, she refuses to be taken by a middle-aged woman in Mexico claiming to want to fatten her up and bring her back to health. But for Flor, jumping the fence proved to be the enormous physical challenge: "*La migra* (INS) is right there. And there are cameras there. They told me to go and jump the wall. The first time they sent me with two *muchachos. Nomás me brinqué,* I jumped over, and down there, there is dust. When you land, it suffo-cates you, and I fainted. And that's where I stayed. The *muchacho* dragged me, but there were ten cars from *la migra....* I jumped *la barda* (the fence) nine times."

Flor, product of an FMLN battalion leader who was killed in battle, daughter of a waxing and waning activist mother, Salvadoran national born in Honduras (in the Mesa Grande refugee camp)—her life cycle and her socialization are steeped in marginal citizenship, if not clandestinity. Flor grew up with a history of surveillance, of violent exclusions, threats of violence, and a history of pseu-donyms.[37] This is a clandestinity policed, disciplined, routinized in its visibility and practices of documentation (see also Stephen 2007), and evidenced in Flor's reflections on her multiple experiences of capture. She explains, "When they get you they put you in a car. They take your fingerprints and they take your picture." Eloquently, she analyzes, "Le tienen bien afichadas." (They have you really controlled, on file.) Young, pretty, quiet, and darker than many Salvadorans, she passes as Mexican and the process begins again: "They take you back to Mexico because I said that I was Mexican. And there are people waiting for you on the other side. And so again in the night I would try again and the same thing would happen."

Can we read Flor's, her kin's, and her neighbor's border crossings as a continuity of "the struggle?" Avel's analysis above would answer yes. Like the naming of the dead, Flor's stories are reminiscent of the wartime *guindas,* the flights through the mountains, escaping the Salvadoran military. More than a decade later, it is not Elsy narrating midnight flights but Flor traversing new ter-rain. In less than fifteen years she has moved from escaping through mountains to seeking passage through vast deserts. I am not making an argument for the celebration of resistance. On the contrary, the contradiction of pain and agency, individual *and* collective, is socially reproduced because of the limits of postwar democracy. Finally, after being caught in the desert, Flor jumps the fence on her ninth attempt.

OK. It was me and Margarita, Esmeralda also from Chalate, and the *mucha-cho* that if he lost his glasses he couldn't see a thing. I had the cell phone on vibrate and they were going to tell us when to jump. And we did. We also had a code, for the other side, and it was "baby baby." OK. So we threw ourselves over, and the *muchacho* says, "My glasses, my glasses." So we found them. I said to the woman from Chalate, "They saw us; they saw us." So we threw ourselves down. And then we ran and heard the car screaming, "Baby, baby." Ay, we were crying. I couldn't believe it. I had struggled for so long.

We can juxtapose these narratives of migration with the narratives of war described earlier in the book: Hugo's organizing, Rolando's ongoing militancy, Chayo's description of Chico's slim escape from the armed forces, and Kasandra's story of a neighbor's torture. An emphasis on the collectivity is one key continuity with the past. Flor's analysis of migration is one of community. Consistently, she narrates her trajectory within the trajectory of others, and her form reminds me of the *testimonios* of war. Much has been written on the importance of the testimonio, co-constructed and consumed by particular audiences as a wartime ideological tool. Among the questions asked, scholars pondered the testimonio's significance during peace and in a post–Cold War political economy. These migration stories, silenced yet circulated, resuscitate the legacies of collective action, but the consuming public is much less clear.

From the death of her young son, to the naming of the dead, to crossing borders, Flor ends our conversation by wondering about the future, specifically, for her son in El Rancho. She invokes the word *mentiras,* lies. As we have seen throughout the book, this is a trope I unmasked in Chalatenango in the intermediate postwar period that referred to the past, specifically, to how people felt burned by their sacrifices. In this framework, lies are at the core of everyday suffering. Like the deception in Chalatenango, targets of blame are elusive, unclear. The contours of accountability are not discrete. Uncovering who lies is the central entanglement of contemporary El Salvador. This is echoed in Flor's anger and sadness regarding the possibility of bringing her at the time eight-year-old son to Los Angeles, a son who no longer runs to speak to her when she phones El Rancho: "Son mentiras lo que te dicen. (They tell you lies.) Imagine making a child walk like that through the desert, and that's how they make them do it." Flor's worries, however, are part of a broader contemporary phenomenon of what Stephen describes as "transborder mothering" (2007, 33).[38] With heightened border security, men's back-and-forth moves have declined and, as a result, women and children have increased their migration in efforts to unify families, often under increasingly vulnerable circumstances.[39] For example, of the forty-three thousand children captured by the U.S. Border patrol in 2003, over six thousand minors were unaccompanied by adults (Stephen 2007, 201). Flor, like many migrant mothers, worries about her children across borders, living in different political and economic contexts, living with different rights and unequal access to resources (Stephen 2007, 205).

Aftermaths and Possibilities

In the Salvadoran diasporic context, the entanglements and possibilities of war and postwar, of development and democracy, and of justice and reconciliation emerge in the continuities of ever-unfolding deceit and in the unexpected joys of everyday life. Lies root (route) suffering, hopes, and dreams. An unanticipated arc erupts in the form of obligated migration by the revolutionaries of the past and their now young adult children. Stories and experiences like Avel's and Flor's unmask a paradox of neoliberal democratization: the postwar inability to survive under democracy, the disillusionment this fosters, and, to use Tsing's analysis, the "zone of awkward engagement" (2005) created that produces insecure, clandestine, precarious, violent, yet at times productive possibilities in migration.[40] In searching for the possible, Tsing reminds us to ponder the "central dilemmas of our times," such as "Why is global capitalism so messy?" and "What kinds of social justice make sense in the 21st century?" (2005, 2). Do the answers lie in Flor's pained "better" life, in Miguel's hopeful move to kitchen manager, in Avel's ironically more secure legal standing as an unauthorized worker, away from the unknown of the Salvadoran courts, or in houses rebuilt in El Rancho, vacant in bodies but full of expectation for an impossible return? The answer is not clear, the entanglements through time will never be complete and neither fully positive nor negative as lived by so many sacrificing Chalatecos.

Veena Das's methodological attention to temporality serves well here as it begs the question of what constitutes the eventful and the ordinary in the Salvadoran experiences of aftermath and displacements. For Chalatecos, death is a continuity from war to phases of postwar. Think about Chepito's violent "accidental" death in postwar and Robertillo's near death from possible dehydration. A continuum of violence entangles the extraordinary and the ordinary and is articulated through a language of obligation too often predicated on a wartime survivor's analysis of the lies of revolution and now democracy. This is an everyday obligation that some migrants describe as impossible to translate.[41] As such, it resonates with this war refrain: "Uno como ya lo vivió en carne propia le da corazón duro." (Because you have lived it in flesh and blood, your heart gets hard.)

Underscoring and compelling this story is a hegemonic metanarrative of a past activism rooted in a local over national identification—the maintaining of revolutionary Chalatecos. As demonstrated in earlier chapters, residents of Chalatenango who repopulated destroyed communities or who never left during the war created communities that operated outside of the nation-state, under FMLN and popular organizing leadership. While in the early to intermediate postwar period debates emerged about these experiences, undeniably, living in a war zone placed residents in a particular relationship to government practices and policies. Ultimately, many Chalatecos have ample practice thinking and living through the larger structures that constrain their lives. Histories of exclusion from FMLN war zones to the Mexican and U.S. borders constitute another continuity through time. Past practices of solidarity continue to be expressed in the narratives of collectivity above and are framed by the disillusionment of postwar.

Flor, Avel, Miguel, Chico, and so many Chalatecos are, as Coutin elegantly theorizes, simultaneously present and absent in their suffering, joy, and clandestine citizenship stretching across nations—"residents, and economies travel, nations leak" (2007, 203). Today, like so many migrants, Flor symbolically recreates her past and documents her present. During fieldwork, one of the first things Chalatecos I have met in the United States do is show me their photo albums. Flor's, for example, records her life in El Rancho and extends her transnational social field in images produced through her absence. Elsy over time has sent these images of the past to her—a few photographs of her striking father in full guerrilla uniform, rifle at his side; Flor's first pregnancy at fifteen, when she was *bien cipota* (just a girl), and photos of her son Robertillo playing with enormous toy trucks sent from Los Angeles. Other photographs show how she is living her young adult life in the United States: in tight jeans, sitting on a rock, wind through her hair, the Pacific Ocean in the background, Flor is gazing coquettishly at the photographer; and later, images of her baby shower, gifts everywhere.

Flor defies legality as she buys a five-hundred-dollar car, repaired by her partner, and drives without a license. However, she abides by laws as she buckles Jennifer (who typically wails) into her new car seat and takes her immunization chart to monthly well-baby visits made possible by Medicaid. I ask her about her visible yet clandestine movement through Los Angeles, and her response is a shrug. Flor tells me she is not terrified of *la migra,* though Raul has a pending deportation hearing. "You just have to do it," she tells me. Perhaps in part this is a generational response, a youthful hopefulness that allows for the negotiation of fear as well as a different lived experience of the war. Or is that shrug part of a continuum, a deeply socialized experience of gendered agency? Is Flor the third generation of women in struggle? Recall that because of sociocultural assumptions about women's roles, women were able to cross different frontiers of war as armed combatants and as logistical support. Many physically used their bodies in the crossfire. Their bodies were (mis)read as passive, apolitical, mothers, wives, sisters who crossed military checkpoints as they slipped papers, ammunition, guns, and so on in baskets of onions and goods carried upon their backs (see Kampwirth 2002; Shayne 2005; Silber and Viterna 2009).

Trajectories "en route" (Coutin 2007) lead me to return to the role of a public anthropology, one that tells stories like Tsing's that do "not erase the conditions of terror in which agency is sometimes formed." How do we "tell stories of destruction" where agency may be formed? (Tsing 2005, 26). This chapter on new migratory paths of revolutionaries failed by the postwar changes has illuminated transformations of despair and an everyday engagement with the possible. The transformations are not resounding and do not eclipse the memories of violence or the anxieties of unknowable futures. But, like Tsing, I wonder if we can underscore tempered hope. Tsing documents the strange bedfellows in environmental justice movements and looks for the positive frictions that emerge: "Occasionally, this alliance has kept the forest from being destroyed for a few years, here and there. This is not so bad: Public forests worldwide are threatened and at best tentatively preserved. Meanwhile the alliance itself revives the promise of democracy" (2005, 268). I conclude with my own question: Is there a "not so bad" story for El Salvador? Can it be found in the productive friction of Chalateco transborder communities? For a place like El Salvador, and in the post-9/11 conflation of a war on terror and a war on migration, questions such as these through the lives of undocumented oppositional migrants are timely and have global resonance.

Epilogue

Amor Lejos, Amor de Pendejos

Writing in 2007, Veena Das, ethnographer-philosopher, locates her project on violence in the everyday. In *Life and Words,* she juxtaposes different moments, kinds, and narratives of violence through time and in doing so theorizes violence not as the fantastic but rather as the ordinary. This book has been inspired by Das's reflections and, in particular, by the ways in which she structures her questions. She writes, "I ask whether a different picture of victims and survivors is possible in which time is not frozen but is allowed to do its work" (Das 2007, 211). I have sought to answer this question by complicating the categories of victim, survivor, revolutionary, activist, and even ethnographer by unpacking the ethnographic present and showing the arcs as well as the stops and retreats of postwar. Das also contemplates "what it means to engage in an ethic of responsibility or to speak responsibly within the anthropological discourse" (2007, 211). As should be evident, this is one of my central concerns as well. Like Das, "I try to defend a picture of anthropological knowledge in relation to suffering as that which is wakeful to violence wherever it occurs in the weave of life, and the body of the anthropological text as that which refuses complicity with violence by opening itself to the pain of the other" (Das 2007, 211).

Opening up to the "pain of the other" happens in various ways and in different social relations. It takes place in the practices of witnessing, in listening to the entangled stories of sick and injured babies of war and postwar, in the politics of accountability, and in the everyday accompaniment of new cattle or new cars. Opening up to the pain of the other moves across class and regional lives beyond Chalatenango to the multiplicity of stories of injury that circulate in and out of El Salvador. There are countless stories yet to tell. This chapter will end with a few more.

Part of research in Chalatenango involved "break" trips to San Salvador, where I rented a small room in a house shared with several middle-class Salvadoran friends and several European international development volunteers. Here I would unwind, reflect, and write up fieldnotes. One afternoon, dusty and weary from the bus trip, I arrived "home" to find Carlos brewing espresso shipped back to El Salvador from my younger brother in the United States. Good coffee in El Salvador was ironically hard to come by at the time, the best of the crop exported out of the country. Carlos was home, unemployed despite his English fluency, a marketable skill, and still locked out of the university because of credit transfer problems—his Cuban education rejected by the university administration.

We had spoken often about his struggle to adjust to life in El Salvador. Self-raised in the safety of exile (his father was an important FMLN military commander and had his children protected out of the country), that afternoon he pondered the war and his separation from his *guerrillero* parents through a metaphor: the hands of his mother. In trying to explain his location of postwar and make his own peace (of sideline participation, of friends and family killed, of childhood loneliness and neglect), he wonders where are those soft hands of youth, of a young, sweet, attentive mother, the ones he last held as a small boy? When were they replaced by the rough, spotted, browned hands of middle age? These were the ones he met again, this time as a young man. The hands of his mother evoke deeply the losses of war and its shadowed reconciliation.

In the embodiment of time, of age, he feels the losses of war. His reflections are also part of a larger story of reconciliation with its attendant disillusionment and hope. Today, Carlos and I speak twice a year. Like so many Salvadorans before him, though with much more privilege, Carlos made his way out of El Salvador in the late 1990s. He moved to Europe and married a former international development volunteer. He graduated from a university there, practices his profession, has two children, purchased a home and a car, and has traveled back to El Salvador once in the last decade.

Carlos's reconciliation takes place in departures and in making himself anew rather than in searching for truth or justice. These departures can be read as simultaneously thwarting El Salvador's reconciliation or deterritorializing and individuating the process. This seeming contradiction is what entangles Salvadorans further. Writing on Argentina's Dirty War, Marguerite Feitlowitz's (1998) analysis provides comparative insights on reconciliation. Her focus on how language terrorizes during and after the military dictatorship also uncovers how "the most castigated Argentines manage to maintain deep reserves of courage, clarity and tenderness," evidenced in the "popular volition to meet the danger at its source, by exposing and resisting the entrenched politics of impunity and amnesia" (Feitlowitz 1998, 255). Quoting Argentine Bishop Miguel Esteban Hesayne, a human rights proponent, Feitlowitz's work provides an operating definition of reconciliation: "Reconciliation does not mean covering [history] with a blanket of oblivion. . . . Reconciliation means truth, justice, and love. Justice without love can degenerate into vengeance. We need to know the truth for medicinal reasons, so that what happened during the *Proceso* will never happen again" (1998, 222).

Never again, *nunca más,* is a resounding call across the globe as societies build from the destruction of civil war and genocide. Work that documents the emerging field of transitional justice (i.e., Hayner 2002; Minow 1998; Theidon 2007) elaborates the important spaces created by Truth Commissions and other structures that create the avenues for reconciliation. While I have documented the spaces of disillusionment in community, in NGO and grassroots practices, and in circulating discourses of "what should have been," ethnographic data also reveals localized attempts to heal, to commemorate this call for never again. In El Rancho I was asked to participate and observe community attempts to commemorate, to root memories about place and produced in displacement.

Tears That Thunder

Folks from El Rancho wanted to build a memorial site with a plaque listing the dead. Few communities had such memorials. The municipal seat of Las Vueltas had recently constructed a commemorative park with a small monument and a plaque with the list of names of fallen combatants. This was a source of envy for many Rancheros as the memorial had been funded through a U.S. sister-city affiliation, a coveted status (and economic relationship) El Rancho had never been able to garner. I was approached by El Rancho's *directiva* members who expressed an interest in building a memorial in their community, as the small plaque in Las Vueltas listing only combatants was not an accurate representation of war deaths. Trained during a time where the anthropological project was undergoing a deep period of reflection and self-critique, I was motivated to "give something back" to the people who had shared their time, experiences, and analysis with me. I promised to help in fund-raising. I was also curious about what this site, the process of designing it, the inspiration behind it, the discussion about it, and the memories surrounding it would mean in the community.

By the end of November 1997, organizing for the community historical memory site was in motion, though community organizing itself was dysfunctional. Finally, after months without a communal governing body, El Rancho had a new directiva. Because this was a time of transition in community politics, members from the new directiva as well as former (resigned) members participated in the first meeting for the monument. The task involved qualifying and quantifying the dead. Given that El Rancho is a repopulated community, representing wartime loses is a difficult issue. Which people, what community? Who were the fallen to be commemorated? Was it El Rancho's original residents who died in the struggle? The combatants born here who died in battle? Should civilians and combatants be included? How about repatriated residents' kin? Was there a limit to the number of names to be remembered? What about current residents of outlying *caseríos?* Clearly, there are no "right" answers to this question. I am more interested in positioning the process that memory work yields. For in trying to make sense of enumerating and honoring the dead, council members were in essence attempting to define community through acts of social memory. The importance of the site was not debated.

During the meeting, Aquilino, local intellectual, former combatant, municipal council member, former vice president of the directiva, and whose words open up this book, explained why he and the former president had approached me in this endeavor.[1] As he spoke to the group about the importance of creating a commemorative site, he was actually quite vague about the past. Salient is that he marked the unforgettable suffering that was common to all present, yet highly personal and nearly impossible to share.

> The idea is to build a monument in memory of those who have fallen and died because of the struggle, for a cause that we all really defended during that time and that many of us still remember. We keep it in our hearts and for many we are in mourning. For that reason we reflect, and for me it is unforgettable. For all that epoch that all of us present here suffered in one way or another, right, very dearly. Because we were together, some of us suffering in one place and others suffering in another, which for me was a large and long history that is unforgettable. It is something that I hold very dear, although I don't share it with anybody. Right? For me it is unforgettable.

These opening words highlight postwar silences. Note how three times he remarked how the past is unforgettable.

Part of this memory work involved the logistics of constructing a site. And, indeed, during the meeting much time was spent deciding how to best make use of the resources I was to garner, where to erect the monument, what sorts of representations or images to design, who to hire, and, most important, who to commemorate. A longtime Swiss solidarity activist, known for his artistic abilities, was to be approached to draw a representation of the past and to etch the names on a plaque. Aquilino suggested a symbolic representation for the plaque: "He can draw you a picture that reflects the past: the struggle of the masses, the armed struggle where there is a National Guardsman over a cemetery, a guerrilla over a guardsman, right, that means that the guerilla was more powerful than the national guard at the end, right. So there are three drawings."

Aquilino spoke for a long time. He highlighted the early wartime activism, re-periodizing the war before 1980 and asking for the recollections of the three original families from El Rancho whose community history he wanted to glean:

> We need to invite the original residents of the community because they know all about the political struggle; FECCAS started in '78, '79, until '80,

right? There were leaders that died from this community; for example, Justo Mejía, right? Many died in those three years, from 1980, when the guerilla forces united, until '92, when the war ends with the peace accords in Chapultepec, Mexico. [We need to] compose a list of names of the people who died in the armed conflict, people who died because of a struggle, who died massacred. So we should do an assembly with the entire community to see if we have forgotten a name, read off the list of names we have, and there people will be able to say, "You have forgotten my son; my wife is not on the list." That is what we were talking about with Lotti.[2]

This commemorative attempt can be interpreted as a building of community from the ashes of the past. All meeting participants agreed that the plaque needed to be displayed in the center of town, preferably on the church's wall or near by. In his long speech, Aquilino voiced the idea of "history in memory." He stated, "We should put it in a very visible spot, so that every one of us in the community can see it, as well as folks visiting us. And it is a history in memory for those from here who have fallen, for real causes, for just causes that we found ourselves involved in." In his organizing discourse, Aquilino's position was clear. Commemorating history in memory served to memorialize the political struggle, for "real causes, for just causes."

As he continued in his organizing speech register, the site also became for Aquilino a place to mark the incomplete victory of a negotiated revolution. Through the names of the dead, he sought personal closure for the painful costs of the transition to democracy, where reintegration into the nation was, as he himself told me a few weeks earlier, spectral because of a powerful political economy that continues to marginalize rural places and peoples. "We had no choice but to study the situation and say, 'Yes, we are in agreement [with the peace accords],' although we had tears in our eyes that streamed down our face and fell as if they were thundering balls. But say yes, with clarity and conscious that this was going to be a spectral reintegration. . . . Here in the community there are people who painfully say, 'My son died. My father died. My father-in-law died. My mother-in-law fell.' For me it is an inspiration to see that name engraved and remembered, that for someone else may be pain."

After Aquilino's mobilizing conversation, he opened the floor for discussion and people began the difficult discussion of naming names. How would this selective process of remembering be handled? For many, the issue of limiting the names and, by default, silencing the memories of their neighbors was hard and painful, but part of the process as there were simply too many dead. In the debate over how to limit names, José, a recent arrival to El Rancho (and Elsy's distant cousin) and a new member of the *directiva,* raised the question of place: How were *aquí* (here) and *la comunidad* (the community) to be defined? As a newcomer, he was still making sense of El Rancho's community politics and history. Below, I include a transcript of how the memory committee addressed these issues. Ultimately, I suggest that this effort was as much about the past as it was about the present attempts to rebuild El Rancho, which, as documented in other chapters, was experiencing and was seen as a community in crisis.

JOSÉ: I have a question. What's being done here will it be only for the community of El Rancho? For the people that died here? Or will surrounding communities be included? That is my question.

AQUILINO: That's why I say, let's start with the people who fell during the time of UTC, FECCAS. Then continue with the original residents of El Rancho. Then start a list of the people who died during the repopulation phase from '87 to '92. Now, in coming up with the list, depending on the number of names, we can continue and extend the listing to surrounding communities.

ELMER: I think it should be the community, although everywhere is important. But the names will be huge. You know that in order to include all the fallen in the community we would cover the entire wall of the church. There won't be space to include folks from surrounding places. It should be those who are living in El Rancho, who lived here and are living here.

DON LUPE: But during that time I lived down there a ways.

ELMER: But now you live here!

DON LUPE: I have three—my son, my son-in-law, and my cousin.

ELMER: Let's put the family member, the dead who has family living here. There are people who died from other places but if there is no room even if we would like to include them . . . the original residents perhaps should go first, they should be the first ones on the list.

ELSY: I have to put my daughter's father. Maybe we should only put one name per family. Or else the list is going to be very long. Just imagine how many names we have of only the community council.

ELMER: If we only put one name per family people will feel bad not to have everyone included.

ELSY: Well, if we include more names, then we have to put my brother.

ELMER: Look, we have to make a list of everybody and depending on how much they will charge us [to engrave the names].

ELSY: It should be two names per family. Because my daughter's father doesn't appear in any place, and I have my brother.

CHEPE: Well, I'm going to read the list of names that I already have. I have fourteen.

By the end of the meeting, thirty names were collectively remembered and recorded in a notebook. So much for people having "forgotten" the struggle.

While the energy to remember was palpable in the room, the more tedious task of transforming the idea of rescuing the past into a site for community residents was less inspiring—no community council member volunteered for managing this project. The issue remained unresolved until the week before my departure. My last day in Chalatenango, the president and the vice president of the directiva, a man and a woman, opened a joint bank account with the first funds I made available to them that came from a grassroots development fund earmarked by one of my scholarships. They handed me a list of eighty-two names, a partial list of the dead which was collected by the president in his preliminary compilation as he went from house to house.[3] From New York, I raised funds and sent them more money, eight hundred dollars in total. A phone call to El Rancho in 1998 verified that they received the wired money but that construction was not underway. Correspondence a year later, a letter from Elsy, admonished me to not send more funds, as had been recently requested of me. She claimed that the original amount was misspent.[4] The plaque was made within the year. I include here the partial list of El Rancho's eighty-two dead, combatants, supporters, civilians, men, women, elderly, and children, in order to acknowledge this desire to remember (see figures 7 and 8). As Elsy stated regarding her daughter's father, it is important to have names appear and be memorialized somewhere.

Coda

Time and place, distance and displacement, these appear as themes in this ethnography of postwar El Salvador saturated by states of disillusionment. My focus on grassroots experiences of development under neoliberal democracy and the unanticipated journey from wartime warriors to postwar migrants exposes the messiness of postwar times, as the meaning of transition can illuminate. This has been a book about the men and women who self-identify as past fighters, politically and armed. In the postwar landscape they negotiate oppositional identities with a "new" Salvadoran citizenship within a nation-state that is increasingly transnationalized (Baker-Cristales 2008). In everyday life Chalatecos embrace peace while they confront the increasingly difficult prospect of make a living, building a home, and raising and schooling their children beyond bare existence. In the municipality of Las Vueltas with an increasing number of households sending at least one member to the United States, the impact of this "development" strategy is still unfolding (Gammage 2006; UNDP 2005). Increasing stratification, further degradation of land, new circuits of production and consumption, and strains on practices of kinship are just some of the issues to explore.

Distance is productive and I seek to make it transparent. Unable to return to El Salvador for both personal and professional reasons—a medically fragile young child and the demands of finding academic employment—by the early

1	Cristoval	Guardado			
2	Arnulfo	Guardado	53	Maximino	Allala
3	Lucid	Guardado	54	M. Guel	Guardado
4	Mirian	Guardado	55	Inacio	Ramires
5	Consecion	Guardado	56	Jesus	Ramires
6	Reina	Ortiz	57	Salvador	Melgar
7	Miguel Antonio	lopes Alas	58	Jose	Calles
8	Maria servacia	Alas	59	Nicolas	Guardado loper
9	Armando	Orellana	40	Guadalupe	Guardado lopez
10	Elia	Alvarado	41	Jose Alfredo	Calles
11	Bernaldina	delgado	42	Maurisio	nunes
12	Misael	palma	43	Maria lisec	allala loper
13	Antonio	Calles	44	Martin	Mejia palma
14	Nicolas	Calles	45	Salvador	Ramirez
15	Fermin	Miranda	46	Sesar	Ramires
16	Jose victor	Calles	47	Katalia	Ramires
17	Moyses	Calles	48	Benites	Ramirez
18	paubla	Alas	49	felipa	Guardado
19	Venito	Calles	50	Teresa	Guardado
20	Isrrael	Miranda	51	Tiofilo	Guardado
21	Morena	Calles		Wuilian	Ortiz
22	Eduardo	pineda			
23	Osmaro	Orellana Ortiz			
24	Maria	Guardado Calles			
25	Luisa	Mejia Allala			
26	Oscar	Mejia			
27	Saul	Mejia			
28	Mardo puro	Mejia			
29	Ana	Mejia			
30	Carlos	Martines palma			
31	Carmen aluerto	palma			
32	Juan Ramon	Orellane			

FIGURE 7. List of the dead compiled by a historical memory committee in December 1997.

years of the twenty-first century I came to realize that my attention to postwar disillusionment had to take into account new experiences of the Chalatecos who migrated from Las Vueltas to various cities across the United States. Traversing time and place are critical components of my theorizing because this traversing is embodied in the lives of Chalatecos. My entrance into this social network stemmed from my relationship to Elsy, and it is for this reason that much of the analysis in this book spins out from this relationship as well.

Listado de personas Caidas en la Guerra

52	Guadalupe	Guardado
53	Marcos	Guardado
54	Efrain	Guardado
55	Morena	Guardado
56	Luisa	Guardado
57	Mirtala	Guardado
58	Mirian Eva	Magar
59	Salvador	Orellana
60	Osmaro	Orellana
61	Armando	Orellana
62	Sevastian	Miranda
63	Adan	Miranda
64	Jesus	Calles
65	Servelio	alas
66	Elias	alas
67	Juan	calles
68	Agustin	alas
69	Maria de Jesus	delgado
70	Salvador	Orellana Ortiz
71	Amando	Orellana
72	Martin	lopez
73	Manuel Antonio	lopes Mejia
74	Juan francisco	Mejia
75	Rafael	lopez
76	Simon	Mejia
77	Berta Idalia	alas
78	gilverto	Mejia
79	Misael	Mejia
80	lilian	Mejia
81	Elias	Mejia
82	Sevastian de jesus	palma
83		

FIGURE 8. List of the dead, Continued.

It is fitting that in closing, I return to Elsy and her family. Shortly before the U.S. presidential elections, Elsy phoned me one night to discuss whom I was voting for. This was international news, and after years of knowing me she wanted my positioning. The elections in El Salvador, to be held in March 2009, were not quite on the international mapping. Both elections have made history. However, in talking a bit about politics, I was not aware that she had recently voted for an ARENA mayoral candidate in Las Vueltas, voting against her own kin ties. Only later did the rumor reach me, from my one remaining international development worker friend living in El Salvador, that Elsy's voting practices have marginalized her in El Rancho. This is a delicate matter and Elsy has refused to speak about her political participation. She did call me on the eve of the FMLN presidential victory, with the words "*Ganamos Lotti.*"

But in this story of shifting politics, which have occurred in former FMLN territories in a few communities in Chalatenango and in other departments, there is also a story of love and struggle. Elsy's life has been one of struggle, defined by war and postwar with love and joy found along the way. I have always found her words sobering and have quoted them in much of my published work and in the presentations I give to multiple audiences. Thrown into war by age eleven, by the mid 1990s, recall how she remarked that one of the battles won included being alive. It took her years to tell me the story about the death of her first love at fifteen, a *guerillero,* and how she went to find the remains of his body: "I picked up a handful of his curly hair and some bones from his feet and others from his hands and like that, little bits of bone. And the shirt, the shirt was red and well-toasted by his own blood. I cut a piece of the shirt and put all of that in it, put it in a bag, and I carried that bag with me in my knapsack. No one knew. Only my friend Lupe. And I carried them with me until I met Rolando, and then I went to bury the bones in the cemetery."

These are precisely the sacrifices of happiness that the anonymous NGO director I quote at the beginning of the book suggests. These are the sacrifices that a counter-hegemonic development seeks to build from in order to combat neoliberal democracy which continues to exclude. But on that night, talking about U.S. and Salvadoran politics, Elsy confided previously masked stories. I apologized that I had yet to visit her son Wilfredo in Virginia and asked how he was doing living with his younger brother and Elsy's partner, Avel. After a pause Elsy responded that "*ya días*" (it had been days), that she and Avel were no longer together. She calculated that seven months had passed since they last spoke and longer still since he stopped sending money back home. Her conclusion was, "Amor lejos, amor de pendejos," which loosely translates as "Long distance love is for fools." Elsy's boys knew, she told me, but her daughter Flor did not. She emphasized that I should not tell her. Flor continues to send money and goods back to El Rancho for her son Robertillo, and Elsy worries that Flor will question her expenditures, knowing that now she no longer receives remittances from other sources. Elsy's past love of Avel, rooted in wartime repression and their work with CRIPDES, is disentangled in unforeseen migrations, the threads are frayed. I am struck by the image of Elsy, forty-five, alone with her nine-year-old grandson, with three of her young adult children in the United States and her teenage daughter living in Las Vueltas with her mother-in-law while her young husband works in the United States.

Within a few minutes, my image, my assumptions, were shattered. Was I looking for more loss and constructing despair? I asked if she was lonely and Elsy responded with another refrain: "Nunca falta un zapato roto para una pata podrida." (You can always find a broken shoe for a rotten leg.) For an undisclosed amount of time, Elsy explained that she had been with a young, decent man from the capital of Chalatenango. He was even tilling the land for her. She was happy and not alone. Later, through correspondence with other community members, I learned about the rumors circulating not only about her politics but about her sexuality. Her infidelity, according to these accounts, prompted Wilfredo, after he punched his mother's new lover, to migrate and her youngest daughter to marry and move out. This story tweaks and complicates my first findings on this particular case of migration. Infidelity produces an affective travel that propels bodies out of homes, to other communities, and, ultimately, across borders. I am still unpacking the sadness, anger, and "lies" that circulate via cell phone calls and emails about the discarding of old lovers, taking on of new lovers, and, ultimately, a mother's shifting loyalties and political commitments. These journeys are physical and moral. This is difficult terrain, made all the more difficult by Elsy's refusal to engage. Like in my work with Chayo (see "Stitching Wounds and Frying Chicken"), I will not ask.

Our conversation ended as Elsy put Robertillo on the phone to speak with me. Flor has often told me how Robertillo desires to meet his little sister born in Los Angeles, calling his mother a liar when he sees a plane fly overhead. He refers to the broken promise to send his baby sister back for a visit to El Salvador. I asked Robertillo ultimately inane questions, questions my own nine-year-old son would find annoying: How is he doing in school, which are his favorite toys sent by his mother, and what does he like to do and think about? But Robertillo was animated and eager. Passionately, he told me he loves rockets and that he will be an astronaut to see the moon. In the background I heard Elsy cackle. What is in a grandmother's laugh? The impossibility of his dream? Awkwardly, I did not laugh and told him to keep doing well in school.

A little boy in the countryside in a nation on the periphery of globalization, Robertillo will more than likely not become an astronaut, let alone finish high school. The odds are structured against his imagination. However, his answer challenges my original thinking on the deceit of everyday life. In the mid to late 1990s I uncovered a striking absence of "hopeful talk," conversations about future dreams, desires, and aspirations. Conversations converged on nightmares, a commingling of past violence in the present, of phantom-like soldiers, of guindas, of bags of bones found beneath cement floors, of apparitions of the dead. "Dreaming" appeared to be on hold. However, the spaces for hope are in children, a mother voicing her son's desire to make it past the ninth grade, and another mother voicing her son's "ludicrous" dream to become a rock star. It is also now found in that ubiquitous search for the American Dream, articulated in Miguel's growing English and his aspiration to become a manager at his fast-food chain, and in Chayo's "American" home in El Rancho, the second floor already under construction.

I offer this account of a small place in a small country (Kincaid 2000) as a form of "public anthropology." Veena Das suggests that we act "on the double register in which we offer evidence that contests the official amnesia and systematic acts of making evidence disappear" and that we also witness "the descent into the everyday through which victims and survivors affirm the possibility of life by removing it from the circulation of words gone wild—leading words home, so to speak" (2007, 221). My tracing of the "tears that thunder" to the *"amor de pendejos"* is an attention to making evidence appear while supporting spaces of possibility. I root this in underscoring the complexities of individual lives and exchanges.

Lessons can be gleaned from the contradictions of postwar realities. For even with the historic election of Mauricio Funes, the first FMLN president of El Salvador, and the anticipation for policy changes that this victory has brought, the grassroots calls for ongoing political participation, both distant and imminent, have not disrupted the ongoing postwar migration of Chalatecos, which is also the Salvadoran story of that search for democracy. In part this book calls attention to problematizing assumptions about the trajectories of social mobilizations, changed consciousness, the strength of "community," the place of violent memories, and grassroots and political development in transitions to democracy. As we move forward in the twenty-first century, being mindful of the Salvadoran experience will be invaluable. For the construction of Cold War terrorists has been replaced by new constructions and conflations of the radical (Mamdani 2005). When I first embarked on this project, it was with an attention to the particular, to the specificity of localized postwar processes that could engage in broader interdisciplinary conversations on societal reconciliation. The intention was to raise sobering questions about El Salvador as a success story. To do so, I have provided evidence of Chalateco agency amidst ongoing injustices that, taking again from Das, too often are made to "disappear," are invisible. Contexts have shifted. My original analysis of postwar realities sought to generate balanced lessons for the region (Nicaragua and Guatemala, particularly), for other model transitions to peace (South Africa and Mozambique), and for peace building in crisis (Gaza and the West Bank).

However, since September 11, 2001, the United States embarked on a series of wars in Afghanistan and Iraq that reinscribed an orientalist gaze and violence along with it. The ultimate impact of these wars, and questions of accountability, will be long unfolding. Of interest for this account are the ways in which the "Salvador option" emerges as a possibility for the war in Iraq. This refers to deploying the modes of U.S.-funded counter-insurgency (i.e., the creation of death squads and the terror this unleashed) used in El Salvador. This is a strategy of terror that exacerbated the civil war. For El Salvador, the legacies of that option are also still unfolding, more than fifteen years into a "transition" to peace. My focus on the everyday "revolutionaries" of Chalatenango, El Salvador, may be one way to think about the place, politics, and imaginings of today's "religious revolutionaries" in the "war on terror." For in an attention to these spaces we can write about emergent possibilities, an astronaut-boy's dreams, and reach across the distance.

NOTES

INTRODUCTION

1. I typically had access to women's evening socializing rather than to men's practices.

2. People who live in the department of Chalatenango call the department Chalate for short. They also self-identify as Chalatecos (males) and Chalatecas (females).

3. Documentation proving legal residency includes a social security card, valid foreign passport with visa, or U.S. Permanent Residency Card. See the Maryland Department of Transportation Motor Vehicle Administration, "Real ID Act Information," http://mva .state.md.us/DriverServ/RealID/default.htm (accessed January 5, 2009). Throughout the United States, most states have already implemented the federal Real ID Act of 2005. New guidelines were issued by the Department of Homeland Security, in effect nationwide beginning on May 11, 2008. Maryland, however, requested and received an extension to January 1, 2010. Arguments abound across the political spectrum; the most anti-immigration, restrictionist, and right-wing conflate undocumented status with terrorism, suggesting that by not complying with this federal guideline, Maryland opens the opportunity for fraud and illicit activities. See, for example, the recent critiques by the Center for Immigration Studies, a "conservative" think tank based in Washington, D.C. (http://www.cis.org/).

CHAPTER 1   ENTANGLED AFTERMATHS

1. Definitions at http://www.m-w.com/dictionary/entanglement and http://dictionary .reference.com/browse/entangle (last visited January 23, 2008).

2. Bourgois defines his theory as follows: "I proposed that violence operates though an overlapping continuum of forms. These range from the bloody guts and gore of politi-cally directed bullets and machetes (i.e. political violence); to the words that hurt more than sticks and stones (i.e. symbolic violence); as well as to the impersonal, political economic forces that make children die of malnutrition (i.e. structural violence) and which fuel interpersonal and institutional violence (i.e. everyday vio-lence). My hope was to contribute, not just to a documentation of human pain and social injustice, but also to a clearer political critique of how power relations maintain inequality and (useless) social suffering under neo-liberalism" (2002, 229).

3. This source agreed to an interview if he and the organization he directs remained nameless. He maintains a "neutral" face in Chalatenango and pursues his political work in San Salvador, as required by his agency. It is precisely because he does not have a past in Chalatenango that he can do his work on coalition building in the NGO sphere. However, he is continually questioned because it is so rare to not have an ideological stance in El Salvador.

4. This section builds from leading sources on Salvadoran migration such as Baker-Cristales (2004), Coutin (2007), Gammage (2006), Mahler (1995), and Menjívar (2000) and the policy work of the UNDP (2005). The stages can be periodized as follows: 1920–1969, a migration into neighboring countries such as Honduras and by a more entrepreneurial class into the West Coast of the United States (see Menjívar 2000); 1970–1979; 1980–1991, a migration produced by war; 1992–present, postwar migration in the context of neoliberal democracy.

5. See Baker-Cristales (2004), Mahler (1995), and Coutin (2007), among other texts, for a comprehensive history of U.S. immigration laws that impinge on Salvadoran immigrants. Important among these are the Immigration Reform and Control Act of 1986; the lawsuit by solidarity movement activists that highlights the discrimination against Salvadoran applicants for political asylum during the war period; the development of temporary protected status (TPS), which creates ongoing and liminal legal status in the lives of migrants; and, finally, the Nicaraguan Adjustment and Central American Relief Act (NACARA) of 1997, created to address (adjust) the ways in which U.S. foreign policy dictated immigration laws during the Cold War.

6. See Manuel Orozco, Draft, March 22, 2006, "Diasporas, Philanthropy, and Hometown Associations: the Central American Experience," http://www.iadb.org/document.cfm?id=812580 (accessed January 20, 2009).

7. Nugent's work on what happens to a revolutionary community after a revolution also informs my theorizing. He explains the historical processes of community formation and suggests that Namiquipan ideology must be heard. He privileges their "alternative periodization" that challenges the centrality of the Mexican revolution and demonstrates a history of resistance to the state in their struggle for community (1993, 4, 9).

8. See Roseberry (1988, 1995) for an analysis on the historical development of this field, tracing it to Mintz's (1973) and Wolf's (1955) "cultural historical approach." In peasant studies, by problematizing peasant consciousness and mobilizing, history and anthropology are linked (Roseberry 1989). Also see Silverman (1979) for a review of the peasant concept in anthropology.

9. See Field (1995), Gould (1990), Hale (1994), and Nugent (1993).

10. One *manzana* is approximately 1.7 acres; 1 hectare is approximately 2.4 acres.

11. Figures indicate that 30 percent of FMLN forces were women, the highest participation in Latin American history (Binford 1998, 38). Some were all female battalions (Mason 1992), and Ready estimates the number of female troops to be between ten thousand and twenty thousand (1994, 196).

12. See Ramos (2000) for a discussion on how anthropologists create "expert reports" and how at times these can enter into the hands of progressive politics.

13. Interview with representative of Plan Internacional, December 1997.

14. Many repoblaciones have garnered sister-city relationships with cities in either the United States, Canada, or Europe, which bring in international assistance for particular projects.

15. CODEM, 1996, Plan de Acción para el Desarrollo: Municipio de Las Vueltas: Chalatenango, El Salvador.

16. Author interview, December 1997.

17. Throughout the book, I have "cleaned up" the transcribed material, making the narratives appear "neater" than the spoken words. For example, I have cleaned up the

repetition and some of the "messiness" of naturally occurring speech, some of the stopping and starting of phrases. The translations into English are mine.

CHAPTER 2   HISTORIES OF VIOLENCE/HISTORIES OF ORGANIZING

1. Gould and Lauria-Santiago define *mestizaje* as emerging in the early twentieth century, "as a nation-building myth of race mixture and a cultural process of 'deindianization'" which became by the 1920s "a dominant national discourse [that] interacted dialectically with the simultaneous disarticulation of the indigenous communities" (2008, xv).

2. For the first synthesizing account see Anderson 1992 (1971); see Zamosc (1989) for a class analysis of the massacre; and for a more complex reading that looks to the relationship between Indian peasants (i.e., the role of *cofradías*) and communist leaders, see Pérez-Brignoli (1995).

3. For a discussion/debate on landlessness versus land poor see Seligson (1995) and responses in that same journal *LARR* 30 (3) (1995).

4. Almeida (2008), in a comprehensive examination of Salvadoran collective action from 1925 to 2005, explores the dialectic between regime liberalization and de-liberalization and the modalities of collective action that emerge in different political environments.

5. Briefly, a shift in the church's teaching emerged from the second Vatican Council of 1964. Particularly, the Conference of Latin American Bishops in Medellín in 1968 was groundbreaking, defining liberation theology as the practice of a "'preferential option for the poor' that legitimized struggles for better wages and working conditions, and for land reform" (Binford 1998, 16). In El Salvador, sectors of the Salvadoran clergy were committed to liberation theology and through CEBs (the first one established in 1969) began working with small groups of poor people. Through religious study, reflection, and action, the aim of priests and lay catechists was to transform people's ideology of poverty as their fate on earth and to remove their sense of powerlessness. The aim was to create a "Kingdom of God" on earth, in the present. Critically, the intent was to make individuals aware of processes of exploitation (Binford 1998).

6. See Binford 1996 on the organizing and transformative processes of lay catechists.

7. Archbishop Oscar Arnulfo Romero's funeral celebration in San Salvador was also repressed with open gunfire into the crowd.

8. For a good synopsis of targeted land reform and the limitations of the reform in design and execution (for example, problems included poor soil quality of the land to be distributed and the failure to address the issue of the landless), see Pearce (1986, 292–302). For a comprehensive analysis of political environment in El Salvador in the 1960s see Almeida (2008).

9. Other groups included the LP-28 (Ligas Populares 28 de Febrero), which was urban based and student controlled; Andes (Asociación Nacional de Educadores Salvadoreños); UPT (Union de Pobladores de Tugurios); MERS (Movimiento Estudiantil Revolucionario de Secundaria); and FAPU (El Frente Popular de Acción Unificada). These groups joined to coordinate under the CRM (Coordinadora Revolucionaria de Masas).

10. McClintock (1998) provides a useful comparative analysis of the FMLN and Peru's Shining Path. She describes the FMLN as fractious, comprised of members of Marxist and social democratic positions whose goal was to overthrow the regime and reform the political and economic system. Her book explores both leaders and rank-and-file members of the various groups and suggests that the war took place where it did more

out of the potential for political organizing and for strategic reasons (i.e., accessible borders) rather than for poverty—which existed everywhere in the country. Her analysis of the FPL is important. She indicates how many campesinos that joined the FPL achieved mid-level leadership positions, which contrasts with the other groups, which were urban and student led. She suggests that FPL peasants joined because of the work of the progressive church in organizing and that most rank-and-file members would not make reference to FMLN in terms of Marxist ideology (McClintock 1998, 267). In fourteen months of ethnographic study I suggest that if Marxist ideology is understood as class consciousness and class struggle, then, indeed, former combatants and sympathizers engage in theories of explanation with this at the core, though people rarely if ever made reference to Marx himself.

11. Also known as FARN.

12. Data from CAMINO (1982, 124) and Montgomery (1995).

13. For an ethnographic analysis of pre-massacre organizing, see Binford 1996.

14. Data for this section is compiled from MSI (1996); United Nations (1993); Montgomery (1995); and Servicio Jesuita para el Desarrollo "Pedro Arrupe" (1994).

15. Survivors and repopulated residents who did not experience this day tell of this event. It represents the horrors of the war in Chalatenango. Hundreds of testimonies documenting this massacre were collected for the Truth Commission report, and a narrative commemoration is part of a permanent collection on human rights abuse at the museum of the war at the Central American University, Simeón Cañas, that honors the six Jesuit priests and scholars killed in the war. On May 14–15 the Destacamento Militar No. 1 of the National Guard and the paramilitary forces ORDEN deliberately killed three hundred people, including civilians, women, and children, who where attempting to cross the Sumpul River from the caserío de Las Aradas in Chalatenango, where a military operation was in progress, to get to Honduras. The Salvadoran forces were assisted by the Honduran army as Salvadorans were caught between two armies, and many died in the river, unable to cross and not able to swim. The massacre was denied (even by the OAS, Organization of American States) and in 1981 José Napoleón Duarte claimed that all who died were "communist guerrillas" (United Nations 1993).

16. For an interesting text that documents the U.S. Central America Peace Movement, see Christian Smith (1996), who explores solidarity as a social movement led mostly by Christians in the 1980s and how they were contesting U.S. government policy.

17. In interviews with low-level to mid-level members of the military leadership of the FPL, many made reference to the economic assistance from Nicaragua and Cuba.

18. The party was founded by Roberto D'Aubuisson, one of the central protagonists of the death squad systems.

19. In the transition to peace there have been shifts in the five branches of the FMLN, dissolution of some (ERP), turns to neoliberal and conservative positions, and tensions between the different tendencies.

20. During an interview with a USAID representative, he critiqued the credit programs. He described the programs as torn between two philosophies that impeded the creation of strong institutional structures: a European model that emphasized social programs that would then lead to income generation and a U.S. model that placed income-generating projects first with the vision that then social progress/programs would follow. He went as far as to critique the very existence of credit programs. He offered that rather than

promoting integration, the FMLN-backed program of the different credit rates for former combatants and *tenedores* created social disintegration.

21. The NRP estimated reconstruction costs at $1.528 billion. The government of El Salvador has the actual number at $20.8 billion.

22. Japan is the second largest donor, pledging $207 million in loans and grants aimed primarily at infrastructure projects. The third largest donor is the Inter-American Development Bank, pledging $145 million, followed by the European Economic Community with $90 million. Individual countries also made direct contributions, such as Germany, giving $29 million. Many international (such as Catholic Relief Service, CARE) and more than 120 Salvadoran NGOs were also involved in implementing the NRP. The GOES implemented the program through such institutions as Secretaría de Reconstrucción Nacional, Banco de Tierras, Banco de Fomento Nacional, Dirección General de Caminos, Fondo de Inversión Social, and the Centro Nacional de Tecnología Agropecuaria (MSI 1996, 22). Research conducted at the Center for International Cooperation at New York University explored the impact of gaps in pledged donations. Recent work focuses on the role and accountability of international financial donors in rebuilding of war-torn societies (Forman and Patrick 2000).

23. The amount given up until December 31, 1995, in the department of Chalatenango totaled 45,977,540.50 colones. The municipality of Las Vueltas, the primary site of my fieldwork, received the least amount in Chalatenango: 1,817,673.30 colones (MSI 1996, Annex J1). Colones were the Salvadoran currency before dollarization in 2001. The exchange rate was 8.75 colones to the U.S. dollar.

24. See Boyce (1996) for an analysis of El Salvador's economic policy.

25. The service sector is the largest sector of the Salvadoran economy, with women as the primary laborers (World Bank 1998).

CHAPTER 3   RANK-AND-FILE HISTORY

1. Recall that in this book I provide pseudonyms for everyone.

2. In Spanish, *historia* can simultaneously mean "history" or "story," and I suggest in the reconstruction of social memory it can mean both.

3. See Abercrombie for an interesting analysis on the intersection of ethnographic and historical research and writing as one of being "a journeyman of the frontier practice of ethnography, the act of entering into the space of another culture in order to write about it for people like myself, I entered into contexts that were already frontiers, in which many generations have engaged in delicate communicative negotiations between local society and more global state forces" (1998, 10).

4. Salvadoran currency.

5. It was unclear who these exactly were. They appear to be early FPL participants.

6. In December 1997, however, the mayor of Las Vueltas along with his municipal counsel (*consejo municipal*) proposed to increase the span of this crafts projects for the region, the idea being to incorporate many more women from other *cantones* in the municipality. They were aware that a market had to first be identified (interview with Gilberto Mejía, November 1997).

7. For example, from October 1996 through December 1997, the *taller* operated through a loan of two thousand colones ($230) from Jennifer, the international development worker overseeing the project. That same December they were still waiting for payment

for three of their last orders, a four-month delay. Moreover, the workshop's petty cash had been "robbed" several times in the night—Lucía's adolescent boys the culprits. Upon confession Lucía was democratically allowed to continue working at the *taller*, the five other women understanding her dire need for money. She did not return the money.

8. Because of their positioning, backs to each other, the tape recorder did not pick up their voices very clearly. I am relying on detailed context notes.

9. *Tatús* were deep holes, small, like caves, that the guerrillas and civilian population dug out of the earth to protect people during military air strikes.

10. The *testimonio* gained official status as a literary category in 1970, in Cuba when Casa de Las Américas created the category for literary competitions.

11. For example, in early 1997 I was contracted by a progressive NGO working in the FMLN (FPL) municipality of Nejapa outside of San Salvador to lead a series of community workshops on the collection of oral history, the importance of historical memory, and how to collect a *testimonio*.

12. This title makes reference to the theme from the first historic interdepartmental Tenth Anniversary Celebration of Return from the refugee camps, to be discussed in this chapter. Its translation immediately raises important semantic questions that guide this chapter. As it is written (*Haciendo lo*) on texts that circulated throughout Chalatenango, it means remembering the past and *doing* the present. However, I suggest that there is an (intentional) double meaning to this rallying call. When spoken, the difference between "*haciendo lo*" and "*haciéndolo*" is not very distinguishable. The meaning, however, is different: "*recordando lo pasado and haciendolo presente*" translates into "remembering the past and *making it* present." This fits well with my thesis on addressing the postwar call to remember.

13. Grassroots organizations in the department of Morazán were invited to attend but did not organize the event because repatriated refugees were not based in Mesa Grande.

14. Data for this section on demobilized combatants was garnered through multiple discussions with three former long-term combatants, Rolando, Hugo, and Aquilino.

15. At the time of my research, for example, the credit received through a government-contracted housing project through FUNDASAL was being debated. Former combatants had to pay back less of the loan than non-combatants (interview with Aquilino, November 1997).

16. Much of this thinking on the contradictions within the movement I developed through many conversations with a National University student originally from a small community in Chalatenango who had lived in Mesa Grande, was a popular educator during repatriation, and had witnessed FMLN practices during different phases of the war. It also builds from interviews with Chayo and Kasandra.

17. *Compa* is short for *compañero* meaning "comrade," a marker of former combatant.

18. This situation is not particular to El Salvador. In the democratic transition following the Argentine Dirty War, for example, a phenomenon occurred in which a series of army officers testified, and through mass media peddled their testimony, leaving some conservatives (i.e., the church) to ask, "Why do we need to know the whole truth? For the purpose of conflict or reconciliation?" (in Feitlowitz 1998, 220).

19. Gal (1995) talks about the linguistic ideologies underlying these practices. See Woolard and Schieffelin (1994) for a review of language ideology's disparate and growing field.

20. The Holocaust literature explores the delicate balance between silence and documenting the horrors of genocide by the generation of survivors (see Boyarin 1994).

CHAPTER 4   NGOs IN THE POSTWAR PERIOD

1. The role of the FMLN is peppered throughout the book and narrated in a forthcoming interstitial.

2. Binford reports that the United States increased spending from $25 million in 1980 to an annual assistance of $500 to $600 million by the mid 1980s (1998, 11–12). After a decade this figure totaled $6 billion (Murray 1997, 15).

3. Or, as a director at USAID explained it to me, the European model emphasized social programs as a way to promote income generation while the U.S. model emphasized income generation as a way to promote social progress (author interview, November 1997).

4. For example, see Chayo's comment in the interstitial "Stitching Wounds and Frying Chicken."

5. See Silber 2007 for my analysis of the shift from solidarity work to the ambivalent activism and professionalization of solidarity in the postwar period through the lives of foreign community-development volunteers.

6. Because I focused on understudied regional grassroots spaces, this account does not focus on the national body of CRIPDES per se.

7. Interview with a CCR representative for Las Vueltas, November 1997.

8. Sister city relationships refer to international ties of solidarity between particular Salvadoran communities and communities in North America or Europe. Often these relationships involve funding and can be faith based.

9. U.S.–El Salvador Sister Cities Network at http://www.us-elsalvador-sisters.org/ (accessed June 23, 2008).

10. For CRIPDES Web sites, see http://www.cripdes.org/English.html, created in 2006; http://www.cripdes.org/ (accessed June 25, 2008), from 2008; and http://www.cripdes.net/ (accessed January 11, 2010), from 2010. Unpublished documents gathered in the mid to late 1990s match up with expanded and detailed mission (organizing rural communities), vision (placing local participation in the national), strategy (popular education, broad definition of development), and objectives (to empower, to create participatory democracy) articulated in CRIPDES Web sites.

11. For these statements, see, from the president of CRIPDES, http://www.elsalvadorsolidarity .org/joomla/index.php?option=com_content&task=view&id=158&Itemid=65 (accessed June 23, 2008); from sister-city organizations, http://www.us-elsalvador-sisters.org/; and from the CRIPDES official Web site, http://www.cripdes.net/ (accessed January 11, 2010).

12. Its first Web site was at http://www.geocities.com/lia_hernandez/Perfil.html (accessed June 23, 2008).

13. These municipalities are Agua Caliente; Arcatao; Citalá; Comalpa; Chalatenango; Dulce Nombre de Jesús; Dulce Nombre de María; El Carrizal; El Paraiso; La Laguna; La Palma; La Reina; Las Vueltas; Nueva Concepción; Nueva Trinidad; Ojos de Agua; Potonico; San Antonio de la Cruz; San Antonio los Ranchos; San Fernando; San Francisco Lempa; San Francisco Morazán; San Ignacio; San Isidro Labrador; San José Cacasque; San José las Flores; San Miguel de Mercedes; San Rafael; Santa Rita; and Tejutla.

14. Stephen et al. (2001), indeed, suggest that in later postwar years mixed NGOs have successfully learned the funding language of gendered development from national women's organizations. Mixed and women's organizations now compete for the same funding.

15. See http://www.cordes.org.sv/ (accessed June 23, 2008).

16. See http://cordes.org.sv/index.php?option=com_content&task=view&id=13&Itemid=40 for the full document (accessed June 23, 2008).

17. See http://cordes.org.sv/index.php?option=com_content&task=view&id=17&itemid=26 (accessed June 23, 2008).

18. CORDES Web site, dated from 2000, http://www.geocities.com/lia_hernandez/Perfil .html (accessed July 31, 2008).

19. CODDICH (Coordinadora de Desarrollo de Chalatenango) emerged from the UN relief institution PRODERE, and its aim is to strengthen local institutions through concerted coalition efforts, linking different NGOs, political sectors, local and regional government bodies, and central government ministries like Education and Heath in order to be "the voice of Chalatenango" for the international community (interview with director, November 1996). Subsequent research indicates a portion of its funding source. In 1998, it was an InterAmerican Foundation (IAF) grantee and received "$180,500 over two years, to provide its public and private sector member organizations with technical assistance to produce local development projects to address local problems, identify resources to implement these projects, and facilitate a participatory democracy throughout Chalatenango (ES-177)" (http://www.iaf.gov/grants/awards_ year_en.asp?country_id=9&gr_year=1998 [accessed July 13, 2007]).

    PROCHALATE emerged as a government-affiliated project with the signing of the peace accords and was intended to oversee Chalatenango's reconstruction. Early on it encountered difficulties because of gaps in pledged funding. It operates on a model of *co-ejucación*, meaning it works directly with local NGOs rather than directly with beneficiaries.

20. It is known to residents as Procap but also has the name FUNDAMUNI (Fundación de Apoyo a Municipios de El Salvador–Programa de Capacitación y Apoyo para el Desarrollo Local). As explained to me in 1997, Procap emerged in 1992 with the objective to strengthen the relationship between the wartime absentee mayors and FMLN communities. Their mission has continued to focus on municipal-level strengthening as local development (http://www.sa.diakonia.se/fundamuni.html [accessed April 15, 2010]).

    Plan Internacional has been working in Chalatenango since 1978. It operates through fostering children at the community level, and projects are directed toward building homes, providing school supplies, and so on. It is a nonpolitical NGO that gained entrance into repopulated communities in July 1993 through the FMLN. See also its Web site, which depicts its commitment to El Salvador (http://www.plan-international.org/wherewework/americas/elsalvador/ [accessed July 31, 2008]). Note that their "detailed map" of where they work in El Salvador names only departments rather than communities or municipalities.

21. See Servicio Jesuita para el Desarrollo "Pedro Arrupe" (1994), where testimonies, such as Niña Dora Chicas's, from Guarjila, a nearby and larger community, talk about the importance of organization and the importance of community work. Niña Dora Chicas states, "Si no hay un trabajo comunitario, no habría nada. No se llamaría comunidad, sino montón de casas con gente (If there is no communal work there

would be nothing. It wouldn't be called a community but rather a bunch of houses with people)" (quoted in ibid., 1994, 22).

22. Interview with PROCHALATE director, October 1997.
23. Interview, December 1997.
24. Interview, November 1997.
25. Interview with Irma, December 1997.
26. Interview, September 1997.
27. See Petras (1997) for a more anecdotal and generalizing analysis of the relationship between NGOs and imperialism that critiques "former Marxists" for having led their social movements astray.
28. Some have attempted to make sense of this field by pointing to the differences within NGOs, for example, by creating typologies sensitive to difference (i.e., Korton 1990).
29. See http://www.simpatizantesfmln.org/index.php?name=News&file=article&sid=3090 (accessed July 28, 2008). This announcement was dated May 26, 2007.

FMLN SNAPSHOTS

1. McClintock (1998) characterizes the FPL's leadership, the branch of the FMLN operating in Chalatenango, as unique in that much of the leadership was drawn from the campesino population.
2. In Morazán, where the ERP branch of the FMLN operated, revolutionary supporters ceased their support as historic leaders (i.e., Joaquín Villalobos) ultimately abandoned them in postwar times.

CHAPTER 6   CARDBOARD DEMOCRACY

1. I thank Marlene Clark for making this connection for me.
2. This is common to social movements and NGO practices. For example, in Nicaragua the women's movement waged an educational campaign focused on raising consciousness across the nation on the importance of women's health issues. This educational campaign influenced state health policies (Ewig 1999, 92).
3. Baker-Cristales further highlights the ways in which governmentality is a changing social process (2008, 351).
4. For example, Hammond (1998) describes the power of a Freirean-inspired popular education project in El Salvador. He documents how individuals became grassroots teachers under an oppressive context and how this engagement and the Catholic Church's teachings of liberation theology were crucial factors in explaining people's participation in the civil war (Hammond 1998, 8).
5. Popular education efforts during the war have been discussed in terms of a two-pronged extra-official project, one aimed at empowering community residents and the other focused on guerilla troops (Guzmán et al. 1994, 29). See Guzmán et al. (1994) and Hammond (1998) for detailed analyses of the popular education movement, its development, operation, phases, structures, relationship with community practices, and educational material and methodologies.
6. My discussion on popular education is ethnographically based on participant observation of teaching practices in El Rancho and interviews with several popular teachers in December 1997.

7. This program began in 1995 in 124 schools in 20 municipalities and benefited 26,000 students from preschool to the sixth grade. It then reached 148 municipalities, 1,450 urban schools and rural schools, and 239,000 students in primary education (Blandon Castro 1998).

8. Blandon Castro documents that there was a 16.5 percent decrease in illiteracy rates throughout the country as a result of national efforts (1998, 12), though in "rural areas" women's illiteracy rates remain higher. In 1996, the adult education completion rate for male heads of household was 7.74 percent as opposed to female heads of household, which was 1.83 percent (1998, 13). Blandon Castro's study, though useful in pointing out the significant gender disparity that continues in education and how this has implications for gendered democratization, limiting women's participation in various social, political, and economic spheres, unfortunately homogenizes all of "rural" El Salvador. Thus she ignores the important advances of popular education movements in departments like Chalatenango and Morazán. Additionally, she tends to describe limitations to education in terms of "cultural barriers"—rural people's practices as being resistant to education.

9. First, by receiving the *bachilerato* (equivalent to U.S. high school diploma), and then the *profesorado* (university-level teachers certificate). Indeed, college-level courses are offered in the unprecedented existence of a Chalatenango branch of the Salvadoran National University. Important critical work by Davies has been done on this topic that illustrates the ways in which MINED practices discriminate, their standardizing policies an example of neoliberalism that competes against the historic participatory democracy of the region (http://forlang.edgewood.edu/ian/Education.htm).

10. In retrospect, the year's discourse had set this into motion. Indeed, in late 1996 CORDES renamed its Women's Branch to the Gender and Training Team.

11. These women are labeled leaders by CCR and CORDES and many self-identify as "*líderes de la comunidad/mujeres*." In practice, the meaning of leadership is up for debate. The invited women participants are members of community-level women's councils (*directivas de mujeres*). Some also served on community councils (*directivas comunales*).

12. During the war, communal days (*días comunales*) to work the land, work on construction projects, and so on, were the norm. In postwar times, individual labor has replaced communal projects.

13. Recall that CCR is one of CRIPDES's regional branches.

14. It is unclear if a sixth-grade education is required. Basically literacy, however, is essential.

15. For a comparative analysis of micro-credit models, those that are minimalist versus those that incorporate training, gender, and so on, see Cosgrove (1998).

16. In a speech made by a leading CORDES credit officer at the annual grassroots credit meeting and attended by hundreds of residents from repopulated communities, he discussed the 38 percent non-recuperation rate for 1997. His point was that this credit failure harmed communities, the future of Chalatenango, and the next generation.

CHAPTER 7   CONNING REVOLUTIONARIES

1. I do not include the Ingeniero's last name and have changed the other name to Patricia. I have kept the title of Ingeniero for it is this educational title that was intended to legitimize the organization and created the hierarchy and authority for

the new organization. It was never clear whether or not the Ingeniero had such a degree.

2. "Revolutionary feminism" is defined as "a grassroots movement that is both pluralist and autonomous in structure. It seeks to challenge sexism as inseparable from larger political structures not explicitly perceived to be patriarchal in nature, but from the perspective of feminists, entirely bound to the oppression of women" (Shayne 2004, 9).

3. See Cosgrove (2010) for a recent comparative analysis of the possibilities for women's leadership in postwar contexts.

4. See also Silber (2006) for a juxtaposition between platforms created by the women's coalition, which delineates areas for structural change, and the platform proposed by ISDEMU.

5. For abortion issues, see Hitt (2006).

6. Max Gluckman's extended case study follows a sequence of events over a long period of time and focuses on social actors in a series of situations. See Mitchell (1983) for a cogent discussion of Gluckman and the Manchester School's theoretical and methodological orientation. Note also that Gluckman was one of the first to think about the position of the anthropologist when discussing social change.

7. See Mo Hume (2009) for a feminist discussion on violence in El Salvador that takes up what she terms "subaltern vocabularies."

8. I provide pseudonyms for the lawyer, MOLID representatives all subjects involved.

9. Translation by author.

10. Author interview, November 1997 with MAM director.

11. She had the resources to travel to San Salvador and conduct the investigation.

12. Many "legitimate" NGOs have a hard time gaining legal status. This is a very bureaucratic procedure that in and of itself does not indicate whether or not an organization is legitimate, but it can interfere with getting external funding.

13. The issue of the lawyer's fee was always vaguely addressed by Virgilio. In this case, he never charged for his services.

14. The survey he refers to is the one that women filled out in Elsy's home, the same survey that many had to resubmit several times, the same survey women said he angrily destroyed.

15. This was never verified.

16. Often Patricia presented herself as a Christian, not a Catholic, an important difference. Although she claimed that MOLID "*no tiene color ni religión*" (doesn't have a political or religious orientation), it is precisely MOLID's political and religious differences (Patricia's evangelical exclamations) that are a factor in people's suspicions. Moreover, in many meetings Patricia engaged in a narrative strategy that othered the *repoblaciones* as she remarked how she was not scared to travel to these sites, for although these were FMLN supporters and past combatants, they were also human beings. In these comments she clearly positioned herself on the right.

17. The Ingeniero was received in a similar manner. In El Salvador, as in much of Latin America, education is a marker of class and hegemony.

18. Because it took place in the CCR offices, I was able to tape record this meeting.

19. April 2, 2009, New York University, Annette Weiner Memorial Lecture.

20. They define these terms as follows: dissent is "a conscious and public opposition to the status quo, whether by an individual or group. Direct action refers to public and

active protest against the existing state of society. If dissent represents the social learning processes by which people come to disagree with their circumstances, then direct action stands for the agency of individuals and small groups to activate opposition into larger movements for change" (Fox and Starn 1997, 14).

CHAPTER 8   THE POSTWAR HIGHWAY

1. The epigraph is from an author interview with eighteen-year-old Miguel, December 2007, Virginia, United States. (As throughout the book, the author has used pseudonyms. Audio-taped interviews were conducted in Spanish with author's translation into English. Readers will find in some excerpts the verbatim Spanish and the English translation.)

2. I juxtapose this to Quesada's poignant (1998) analysis of childhood suffering in Nicaragua.

3. Across Chalatenango and other former conflict zones there are significant cases of families that did not qualify for postwar benefits for reasons such as not participating in demobilization efforts. There are also cases of families that did not receive international development assistance regarding housing. In such instances, men and women attempt to rebuild homes through kinship networks, entrepreneurial enterprises, and wage labor.

4. In this conversation, Miguel is conscious to translate his experiences in the fast-food industry into a meaningful language for friends and family back home in El Rancho. He called Elsy first, telling her of the store manager's intention to send him to language school so that he could be promoted to supervisor, a concept, Miguel explains, that makes more sense to *campesinos* who have no experience in the fast-food industry.

5. See Tsing (2005) for an analysis on the wildness and taming of frontiers, in her case the frontiers of the forest that are pillaged by logging companies and all that is displaced.

6. See the introduction, where I discuss my positioning as a "young South American gringa." For the struggles of engaged research praxis, see chapter 7.

7. For an illustrative case of long-term engaged research praxis, see R. Smith 2006. In what could be described as my "second phase" of research, I employed what Smith defines as "grounded ethnographic interviews" that "involve asking informants about particular events or themes that have emerged in past research with these and other informants" (R. Smith 2006, 356). This methodology could only be employed because of the shared experiences and relationship cultivated during previous research.

8. In this article Coutin borrows from Marilyn Strathern's work. Over the last two decades anthropologists have addressed the ethics of research methodology and the politics of representation often on the heels of feminist theorizing. See Jackson (2005) for a cogent summary of politics of representation.

9. I am indebted to Constance Sutton for elaborating this point more than twenty years ago in among the first articulations of transnational processes.

10. See my discussion on the pained memories articulated by Chayo in New Jersey.

11. Philippe Bourgois's (2002) theory on a continuum of violence provides a complementary analysis.

12. Importantly, Coutin wants to draw attention to studying beyond the process of arrival. See also Beth Baker-Cristales for her discussion on "mobile ethnography" (2004, 2).

13. Here Tsing engages with a debate between the search for universals and the particular. She writes, "Postcolonial theory challenges scholars to position our work between the traps of the universal and the culturally specific. . . . The universal offers us the chance to participate in the global stream of humanity. We can't turn it down. Yet we also can't replicate previous versions without inserting our own genealogy of commitments and claims. Whether we place ourselves inside or outside the West, we are stuck with universals created in cultural dialogue. It is this kind of post- and neocolonial universal that has enlivened liberal politics as well as economic neoliberalism as they have spread around the world with such animation since the end of the Cold War" (Tsing 2005, 1).

14. See Roseberry (1988) for a now classic exposition on political economy and the importance of being attentive to regional formations. See Lauria-Santiago (1999) for a groundbreaking study on the emergence of coffee in El Salvador that illuminates the importance of small-scale producers.

15. For example, see Silber (2004b) and Moser and Clark (2001).

16. This epigraph is from an author interview with Chico, Chayo's husband, from El Rancho, conducted in New Jersey, January 2008.

17. Men and women, and often times nuclear and extended families, migrated to work on coffee and sugar plantations in other regions of the country. Women also have migrated for many generations to Chalatenango and San Salvador as *domésticas*.

18. The UNDP report notes a "pause" in postwar migration in the early 1990s, which picks up again after 1996 when the economy becomes more "sluggish" (2005, 14).

19. Discussion of borders also needs to address flows out of the United States. For example, see Weinberg (2008) for a discussion of the illegal trade in small arms from the United States into Mexico.

20. El Salvador's national territory is comprised of fourteen departments.

21. Some examples include Mary Beth Sheridan, "Acting Locally, Voting Globally," *Washington Post*, March 18, 2004, B1, B4; "A Daughter Stolen in Wartime Returns to El Salvador," *New York Times*, April 5, 2007; Marc Lacey, "Money Earned in U.S. Pushes Prices Higher [in] El Salvador," *Washington Post*, May 14, 2006, A1, A17.

22. UNDP human development reports are significant in their redefinition of what constitutes development, shifting the indicators beyond macroeconomic growth to the lives of people, development as defined as wealth in people in terms of poverty, inequality, education, illiteracy. The authors of this report suggest that "international migration can be seen as the antithesis of human development, or as a hemorrhage of human development" (UNDP 2005, 3). However, the authors reframe the debate by asking what happens if migration is understood as "an opportunity for human development" (UNDP 2005, 5).

23. Some of the departments with the highest level of remittances include Cabañas, Morazán, and La Union—areas of high conflict during the war (UNDP 2005, 10).

24. Author interview with Avel, October 2006. Author's translation into English.

25. This is interestingly juxtaposed with the intermediate postwar apologetic recollections of survivors of the war. I characterize these as apologetic because of the hierarchy of value attached to the deaths caused by the bullets of war, the political violence easily translated and importantly mobilized by a solidarity movement during the war period (see also Dickson-Gómez 2004). Deaths by illness were often narrated as not related to war, more often than not qualified as such, with a pause.

26. Here is a note on translation: *To obligate* means "to bind legally or morally; to commit (as funds) to meet an obligation" (http://www.m-w.com/dictionary/obligate); *obligado* means "obliged, obligatory, compulsory, customary"; *obligar* means "to force, to require, to oblige"; *obligarse* means "to commit oneself, to undertake (to do something)" (http://www.m-w.com/spanish/obligar).

27. The authors of the report argue that a cycle is created. Salvadorans leave because there is unemployment, this leads to a growth in remittances, the appreciation of the exchange rate, an increase in imports, which adversely impacts local production, which then creates more unemployment, which then leads to more migration (UNDP 2005, 14).

28. Coutin further explains, "The features of legal clandestinity in the United States and political clandestinity in El Salvador are strikingly similar. Like undocumented immigrants, individuals who go into hiding within their countries of origin cannot work, be with their families, have residences, move about freely, or fulfill their plans for the future" (1999, 56).

29. As mentioned in the introduction, because of my longitudinal research, my change in status from unmarried to married and then to mother positioned me differently throughout my research agenda. Not only did it shift how I was perceived, but I address how it shapes the very questions that I pose in terms of understanding revolutionary motherhood and what Stephen (2007) discusses as "transborder motherhood."

30. *Bicha*, meaning "little girl," is a frequent term used in the countryside. It translates as "little insect."

31. See R. Smith (2006) and also George (2005) for reviews of this literature as well as Hondagneu-Sotelo (2003) for a synthesizing, edited volume.

32. See also Menjívar (2000) for a comprehensive analysis of the history of migration in San Francisco and the ways in which gender and class are key factors in making or breaking social networks of exchange. In its review of the literature, the UNDP states that in the Washington, D.C., area, men continue to migrate more than women, though in each case 50 percent of male and female migrants indicate that they migrate in search of work (335), while 21 percent of women and 7 percent of men explain their migration in terms of reunification with family members (2005, 336).

33. Critical scholarship in the Salvadoran case exists on this material, indexing as well the centrality of the solidarity movement in the parallel conversation of political asylum. See Mahler (1995), Baker-Cristales (2004), and Coutin (2007, 2003).

34. This is a Salvadoran fast-food chicken chain that in the last five to ten years has opened up branches in the United States.

35. Throughout this region, some residents have purchased pickup trucks, minivans, and buses and gone into the business of transporting people from regional capitals to distant communities.

36. At the time Flor was sixteen years old and followed her mother's experience. The fear of traveling with the police officers reflects the possibility that a pursuit would take place and place them in more danger.

37. See also Silber 2004a for a discussion of the ways in which adolescent girls' sexuality is monitored in a postwar context.

38. Stephen concentrates on Mexican crossings and suggests the term *transborder* rather than *transnational* because "the borders they cross are ethnic, class, cultural, colonial, and state borders within Mexico as well as at the US-Mexico border and in different regions of the United States" (2007, 6).

39. In a post-9/11 context where migration is posited as a security threat, the INS (Immigration and Naturalization Service) was restructured into the Bureau of Citizenship and Immigration Services, which is housed in the Department of Homeland Security (DHS) (see Baker-Cristales 2004, 134).

40. In theorizing how to study globalization, Tsing writes, "My answer has been to focus on zones of awkward engagement, where words mean something different across a divide even as people agree to speak. These zones of cultural friction are transient; they arise out of encounters and interactions. They reappear in new places with changing events" (2005, xi).

41. Interview with Chayo, January 2008, New Jersey.

EPILOGUE

1. This meeting was audio-taped and transcribed.

2. Recall the recent death of Justo Mejía's son in the United States and the fund-raising efforts to bury his body in El Salvador—two generations of death.

3. I am not quite sure why the majority of the thirty names collected on the day of the meeting are not included on this list. More than likely it is indicative of miscommunication between the organizers, and the names were accidentally left out.

4. In the past, because of our relationship, Elsy had shown frustration when I economically assisted other folks rather than herself and her family.

REFERENCES

Abercrombie, Thomas. 1998. *Pathways of Memory and Power: Ethnography and History among an Andean People.* Wisconsin: University of Wisconsin Press.

Aguilar, Ana Leticia, Blanca Estela Dole, Morena Herrera, Sofía Montenegro, Lorena Camacho, and Lorena Flores. 1997. *Movimiento de Mujeres en Centroamerica.* Managua, Nicaragua: Programa Regional La Corriente.

Alegría, Claribel. 1987. *They Won't Take Me Alive: Salvadorean Women in the Struggle for National Liberation.* London: Women's Press.

Almeida, Paul. 2008. *Waves of Protest: Popular Struggle in El Salvador, 1925–2005.* Minneapolis and London: University of Minnesota Press.

Alonso, Ana María. 1995. *Thread of Blood: Colonialism, Revolution, and Gender on Mexico's Northern Frontier.* Tucson: University of Arizona Press.

Alvarez, Sonia E. 1998. Latin American Feminisms "Go Global": Trends of the 1990s and Challenges for the New Millennium. In *Cultures of Politics/Politics of Cultures: Re-Visioning Latin American Social Movements,* ed. S. Alvarez, E. Dagnino, and A. Escobar, 293–324. Boulder, CO: Westview Press.

Anderson, Thomas. 1992. *Matanza: The 1932 "Slaughter" that Traumatized a Nation, Shaping U.S. Policy to This Day.* Connecticut: Curbstone Press.

Angel-Ajani, Asale. 2006. Expert Witness: Notes toward Revisiting the Politics of Listening. In *Engaged Observer: Anthropology, Advocacy, and Activism,* ed. V. Sanford and A. Angel-Ajani, 76–89. New Brunswick, NJ: Rutgers University Press.

Babb, Florence. 2004. Recycled Sandalistas: From Revolution to Resorts in the New Nicaragua. *American Anthropologist* 106 (3): 541–555.

———. 2001. *After Revolution: Mapping Gender and Cultural Politics in Neoliberal Nicaragua.* Austin: University of Texas Press.

Baker-Cristales, Beth. 2004. *Salvadoran Migration to Southern California: Redefining el Hermano Lejano.* Gainesville: University Press of Florida.

———. 2008. Magical Pursuits: Legitimacy and Representation in a Transnational Political Field. *American Anthropologist* 110 (3): 349–359

Barry, Tom. 1990. *El Salvador: A Country Guide.* Albuquerque: The Inter-Hemispheric Education Resource Center.

Bergman, Marcelo, and Monika Szurmuk. 2001. Gender, Citizenship, and Social Protest: The New Social Movements in Argentina. In *The Latin American Subaltern Studies Reader,* ed. Ileana Rodríguez, 383–401. Durham: Duke University Press.

Berryman, Phillip. 1984. *The Religious Roots of Rebellion: Christians in Central American Revolutions.* Maryknoll: Orbis Books.

Beverley, John, and Marc Zimmerman. 1990. *Literature and Politics in the Central American Revolutions.* Austin: University of Texas Press.

Biehl, Joâo. 2005. *Vita: Life in a Zone of Social Abandonment.* Berkeley: University of California Press.

Binford, Leigh. 1996. *The El Mozote Massacre: Anthropology and Human Rights.* Tucson: University of Arizona Press.

———. 1998. Hegemony in the Interior of the Salvadoran Revolution: The ERP in Northern Morazán. *Journal of Latin American Anthropology* 4 (I): 2–45.

Blandon Castro, Norma. 1998. Democratization of Education in El Salvador: Examining the Participation of Women. Paper presented at the Twenty-first International Congress of the Latin American Studies Association, Chicago, September 24–26, 1998.

Bodnar, John. 1992. *Remaking America: Public Memory, Commemoration, and Patriotism in the Twentieth Century.* Princeton, NJ: Princeton University Press.

Bonner, Raymond. 1982. Salvador Deploys U.S.-Trained Unit: Troops Back from Fort Bragg Conduct First Operation—Rebel Toll Is Put at 135. *New York Times.* June 13.

Bourgois, Philippe. 2001. The Power of Violence in War and Peace: Post–Cold War Lessons from El Salvador. *Ethnography* 2 (I): 5–34.

———. 2002. The Violence of Moral Binaries: Response to Leigh Binford. *Ethnography* 3 (2): 221–231.

———. 2006. Foreword to *Engaged Observer: Anthropology, Advocacy, and Activism,* ed. V. Sanford and A. Angel-Ajani, vol. 5, ix–xii. New Brunswick, NJ: Rutgers University Press.

Boyarin, Jonathan, ed. 1994. *Remapping Memory: The Politics of Timespace.* Minneapolis: University of Minnesota Press.

Boyce, J. K. 1996. *Economic Policy for Building Peace: The Lessons of El Salvador.* Boulder, CO: Lynne Rienner Publishers.

Boyce, James, et al. 1995. *Adjustment Toward Peace: Economic Policy and Post-War Reconstruction in El Salvador.* San Salvador, El Salvador: UNDP.

Brooks, Ethel C. 2007. *Unraveling the Garment Industry: Transnational Organizing and Women's Work.* Minneapolis: University of Minnesota Press.

Browning, David. 1971. *El Salvador: Landscape and Society.* Oxford: Clarendon Press.

Burton, Barbara. 2004. The Transmigration of Rights: Women, Movement, and the Grassroots in Latin American and Caribbean Communities. *Development and Change* 35(4): 773–798.

Cabarrús, C. R. 1983. *Génesis de una Revolución: Análisis del Surgimiento y Desarrollo de la Organización Campesina en El Salvador.* Mexico: Ediciones de la Casa Chata.

Campos, Orsy. 1996. Somos Una Mezcla de Colores. *Diario de Hoy* (San Salvador, El Salvador), December 1, 1996, 2–3.

Canclini, Néstor García. 2001. *Consumers and Citizens: Globalization and Multicultural Conflicts.* Minneapolis: University of Minnesota Press.

Central America Information Office (CAMINO). 1982. *El Salvador: Background to the Crisis.* Cambridge: Central America Information Office.

Christian, Shirley. 1992. Rebel Villages Weary of War, but Wary of Peace. *New York Times.* January 29.

CODEM. 1996. *Plan de Acción para el Desarrollo: Municipio de Las Vueltas: Chalatenango.* El Salvador: CODEM.

Coles, Kimberly. 2002. Ambivalent Builders: Europeanization, the Production of Difference, and Internationals in Bosnia-Herzegovina. *PoLAR: Political and Legal Anthropology Review* 25 (I): 1–18.

Connerton, Paul. 1989. *How Societies Remember.* Cambridge: Cambridge University Press.

CORDES. 1997. Construyendo el Desarrollo Participativo y la Autogestión Comunal. *Memoria de Labores. Enero-diciembre 1996.* Seventh Asamblea General Originaria. San Salvador, El Salvador, June 1997.

Coronil, Fernando, and J. Skurski. 1991. Dismembering and Remembering the Nation: The Semantics of Political Violence in Venezuela. *CSSH* 33 (2): 288–337.

Cosgrove, Serena. 1998. Give Them the Credit They Deserve. PhD diss., Northeastern University.

———. 2010. *Leadership from the Margins: Women and Civil Society Organizations in Argentina, Chile, and El Salvador.* New Brunswick, NJ: Rutgers University Press.

Coutin, Susan Bibler. 1999. Citizenship and Clandestiny among Salvadoran Immigrants. *Polar* 22 (2): 53–63.

———. 2000. *Legalizing Moves: Salvadoran Immigrants' Struggle for Salvadoran Residency.* Ann Arbor: University of Michigan Press.

———. 2003. Cultural Logics of Belonging and Movement: Transnationalism, Naturalization, and US Immigration Politics. *American Ethnologist* 30 (4): 508–526.

———. 2005. Being en Route. *American Anthropologist* 107 (2): 195–206.

———. 2007. *Nations of Emigrants: Shifting Boundaries of Citizenship in El Salvador and the United States.* Ithaca, NY: Cornell University Press.

Coutin, Susan Bibler, and Barbara Yngvesson. 2006. Backed by Papers: Undoing Persons, Histories, and Return. *American Ethnologist* 33 (2): 177–190.

Daniel, E. Valentine. 1996. *Charred Lullabies: Chapters in an Anthropology of Violence.* Princeton, N.J.: Princeton University Press.

Danner, Marc. 1994. *The Massacre at El Mozote: A Parable of the Cold War.* New York: Vintage Books.

Das, Veena. 2007. *Life and Words: Violence and the Descent into the Ordinary.* Berkeley: University of California Press.

Davies, Ian. The Debate over Popular Education in El Salvador. http://forlang.edgewood.edu/ian/Education.htm#_ftnref1 (accessed January 5, 2009).

DeLugan, Robin Maria. 2005. Peace, Culture, and Governance in Post–Civil War El Salvador (1992–2000). *Journal of Human Rights* 4: 233–249.

Dickson-Gómez, Julia. 2004. "One Who Doesn't Know War, Doesn't Know Anything": The Problem of Comprehending Suffering in Postwar El Salvador. *Anthropology and Humanism* 29 (2): 145–158.

DIGNAS. 1993. *Hacer Política Desde Las Mujeres: Una Propuesta Feminista para la Participación Política de las Mujeres Salvadoreñas.* San Salvador, El Salvador: DIGNAS.

Doljanin, Nicolas. 1982. *Chalatenango La Guerra Descalaza: Reportaje Sobre El Salvador.* Mexico City: El Día.

Dunkerley, James. 1988. *Power in the Isthmus: A Political History of Modern Central America.* London: Verso.

———. 1995. *The Pacification of Central America.* London: Verso Books.

Eade, Deborah, ed. 1998. *From Conflict to Peace in a Changing World: Social Reconstruction in Times of Transition.* An Oxfam Working Paper. [Boston, MA:] Oxfam.

ECA. 1997. La Cultura de la Violencia en El Salvador. *Estudios Centroamericanos* 588 (October): 938–948.

Edwards, Beatrice E., and Gretta Tovar Siebentritt. 1991. *Places of Origin: The Repopulation of Rural El Salvador.* Boulder, CO: Lynne Rienner.

Enzinna, Wes. 2008. Another SOA? A U.S. Police Academy in El Salvador Worries Critics. *NACLA* 41 (2): 5–12.

Escobar, Arturo. 1995. *Encountering Development: The Making and Unmaking of the Third World.* Princeton, NJ: Princeton University Press.

Ewig, Christina. 1999. The Strengths and Limits of the NGO Women's Model: Shaping Nicaragua's Democratic Institutions. *Latin American Research Review* 34 (3): 75–102.

Farmer, Paul. 2001. *Infections and Inequalities: The Modern Plagues.* Berkeley: University of California Press.

Feitlowitz, Marguerite. 1998. *A Lexicon of Terror: Argentina and the Legacies of Torture.* New York: Oxford University Press.

Feldman, Allen. 1991. *Formations of Violence: The Narrative of the Body and Political Terror in Northern Ireland.* Chicago: University of Chicago Press.

Ferguson, James. 1994. *The Anti-Politics Machine: "Development," Depoliticization, and Bureaucratic Power in Lesotho.* Minneapolis: University of Minnesota Press.

Field, Les. 1995. Constructing Local Identities in a Revolutionary Nation: The Cultural Politics of the Artisan Class in Nicaragua, 1979–1990. *AE* 22 (4): 789–806.

Fisher, William F. 1997. Doing Good? The Politics and Antipolitics of NGO Practices. *Annual Review of Anthropology* 26:439–464.

Fitzsimmons, Tracy. 2000. A Monstrous Regiment of Women? State, Regime, and Women's Political Organizing in Latin America. *LARR* 35 (2): 216–229.

Foley, Michael. 1996. Laying the Groundwork: The Struggle for Civil Society in El Salvador. *Journal of Interamerican Studies and World Affairs* 38 (1): 67–104.

Forman, Shepard, and Stewart Patrick, eds. 2000. *Good Intentions: Pledges of Aid for Postconflict Recovery.* Boulder, CO: Lynne Rienner Publishers.

Foucault, Michel. 1991. "Governmentality." In *The Foucault Effect: Studies in Governmentality,* ed. Graham Burchell, Colin Gordon, and Peter Miller, 87–104. Chicago: University of Chicago Press.

Fox, Richard, and Orin Starn. 1997. *Between Resistance and Revolution: Cultural Politics and Social Protest.* New Brunswick, NJ: Rutgers University Press.

Friedman, Elisabeth J. 2000. *Unfinished Transitions: Women and the Gendered Development of Democracy in Venezuela, 1936–1996.* University Park: Pennsylvania State University Press.

Fundación 16 de enero. 1993. *Diagnostico de la Situación Actual de la Mujer Ex Combatiente.* San Salvador, El Salvador: Proyecto Prodepas.

Funde. 1997. *Diagnostico Agro-socioeconomico Microregion VI "Oriente."* Report. Chalatenango, El Salvador.

Gal, Susan. 1991. Between Speech and Silence: The Problematics of Research on Language and Gender. In *Gender at the Crossroads of Knowledge: Feminist Anthropology in the Postmodern Era,* ed. M. di Leonardo, 175–203. Berkeley: University of California Press.

———. 1995. Language and the Arts of Resistance. *Cultural Anthropology* 10 (3): 407–424.

Galdámez, Pablo. 1986. *Faith of a People: The Story of a Christian Community in El Salvador, 1970–1980.* Maryknoll, NY: Orbis Books.

Gammage, Sarah. 2006 Exporting People and Recruiting Remittances: A Development Strategy for El Salvador? *Latin American Perspectives* 151, 33 (6): 75–100.

George, Sheba Mariam. 2005. *Women Come First: Gender and Class in Transnational Migration.* Berkeley: University of California Press.

Gould, Jeffrey. 1990. *To Lead as Equals: Rural Protest and Political Consciousness in Chinandega, Nicaragua, 1912–1979.* Chapel Hill: University of North Carolina Press.

Gould, Jeffrey L., and Aldo A. Lauria-Santiago. 2008. *To Rise in Darkness: Revolution, Repression, and Memory in El Salvador, 1920–1932.* Durham: Duke University Press.

Green, Linda. 1999. *Fear as a Way of Life : Mayan Widows in Rural Guatemala.* New York: Columbia University Press.

Gregory, Steven. 2006. *The Devil behind the Mirror: Globalization and Politics in the Dominican Republic.* Berkeley: University of California Press.

Gruson, Lindsey. 1987. Salvador Refugees Win Test of Wills. *New York Times.* October 13.

Gugelberger, Georg, and Michael Kearney. 1991. Voices for the Voiceless: Testimonial Literature in Latin America. *Latin American Perspectives* 18 (3): 3–14.

Gupta, Akhil. 1995. Blurred Boundaries: The Discourse of Corruption, the Culture of Politics, and the Imagined State. *American Ethnologist* 22 (2): 375–402.

———. 1998. *Postcolonial Developments: Agriculture in the Making of Modern India.* Durham: Duke University Press.

Gupta, Akhil, and James Ferguson. 2002. Spatializing States: Toward an Ethnography of Neoliberal Governmentality. *American Ethnologist* 29 (4): 981–1002.

Gupta, Akhil, and Aradhana Sharma. 2006. Globalization and Postcolonial States. *Current Anthropology* 47 (2): 277–307.

Guzmán, José Luis, Yanci Urbina, and Julio Sosa. 1994. *Las Escuelas Populares de Chalatenango: Un Aporte para el Desarrollo de la Educación en las Zonas Rurales de El Salvador.* San Salvador, Chalatenango: ED-UCA, CCR y PRODERE ELS.

Halbwachs, Maurice. 1992. *On Collective Memory.* Chicago: University of Chicago Press.

Hale, Charles. 1994. *Resistance and Contradiction: Miskitu Indians and the Nicaraguan State, 1894–1987.* Stanford: Stanford University Press.

———. 2005. Neoliberal Multiculturalism: The Remaking of Cultural Rights and Racial Dominance in Central America. *PoLAR* 28 (1): 10–28.

———. 2006. Activist Research v. Cultural Critique: Indigenous Land Rights and the Contradictions of Politically Engaged Anthropology. *Cultural Anthropology* 21 (1): 96–120.

Halsband, Silvia. 1996. *Diagnóstico de los Medios de Vida de las Mujeres de Chalatenango.* UNIFEM-Proyecto ELS/92/W01.

Hammond, John. 1998. *Fighting to Learn: Popular Education and Guerrilla War in El Salvador.* New Brunswick, NJ: Rutgers University Press.

Harvey, David. 2005. *A Brief History of Neoliberalism.* New York: Oxford University Press.

Hayner, Priscilla. 2001. *Unspeakable Truths: Confronting State Terror and Atrocity.* New York: Routledge.

Hemment, Julie. 2004. The Riddle of the Third Sector: Civil Society, International Aid, and NGOs in Russia. *Anthropological Quarterly* 77 (2): 215–241.

Henríquez, Alexis. 2006. Los, 20,000 KM más letales. *La Prensa Gráfica.* January 15. http:///www.laprensagrafica.com/enfoques/394579.asp (accessed February 28, 2007).

Hernández Rodríguez, M., and K. I. Mendez. 1996. *Marco Histórico-Social y Socio-Cultural de Las Vueltas. Dept. de Chalatenango.* IV Año de Lic. En letras. San Salvador, El Salvador: National University.

Hitt, Jack. 2006. Pro-Life Nation. *New York Times Magazine.* April 9.

Holston, James, and Arjun Appadurai. 1999. Introduction: Cities and Citizenship. In *Cities and Citizenship*, ed. J. Holston, 1–18. Durham: Duke University Press.

Hondagneu-Sotelo, Pierrette, ed. 2004. *Gender and U.S. Immigration: Contemporary Trends.* Berekely: University of California Press.

Hume, Mo. 2009. *The Politics of Violence: Gender, Conflict and Community in El Salvador.* Malden, MA: Wiley-Blackwell.

Jackson, John. 2005. *Real Black: Adventures in Racial Sincerity.* Chicago: University of Chicago Press.

Kampwirth, Karen. 2002. *Women and Guerrilla Movements: Nicaragua, El Salvador, Chiapas, Cuba.* University Park: Pennsylvania State University Press.

———. 2004. *Feminism and the Legacy of Revolution: Nicaragua, El Salvador, Chiapas.* Athens: Ohio University Press.

Keane, Webb. 2002. Sincerity, "Modernity," and the Protestants. *Cultural Anthropology* 17 (1): 65–92.

Keating, Christine. 2003. Developmental Democracy and Its Inclusions: Globalization and the Transformation of Participation. *Signs* 29 (2): 417–437.

Kincaid, Jamaica. 2000. *A Small Place*. New York: Farrar, Straus, and Giroux.

Kinzer, Stephen. 1983. Tide of Refugees, and Suffering, Rises across Salvador. *New York Times*. May 8.

Kirsch, Gesa. 2005. Friendship, Friendliness, and Feminist Fieldwork. *Signs: Journal of Women in Culture and Society* 30 (4): 2163–2172.

Korton, D. C. 1990. *Getting to the 21st Century: Voluntary Action and the Global Agenda*. West Hartford, CT: Kumarian.

Kovats-Bernat, J. Christopher. 2002. Negotiating Dangerous Fields: Pragmatic Strategies for Fieldwork amid Violence and Terror. *American Anthropologist* 104 (1): 208–222.

Lacey, Marc. 2007. A Daughter Stolen in Wartime Returns to El Salvador. *New York Times*. April 5.

Lara Martínez, Carlos Benjamín. 2005. Tradición Oral: Formación y Desarrollo del Movimiento Campesino de Chalatenango. Consejo de Investigaciones Científicas Licenciatura en Antropología Sociocultural. Instituto de Estudios Históricos, Antropológicos y Arqueológicos. Universidad de El Salvador, San Salvador.

Latour, Bruno. 1999. *Pandora's Hope: Essays on the Reality of Science Studies*. Cambridge, MA: Harvard University Press.

Lauria-Santiago, Aldo. 1998. "That a Poor Man Be Industrious:" Coffee, Community, and Agrarian Capitalism in the Transformation of El Salvador's Ladino Peasantry, 1850–1900. In *Identity and Struggle at the Margins of the Nation-State: The Laboring Peoples of Central America and the Hispanic Caribbean*, ed. A. Lauria-Santiago and A. Chomsky, 25–51. Durham, NC: Duke University Press.

———. 1999. *An Agrarian Republic: Commercial Agriculture and the Politics of Peasant Communities in El Salvador, 1823–1914*. Pittsburgh: University of Pittsburgh Press.

Lauria-Santiago, Aldo, and Leigh Binford, eds. 2004. *Landscapes of Struggle: Politics, Society, and Community in El Salvador*. Pittsburgh: University of Pittsburgh Press.

Leaman, D. E. 1998. Participatory Outsiders and the Reach of Representation in Post-War El Salvador: The Community of El Jicaro in Changing Political Contexts. Paper presented at the Twenty-first International Congress of the Latin American Studies Association, Chicago, September 24–26, 1998.

Le Moyne, James. 1985. Salvadoran Army Improving, but Rebels Adjust. *New York Times*. January 29.

———. 1986. Guerrillas. *New York Times*. April 6.

Levitt, Peggy. 2001. *Transnational Villagers*. Berkeley: University of California Press.

Levitt, Peggy, and Nina Glick Schiller. 2004. Conceptualizing Simultaneity: A Transnational Social Field Perspective on Society. *International Migration Review* 38 (3): 1002–1039.

Lindo-Fuentes, Hector. 1990. *Weak Foundations: The Economy of El Salvador in the Nineteenth Century*. Berkeley: University of California Press.

Lobato, C. 1996. *La Sociedad Civil en el Proceso de Transformación Social*. El Salvador: Instituto de Estudios Jurídicos de El Salvador.

Luciak, Ilja. 2001. *After the Revolution: Gender and Democracy in El Salvador, Nicaragua, and Guatemala*. Baltimore, MD: Johns Hopkins University Press.

Lungo Uclés, Mario. 1990. *El Salvador en los 80: Contrainsurgencia y Revolución*. San José, Costa Rica: EDUCA.

Macdonald, Laura. 1997. *Supporting Civil Society: The Political Role of Non-Governmental Organizations in Central America*. London: Macmillan Press.

MacDonald, M., and M. Gatehouse. 1995. *In the Mountains of Morazán: Portrait of a Returned Refugee Community in El Salvador*. New York: Monthly Review Press.

Mahler, Sarah J. 1995. *American Dreaming: Immigrant Life on the Margins*. Princeton: Princeton University Press.

Mamdani, Mahmood. 2005. *Good Muslim, Bad Muslim: America, the Cold War, and the Roots of Terror* New York: Three Leaves.

Marcus, George E., and M. J. Fischer. 1986. *Anthropology as Cultural Critique : An Experimental Moment in the Human Sciences*. Chicago: University of Chicago Press.

Marizco, Michael. 2004. Smuggling Children, Part I: Young Immigrants Become Human Cargo. *Arizona Daily Star*. November 21. http://www.azstarnet.org/dailystar/relatedarticles/49066.php (accessed September 7, 2008).

Márquez, Gabriel García. 1996. *Noticia de un secuestro*. Buenos Aires: Editorial Sudamericana.

Mason, T. David. 1992. Women's Participation in Central American Revolutions: A Theoretical Perspective. *Comparative Political Studies* 25 (1): 63–89.

McClintock, Cynthia. 1998. *Revolutionary Movements in Latin America: El Salvador's FMLN and Peru's Shining Path*. Washington, DC: United States Institute of Peace Press.

Menjívar, Cecilia. 2000. *Fragmented Ties: Salvadoran Immigrant Networks in America*. Berkeley: University of California Press.

Merry, Sally Engle. 2005. Anthropology and Activism: Researching Human Rights across Porous Boundaries. *PoLAR: Political and Legal Anthropology Review* 28 (2): 240–257.

Metzi, Francisco. 1988. *Por los Caminos de Chalatenango: Con la Salud en la Mochila*. San Salvador: UCA Editores.

Minow, Martha. 1998. Between Vengeance and Forgiveness: Facing History after Genocide and Mass Violence. Boston: Beacon Press.

Mintz, Sidney. 1973. A Note on the Definition of Peasantries. *Journal of Peasant Studies* 1:91–106.

Molyneux, Maxine. 1985. Mobilization without Emancipation? Women's Interests, the State, and Revolution in Nicaragua. *Feminist Studies* 11 (2): 227–254.

Montgomery, Tommie Sue. 1995. *Revolution in El Salvador: From Civil Strife to Civil Peace.* 2nd ed. Boulder, CO: Westview Press.

Moodie, Ellen. 2006. Microbus Crashes and Coca-Cola Cash: The Value of Death in "Free-Market" El Salvador. *American Ethnologist* 33 (1): 63–80.

———. 2009. Seventeen Years, Seventeen Murders: Biospectacularity and the Production of Post–Cold War Knowledge in El Salvador. *Social Text* 27 (2): 77–103.

———. 2010. *El Salvador in the Aftermath of Peace: Crime, Uncertainty, and the Transition to Democracy*. Philadelphia: University of Pennsylvania Press.

Moreno, María. 1997. La Concertación Como Condición del Desarrollo Regional/Local: Caso Chalatenango. In *Desarrollo Regional/Local en El Salvador: Reto Estratégico del Siglo XXI*, ed. A. E. Villacorte et al., 86–113. El Salvador: FUNDE.

Moser, Caroline O., and Fiona Clark, eds. 2001. *Victims, Perpetrators, or Actors? Gender, Armed Conflict, and Political Violence*. London: Zed Books.

MSI. 1996. *Assistance to the Transition from War to Peace: Evaluation of USAID/El Salvador's Special Strategic Objective*. Washington, DC: MSI.

Murdock, Donna F. 2003. The Stubborn "Doing Good?" Question: Ethical/Epistemological Concerns in the Study of NGOs. *Ethnos* 68 (4): 507–532.

Murray, Kevin, Ellen Coletti, Jack Spence, Cynthia Curtis, Garth David Cheff, René Ramos, José Chacón, and Mary Thompson. 1994. *Rescuing Reconstruction: The Debate on Post-War Economic Recovery in El Salvador*. Cambridge, MA: Hemisphere Initiatives.

Murray, Kevin and Tom Barry. 1995. *Inside El Salvador: The Essential Guide to Its Politics, Economy, Society, and Environment.* Albuquerque: Resource Center Press.

Murray, Kevin. 1997. *El Salvador: Peace on Trial.* London, England: Oxfam UK and Ireland.

Narayan, Kirin. 1993. How Native Is a "Native" Anthropologist? *American Anthropologist* 95 (3): 671–686.

Nordstrom, Carolyn. 1997. *A Different Kind of War Story.* Philadelphia: University of Pennsylvania Press.

———. 2004. *Shadows of War: Violence, Power, and International Profiteering in the Twenty-first Century.* Berkeley: University of California Press.

Nugent, Daniel. 1993. *Spent Cartridges of Revolution.* Chicago: University of Chicago Press.

Ochs, Elinor, and Lisa Capps. 1996. Narrating the Self. *Annual Review of Anthropology* 25:19–43.

Ochs, Elinor, and Carolyn Taylor. 1992. Family Narrative as Political Activity. *Discourse and Society* 3 (3): 301–340.

Ochs, Elinor, Carolyn Taylor, Dina Rudolph, Ruth Smith. 1992. Storytelling as Theory-Building Activity. *Discourse Processes* 15 (1): 37–72.

Ong, Aihwa. 2006. *Neoliberalism as Exception: Mutations in Citizenship and Sovereignty.* Durham, NC: Duke University Press.

Paley, Julia. 2001. *Marketing Democracy: Power and Social Movements in Post-Dictatorship Chile.* Berkeley: University of California Press.

Pampell Conaway, Camile, and Salomé Martínez, with Sarah Gammage and Eugeniz Piza-Lopez. 2004. *Adding Value: Women's Contributions to Reintegration and Reconstruction in El Salvador.* Cambridge, MA: Hunt Alternatives Fund.

Pan-American Health Organization (PAHO). 1998. *Health in the Americas, 1998 Edition.* Vol. 2. Washington, DC: PAHO.

Pearce, Jenny. 1986. *Promised Land: Peasant Revolution in Chalatenango, El Salvador.* London: Latin America Bureau.

———. 1998. From Civil War to "Civil Society": Has the End of the Cold War Brought Peace to Central America? *International Affairs* 74 (3): 587–615.

Pederson, David. 2002. The Storm We Call Dollars: Determining Value and Belief in El Salvador and the United States. *Cultural Anthropology* 17 (3): 431–459.

Pérez-Brignoli, Héctor. 1995. Indians, Communists, and Peasants: The 1932 Rebellion in El Salvador. In *Coffee, Society, and Power in Latin America,* ed. W. Roseberry, L. Gudmundson, and M. Samper Kutschbac, 232–261. Baltimore: Johns Hopkins University Press.

Peterson, Anna. 1997. *Martyrdom and the Politics of Religion: Progressive Catholicism in El Salvador's Civil War.* Albany: State University of New York Press.

Peterson, Anna, and Brandt Peterson. 2008. Martyrdom, Sacrifice, and Political Memory in El Salvador. *Social Research* 75 (2): 511–542.

Petras, James. 1997. Imperialism and NGOs in Latin America. *Monthly Review* 49 (7): 10–27.

Polkinghorne, Donald. 1988. *Narrative Knowing and the Human Sciences.* Albany: State University of New York.

Poole, Deborah. 1994. *Unruly Order: Violence, Power, and Cultural Identity in the High Provinces of Southern Peru.* Boulder, CO: Westview Press.

Popkin, Margaret. 2000. *Peace without Justice: Obstacles to Building the Rule of Law in El Salvador.* University Park: Pennsylvania State University Press.

Quan, Adán. 2005. Through the Looking Glass: U.S. Aid to El Salvador and the Politics of National Identity. *American Ethnologist* 32 (2): 276–293.

Quesada, James. 1998. Suffering Child: An Embodiment of War and Its Aftermath in Post-Sandinista Nicaragua. *Medical Anthropology Quarterly* 12 (4): 51–73.

————. 1999. From Central American Warriors to San Francisco Latino Day Laborers: Suffering and Exhaustion in a Transnational Context. *Transforming Anthropology* 8 (1 and 2): 162–185.

Ramos, Alícia Rita. 2000. Anthropologist as Political Actor. *Journal of Latin American Anthropology* 4 (2): 172–189.

Rappaport, Joanne. 1990. *The Politics of Memory: Native Historical Interpretation in the Colombian Andes.* Cambridge: Cambridge University Press.

————. 1994. *Cumbe Reborn: An Andean Ethnography of History.* Chicago: University of Chicago Press.

Ready, Kelley. 1994. It's a Hard Life: Women in El Salvador's Economic History. In *Hear My Testimony: María Teresa Tula, Human Rights Activist of El Salvador,* ed. M. Tula and L. Stephen, 187–200. Cambridge, MA: South End Press.

Redfield, Peter. 2005. Doctors, Borders, and Life in Crisis. *Cultural Anthropology* 20 (3): 328–361.

————. 2006. A Less Modest Witness: Collective Advocacy and Motivated Truth in a Medical Humanitarian Movement. *American Ethnologist* 33 (1): 3–26.

Riding, Alan. 1980. Salvador Junta Opens Anti-Leftist Drive. *New York Times.* October 25.

Rivera, Ana Kelly, Edy Arelí Ortiz Cañas, Lisa Domínguez Magaña, and María Canadelaria Navas. 1995. *¿Valió la Pena?! Testimonios de Salvadoreñas que Vivieron la Guerra.* San Salvador: Editorial Sombrero Azul.

Rojas Pérez, Isaias. 2008. Writing the Aftermath: Anthropology and "Post-Conflict." In *A Companion to Latin American Anthropology,* ed. Deborah Poole, 254–275. Malden, MA: Blackwell Publishing.

Roseberry, William. 1988. Political Economy. *Annual Review of Anthropology* 17: 161–185.

————. 1989. *Anthropologies and Histories: Essays in Cultures, History, and Political Economy.* New Brunswick, NJ: Rutgers University Press.

————. 1993. Beyond the Agrarian Question in Latin America. In *Confronting Historical Paradigms,* ed. F. Cooper, F. Mallon, S. Stern, A. Isaacman, and W. Roseberry, 318–368. Madison: University of Wisconsin Press.

————. 1995. The Cultural History of Peasantries. In *Articulating Hidden Histories: Exploring the Influence of Eric R. Wolf,* ed. J. Schneider and R. Rapp, 51–66. Berkeley: University of California Press.

Rowe, William, and Vivian Schelling. 1991. *Memory and Modernity: Popular Culture in Latin America.* London: Verso.

Sanford, Victoria. 2003. *Buried Secrets: Truth and Human Rights in Guatemala.* New York: Palgrave Macmillan.

————. 2006. Introduction to *Engaged Observer: Anthropology, Advocacy, and Activism,* ed. V. Sanford and A. Angel-Ajani, 1–18. New Brunswick, NJ: Rutgers University Press.

Sanford, Victoria, and Asale Angel-Ajani, eds. 2006. *Engaged Observer: Anthropology, Advocacy, and Activism.* New Brunswick, NJ: Rutgers University Press.

Schenck, Celeste. 2003. The Human Face of Development: Disciplinary Convergence and New Arenas of Engagement. *Signs* 29 (2): 291–297.

Scheper-Hughes, Nancy. 1992. *Death without Weeping: The Violence of Everyday Life in Brazil.* Berkeley: University of California Press.

Scheper-Hughes, Nancy, and Philippe Bourgois, eds. 2004. *Violence in War and Peace: An Anthology.* Malden, MA: Blackwell Publishing.

Schrading, Roger. 1991. *Exodus en América Latina: El Movimiento de Repoblación en El Salvador.* San José, Costa Rica: Instituto Interamericano de Derechos Humanos (IIDH).

Schuller, Mark. 2008. Seeing Like a "Failed" NGO: Globalization's Impacts on State and Civil Society in Haiti. *PoLAR* 30 (1): 67–89.

Scott, James. 1985. *Weapons of the Weak: Everyday Forms of Peasant Resistance*. New Haven, CT: Yale University Press.

Seligson, Mitchell. 1995. Thirty Years of Transformation in the Agrarian Structure of El Salvador, 1961–1991. *LARR* 30 (3): 43–74.

———. 1996. Agrarian Inequality and the Theory of Peasant Rebellion. *LARR* 31 (2): 410–457.

Seligson, Mitchell, and Ricardo Córdova Macías. 1995. *De la Guerra a la Paz: Una Cultural Política en Transición*. San Salvador: La Universidad de Pittsburgh.

Servicio Jesuita para el Desarrollo "Pedro Arrupe," ed. 1994. *Tiempo de Recordar y Tiempo de Contar: Testimonios de Comunidades Repatriadas y Reubicadas de El Salvador*. San Salvador, El Salvador: Servicio Jesuita para el Desarrollo "Pedro Arrupe."

Shayne, Julie D. 2004. *The Revolution Question: Feminisms in El Salvador, Chile, and Cuba*. New Brunswick, NJ: Rutgers University Press.

Sheridan, Mary Beth. 2004. Acting Locally, Voting Globally. *Washington Post*. March 18.

Shorey, Ananda. 2005. Migrant Smugglers Getting Creative. Associated Press, April 4. http://wireservice.wried.com/wired/story.asp?section=Breaking&storyID=1013627&tw=wn_wire_story (accessed September 7, 2008).

Silber, Irina Carlota. 2004a. Mothers/Fighters/Citizens: Violence and Disillusionment in Postwar El Salvador. *Gender & History* 16 (3): 561–587.

———. 2004b. Not Revolutionary Enough? Community Rebuilding in Postwar Chalatenango. In *Landscapes of Struggle, Politics, Society, and Community in El Salvador*, ed. Aldo Lauria-Santiago and Leigh Binford, 166–186. Pittsburgh: University of Pittsburgh Press.

———. 2006. It's a Hard Place to Be a Revolutionary Woman. In *Engaged Observer: Anthropology, Advocacy, and Activism*, ed. V. Sanford and A. Angel-Ajani, 189–210. New Brunswick, NJ: Rutgers University Press.

———. 2007. Local Capacity Building in "Dysfunctional" Times: Internationals, Revolutionaries, and Activism in Postwar El Salvador. *Women's Studies Quarterly* 35 (3 and 4): 163–183.

Silber, Irina Carlota, and Jocelyn Viterna. 2009. Women in El Salvador: Continuing the Struggle. In *Women and Politics around the World: A Comparative History and Survey*, ed. Joyce Gelb and Marian Lief Palley, 329–352. Santa Barbara, CA: ABC-CLIO.

Silverman, Sydel. 1979. The Peasant Concept in Anthropology. *Journal of Peasant Studies* 7: 46–69.

Skidmore, Monique. 2003. Darker Than Midnight: Fear, Vulnerability, and Terror Making in Urban Burma (Myanmar). *American Ethnologist* 30 (1): 5–21.

Smith, Christian. 1996. *Resisting Reagan: The U.S. Central American Peace Movement*. Chicago: University of Chicago Press.

Smith, Robert Courtney. 2006. *Mexican New York: Transnational Lives of New Immigrants*. Berkeley: University of California Press.

Snyder, Margaret. 2003. Women Determine Development: The Unfinished Revolution. *Signs* 29 (2): 619–632.

Spence, Jack. 2004. *War and Peace in Central America: Comparing Transitions toward Democracy and Social Equality in Guatemala, El Salvador, and Nicaragua*. Cambridge, MA: Hemisphere Initiatives.

Spence, Jack, David R. Dye, Mike Lanchin, and Geoff Thale, with George Vickers. 1997. *Chapultepec Five Years Later: El Salvador's Political Reality and Uncertain Future*. Cambridge, MA: Hemisphere Initiatives.

Sprenkels, Ralph. 2005. *The Price of Peace: The Human Rights Movement in Postwar El Salvador*. Amsterdam: CEDLA Publications.

Stephen, Lynn. 1996. Women's Rights Are Human Rights: The Merging of Feminine and Feminist Interests among El Salvador's Mothers of the Disappeared (CO-MADRES). *AE* 22 (4): 807–827.

———. 1997. *Women and Social Movements in Latin America: Power from Below.* Austin: University of Texas Press.

———. 2007. *Transborder Lives: Indigenous Oaxacans in Mexico, California, and Oregon.* Durham, NC: Duke University Press.

Stephen, Lynn, Serena Cosgrove, and Kelley Ready. 2001. Women's Organizations in El Salvador: History, Accomplishments, and International Support. In *Women and Civil War: Impact, Organizations, and Action*, ed. Krishna Kumar, 183–204. Boulder, CO: Lynne Rienner.

Stern, Steven. 1987. *Resistance, Rebellion, and Consciousness in the Andean Peasant World, 18th to 20th Centuries.* Madison: University of Wisconsin.

Strathern, Marilyn. 1999. *Property, Substance, and Effect: Anthropological Essays on Persons and Things.* London: Athlone Press.

Taussig, Michael. 2004. *My Cocaine Museum.* Chicago and London: University of Chicago Press.

Theidon, Kimberly. 2007. Transitional Subjects: The Disarmament, Demobilization, and Reintegration of Former Combatants in Colombia. *International Journal of Transitional Justice* 1:66–90.

Thompson, Martha. 1995. Repopulated Communities in El Salvador. In *The New Politics of Survival: Grassroots Movements in Central America*, ed. M. Sinclair, 109–151. New York: Monthly Review Press.

Thomson, Marilyn. 1986. *Women of El Salvador: The Price of Freedom.* London: Zed Books.

Todd, Molly. 2007. Salvadorans by Flight: Peasants and Citizen Action on the El Salvador–Honduras Border, 1960–1990. PhD diss., University of Wisconsin, Madison.

Tsing, Anna Lowenhaupt. 2005. *Friction: An Ethnography of Global Connection.* Princeton, NJ: Princeton University Press.

Tula, Maria Teresa. 1994. *Hear My Testimony: Maria Teresa Tula, Human Rights Activist of El Salvador.* Boston: South End Press.

Unidad de Salud Las Vueltas. 1997. Censo Poblacional por Grupos. Document. Chalatenango, El Salvador.

United Nations. 1993. *De La Locura a La Esperanza: La Guerra de Doce Años en El Salvador. Informe de La Comisión de la Verdad para El Salvador.* New York: United Nations.

United Nations Development Programme (UNDP). 2004. *Democracy in Latin America: Towards a Citizens' Democracy.* New York: UNDP.

———. 2005. *Informe Sobre Desarrollo Humano de El Salvador 2005: Una Mirada al Nuevo Nosotros. El Impacto de las Migraciones.* New York: UNDP.

Van Velsen, J. 1967. The Extended-Case Method and Situational Analysis. In *The Craft of Social Anthropology*, ed. A. L. Epstein, 129–149. London: Tavistock Publication.

Vázquez, Norma, Cristina Ibáñez, and Clara Murguialday. 1996. *Mujeres Montaña: Vivencias de Guerrilleras y Colaboradoras del FMLN.* Spain: Horas y HORAS la Editorial.

Viterna, Jocelyn. 2006. Pulled, Pushed, and Persuaded: Explaining Women's Mobilization into the Salvadoran Guerrilla Army. *American Journal of Sociology* 112 (1): 1–45.

Viterna, Jocelyn, and Kathleen M. Fallon. 2008. Democratization, Women's Movements, and Gender-Equitable States: A Framework for Comparison. *American Sociological Review* 73:668–689.

Walley, Christine. 2004. *Rough Waters: Nature and Development in an East African Marine Park.* Princeton, NJ: Princeton University Press.

Warren, Kay. 1993. *The Violence Within: Cultural and Political Opposition in Divided Nations.* Boulder, CO: Westview Press.

Weinberg, Bill. 2008. Guns: The U.S. Threat to Mexican National Security. *NACLA* 41 (2): 21–26.

Whitfield, Teresa. 1994. *Paying the Price: Ignacio Ellacuría and the Murdered Jesuits of El Salvador.* Philadelphia: Temple University Press.

Wolf, Eric. 1955. Types of Latin American Peasantry: A Preliminary Discussion. *American Anthropologist* 57 (3): 452–471.

Wood, Elisabeth J. 2000. *Forging Democracy from Below: Insurgent Transitions in South Africa and El Salvador.* New York: Cambridge University Press.

———. 2003. *Insurgent Collective Action and Civil War in El Salvador.* Cambridge: Cambridge University Press.

Woolard, Kathryn A., and Bambi B. Schieffelin. 1994. Language Ideology. *Annual Review of Anthropology* 23:55–82.

The World Bank. 1998. *El Salvador: Rural Development Study.* Washington, DC: World Bank.

Zamosc, Leon. 1988. Class Conflict in an Export Economy: The Social Roots of the Salvadoran Insurrection of 1932. In *Sociology of "Developing Societies": Central America,* ed. Edelberto Torres-Rivas, 56–72. New York: Monthly Review Press.

Zilberg, Elana. 2007. Gangster in Guerilla Face: A Transnational Mirror of Production between the USA And El Salvador. *Anthropological Theory* 7 (1): 37–57.

Zimmerman, Marc. 1991. Testimonio in Guatemala: Payera, Rigoberta, and Beyond. *Latin American Perspectives* 18 (4): 22–47.

INDEX

Note: Illustrations are indicated by page numbers in italic type.

ABOUT THE AUTHOR

IRINA CARLOTA (LOTTI) SILBER is an associate professor of anthropology at City College of New York's Department of Interdisciplinary Arts and Sciences, which is housed at the Center for Worker Education. *Everyday Revolutionaries* stems from her long-term interest in studying the aftermaths of war and displacement in people's everyday lives.